Beginners' Welsh Reading Dictionary

Beginners' Welsh Reading Dictionary

Common Welsh words together with mutated and other forms, especially for Beginners and non-Welsh speakers

D. Geraint Lewis
& Nudd Lewis

Argraffiad cyntaf: 2023

Cynllun y clawr: Richard Huw Pritchard

Rhif Llyfr Rhyngwladol: 978 1 80099 333 4

Cyhoeddwyd ac argraffwyd yng Nghymru
ar bapur o goedwigoedd cynaliadwy gan
Y Lolfa Cyf., Talybont, Ceredigion SY24 5HE
e-bost ylolfa@ylolfa.com
gwefan www.ylolfa.com
ffôn 01970 832 304

Foreword & Acknowledgements

Introduction 2nd revised edition

A new and updated version of 'Reading Welsh' (Gomer 2014) drawn from a corpus of the 10,000 most frequently used words in Welsh. The distinction between the mutated word form and its base form has been highlighted by printing the mutated forms in blue. Another dimension has been added, turning the original word list into a dictionary by labelling the different grammatical parts of speech of the unmutated wordforms.

Foreword & Acknowledgements

This is a comprehensive list in all their various forms of the most frequently used words in written Welsh. It includes:
- mutated forms,
- plural, and feminine forms
- the most frequently used verb forms
- personal forms of prepositions
- contracted forms

A further innovation is that it sets out these words in English alphabetical order for those not familiar with the (different) order of the Welsh alphabet.
To include all the possible forms for even a limited Welsh vocabulary would result in a tediously long list containing a large number of rarely used word-forms.

The present list draws on those words most frequently used in written Welsh and has been made possible by the work of Professor Kevin P. Scannell of the University of Saint Louis, Missouri, who has compiled a large corpus of Welsh words by electronically combing through a huge range of Welsh texts.

We are extremely grateful to Professor Scannell for permission to draw on this work and also to Andrew Hawke, editor of the University of Wales Dictionary, for making available to us the 10,000 most frequently used forms to appear in Professor Scannell's corpus.

More details on all the entries may be found free of charge in the electronic dictionary _Gweidur.com_

We are indebted to Gwasg y Lolfa for their readiness to publish this revised edition.

Diolch i

Garmon Gruffudd
Carolyn Hodges

Rarely does one have the opportrunity in Welsh
to compile a 2nd Revised edition of a work.

D.Geraint Lewis & Nudd Lewis
Llangwrddon

Introduction

The Welsh language differs in so many respects from English that it is almost impossible to use current dictionaries of Welsh without knowing what these differences are.

The aim of this dictionary is to set out the most commonly used Welsh words in all their bewildering varieties. It has a number of unique features to assist those who are relatively new to reading Welsh:

- It follows the **English alphabet** (which differs significantly from the Welsh alphabet normally used in dictionaries of Welsh)

- The most obvious and potentially confusing change is the way in which the first letter of a word can vary due to **mutation**; for the first time, the most common words are presented here in all their mutated forms

- The use of verb forms is more complex in Welsh than English due to **inflexion**; the most common of these verbs are set down in both their regular and mutated forms

- Many adjectives have both feminine and plural forms, e.g. white has a masculine form 'gwyn' and a feminine form 'gwen' and 'coch,' the Welsh word for 'red, has a plural form 'cochion'

- Plural nouns do not follow a regular pattern such as adding 's' (cat, cats etc,) as in English, and many prepositions (like verbs) have personal forms in Welsh.

None of these individual forms would normally be included in a traditional dictionary of Welsh.

general guidelines for readers new to Welsh:

The order of the words in a Welsh sentence does not follow the same pattern as in English. You will find the meaning of the individual words here but will have to rearrange the order of the words to make sense of the sentence:

1. Sometimes the translation of individual words can produce what looks like a question in English, e.g. 'is John here'; this is due to the different word order in Welsh where it means 'John is here'; so, unless there is a question mark in the text, it would be as well to treat any seeming question as a direct statement

2. For questions, look out for a tell-tale question mark

3. Negative (not) statements are introduced by 'Ni' or 'Na' or include the word 'ddim' (not)

4. There is no impersonal 'it' in Welsh, so sometimes you will need to translate 'he' or 'she' as 'it'

5. There is no 'a' as in *a dog* in Welsh; the stand-alone noun (name) 'ci' means 'a dog'

6. Adjectives which normally appear before a noun in English, e.g. 'the red door', follow the noun in Welsh *y* (the) *drws* (door) *coch* (red)

7. Welsh numerals are followed by the singular form of the noun, e.g. 'tri dyn' which translates literally as 'three man'

8. This listing does not include idioms (e.g. 'going *flat out*' where the meaning of the phrase cannot be understood from the meaning of the individual words)

inflected verb forms

These are forms like 'went' or 'gone' from *go*, 'sat' from *sit*, and '(I) *am*', '(you) *are*', '(he/she) *is*', from the verb *to be*. With the exception of the heavily used forms of *to be* these have largely disappeared in English, however they are more frequently used in Welsh, being particularly important in narrative sequences (i.e. telling of past events).

syntax or sentence order

Most European languages follow the pattern: **Subject** (*John*) **Verb** (*saw*) **Object** (*the dog*).

However the equivalent pattern in Welsh is: **Verb** (*Gwelodd*) **Subject** (*John*) **Object** (*y ci*).

mutation

Welsh mutations alarm both native Welsh speakers and Welsh learners and must prove baffling to anyone coming to Welsh for the first time. However, surprisingly, this phenomenon also takes place in English, for example when 'f' changes to 'v' and *wolf* becomes *wolves*, or when the English 'int' as in *international* becomes 'inn' in the transatlantic *innernational*. Due to the way Welsh has developed from the earlier Brythonic language, these changes occur at the beginning of words in Welsh.

mutated forms of words

a word printed in blue means that the root form of that word begins with a different letter

a	is a mutation of	**g**
b	is a mutation of	**p**
ch	is a mutation of	**c**
d	is a mutation of	**t**
dd	is a mutation of	**d**
e	is a mutation of	**g**
f	is a mutation of	either **b** or **m**
g	is a mutation of	**c**
h	is a mutation of	any vowel (**a,e,i,o,u ALSO W** and **Y**)
l	is a mutation of	either **ll** or **g**
m	is a mutation of	**b**
mh	is a mutation of	**p**
n	is a mutation of	**d**
ng	is a mutation of	**g**
ngh	is a mutation of	**c**
nh	is a mutation of	**t**
o	is a mutation of	**g**
ph	is a mutation of	**p**
r	is a mutation of	either **rh** or **g**
th	is a mutation of	**t**
w	is a mutation of	**g**
y	is a mutation of	**g**

alphabetical order

If you wish to look up words (set down here in the order of the English alphabet) in a Welsh dictionary, you need to be aware of the Welsh alphabetical sequence.

a b c **ch** d **dd** e f **ff** g **ng** h i j l **ll** m n o p **ph** r **rh** s t **th** u w y

The pairs of letters in bold actually signify a single letter (sound) in the Welsh alphabet. The words are arranged in the order of the English alphabet. More details and examples are included at the start of each letter in this dictionary

Warning

This lexicon is made up of the words most frequently used in written material on the Internet over a period of a number of years:

- It is not intended as a basic vocabulary for Welsh learners as it contains some words in a non-standard format; it is intended to provide the general meaning of a written word. The precise meaning of the word will be derived from its context

- The grammatical function of the word is not essential, but may help distinguish between homographs (words sharing the same spelling) e.g. light (weight) *ysgafn (adj)*; (to) light *goleuo*; (a) light *golau (nm)* (noun masculine)

- The parts of speech also indicate the different ways in which Welsh and English work.

If you wish to pursue this, you might like to look at my volume *D.I.Y. Welsh* which provides a basic Welsh vocabulary and an introduction to Welsh grammar.

Here are the parts of speech in this volume for those of you who might be interested in learning more about Welsh:

Nouns have a gender

(nm)	*masculine noun*
(nf)	*feminine noun*
(npl)	*noun plural*

Adjectives have feminine and plural forms

(adj)	*adjective*
(adj/f)	*feminine adjective*
(adj/pl)	*plural adjective*

Verbs have an Infinitive form and conjugated forms

to xxx	*the Infinitive*
(vb)	*verb*
(conj)	*conjunction*
(prep)	*preposition*
(adv)	*adverb*

Numerals have masculine and feminine forms

(num/m)	*masculine numeral*
(num/f)	*feminine numeral*

WELSH
(Cymraeg)
– *English*

A

a word starting with **a** printed in blue means that the root form of that word begins with **g**, e.g. **adael** root **gadael**

a and (*conj*)
    a'ch and your
    a'i and his/her/its
    a'm and my
    a'n and our
    a'r and the
    a'th and your
    a'u and their
a that, which, who, whom
    (*relative pronoun*)
a [introduces a question]
ab son of
abaty abbey (*nm*)
aberth sacrifice (*nm*)
aberthu to sacrifice (*v*)
abl able, rich, strong (*adj*)
absenoldeb absence (*nm*)
absenoldebau absences (*npl*)
absoliwt absolute, complete (*adj*)
abwyd bait, earthworm, lure (*nm*)
ac and (*conj*)
academaidd academic, scholarly (*adj*)
academi academy (*nf*)
academydd academic (*nm*)
academyddion academics (*npl*)
acen accent, diacritic (*nf*)
acenion accents (*npl*)
acennog accented (*adj*)
ach lineage, pedigree (*nf*)
ach ugh! (*exclamation*)
achau family tree (*npl*)
achlysur occasion (*nm*)
achlysurol occasional (*adj*)

achlysuron occasions (*npl*)
achos case, cause (*nm*)
achos because (*conj*)
achosi to cause (*v*)
achosion cases, causes (*npl*)
achosir is/are/will be caused (*v*)
achosodd he/she/it caused (*v*)
achoswyd was/were caused (*v*)
achrededig accredited (*adj*)
achrediad accreditation (*nm*)
achredu to accredit (*v*)
achub to save, to rescue (*v*)
achub holding, piece of land (*nm*)
achwyn to complain (*v*)
achwynwyr complainants (*npl*)
achwynydd complainant, plaintiff (*nm*)
achwynyddion complainants (*npl*)
acrobat acrobat (*nm*)
act act (*nf*)
actio to act, to imitate (*v*)
actor actor (*nm*)
actores actress (*nf*)
actorion actors (*npl*)
acw that, there, those (*adv*)
ad he/she/it will let
adael to leave
adain spoke, wing (*nf*)
adar birds (*npl*)
adawodd he/she/it left
adawyd was/were left
adborth feedback (*nm*)
ad-dâl repayment (*nm*)
ad-daliad repayment (*nm*)

ad-dalu to recompense, to repay *(v)*
addas suitable, worthy *(adj)*
addasiad adaptation, modification *(nm)*
addasiadau modifications *(npl)*
addasrwydd suitability *(nm)*
addasu to adapt *(v)*
addaswyd was/were adapted *(v)*
addawodd he/she/it promised *(v)*
addawol auspicious, promising *(adj)*
addewid promise *(nm)*
addewidion promises *(npl)*
addo to promise *(v)*
addoli to adore, to worship *(v)*
addoliad adoration, worship *(nm)*
ad-drefnu to reorganize, to reshuffle *(v)*
addurn decoration, ornament *(nm)*
addurniadau ornaments *(npl)*
addurno to decorate *(v)*
addysg education *(nf)*
addysgiadol educational *(adj)*
addysgir is/are/will be educated *(v)*
addysgol educational *(adj)*
addysgu to educate, to teach *(v)*
addysgwr educationalist *(nm)*
addysgwyr educationalists *(npl)*
adeg time *(nf)*
adegau times *(npl)*
adeilad building *(nm)*
adeiladau buildings *(npl)*
adeiladodd he/she/it built *(v)*
adeiladol constructive *(adj)*
adeiladu to build, to construct *(v)*
adeiladwaith construction, structure *(nm)*
adeiladwr builder *(nm)*
adeiladwyd was/were built *(v)*
adeiladwyr builders *(npl)*
adeiledd structure *(nm)*
adeileddau structures *(npl)*
adeiledig built-up *(adj)*
adennill to recapture, to regain *(v)*
adenydd wings *(npl)*
aderyn bird *(nm)*

adfeilion ruins *(npl)*
adfer remedial *(adj)*
adfer to recover, to restore *(v)*
adferiad recovery *(nm)*
adferol restoring *(adj)*
adfywiad recovery, regeneration *(nm)*
adfywio to recover, to revive *(v)*
adio to add *(v)*
adlais echo *(nm)*
adleoli to relocate *(v)*
adlewyrchiad reflection *(nm)*
adlewyrchir is/are/will be reflected *(v)*
adlewyrchu to reflect *(v)*
adloniant entertainment, recreation *(nm)*
adnabod to know, to recognize *(v)*
adnabyddiaeth knowledge *(nf)*
adnabyddir is/are/will be known *(v)*
adnabyddus well-known *(adj)*
adnau deposit *(nm)*
adnewyddadwy renewable *(adj)*
adnewyddu to renew, to renovate *(v)*
adnod verse *(nf)*
adnodd resource *(nm)*
adnoddau resources *(npl)*
adolygiad review *(nm)*
adolygiadau reviews *(npl)*
adolygu to review, to revise *(v)*
adolygwyd was/were reviewed *(v)*
adran department, section *(nf)*
adrannau sections *(npl)*
adrannol departmental *(adj)*
adref homewards *(adv)*
adrodd to narrate, to recite, to report *(v)*
adroddiad report *(nm)*
adroddiadau reports *(npl)*
adroddir is/are/will be reported *(v)*
adroddodd he/she/it reported *(v)*
adroddwyd was/were reported *(v)*
adsefydlu to re-establish, to rehabilitate *(v)*
adwaenir is known *(v)*
adwaith reaction *(nm)*
adweithiau reactions *(npl)*

adweithio to react (*v*)
adwerthu to retail (*v*)
adwy breach, gap (*nf*)
aed go! (*v*)
aeddfed mature, ripe (*adj*)
aeddfedrwydd maturity (*nm*)
aeddfedu to mature, to ripen (*v*)
ael eyebrow (*nf*)
aelod limb, member (*nm*)
aelodaeth membership (*nf*)
aelodau members (*npl*)
aelwyd fireside, household (*nf*)
aelwydydd households (*npl*)
aer air (*nm*)
aer heir (*nm*)
aeth he/she/it went (*v*)
aethant they went (*v*)
aethom we went (*v*)
aethon they went (*v*)
aethpwyd was/were taken (*v*)
af I will go (*v*)
afael to grasp
afal apple (*nm*)
afalau apples (*npl*)
Affricanaidd African (*adj*)
affrodisaidd aphrodisiacal (*adj*)
afiach dirty, unhealthy, unhygienic (*adj*)
afiechyd disease, illness (*nm*)
afiechydon diseases (*npl*)
aflan dirty, unclean (*adj*)
aflonydd restless, uneasy (*adj*)
aflonyddu to disturb, to ruffle (*v*)
aflonyddwch disquiet, unrest (*nm*)
aflwyddiannus unsuccessful (*adj*)
afon river (*nf*)
afonydd rivers (*npl*)
afreolaidd erratic, irregular (*adj*)
afresymol irrational, unreasonable (*adj*)
afu liver (*nm*)
ag with (*prep*)
agenda agenda (*nf*)
agendâu agendas (*npl*)

ager steam (*nm*)
agor to cut open, to open, to undo (*v*)
agored open (*adj*)
agoriad key, opening (*nm*)
agoriadol opening (*adj*)
agorodd he/she/it opened (*v*)
agorwch you open (*v*)
agorwyd was/were opened (*v*)
agos near (*adj*)
agosach nearer (*adj*)
agosaf nearest (*adj*)
agwedd attitude (*nf*)
agweddau attitudes (*npl*)
ai if, whether (*conj*)
âi he/she/it went (*v*)
aiff he/she/it goes (*v*)
Aifft, yr Egypt
aig shoal (*nf*)
ail second (*ordinal*)
ailadeiladu to rebuild (*v*)
ailadrodd to reiterate, to repeat (*v*)
ailbrisio to re-price (*v*)
ailddatblygu to redevelop (*v*)
ailddefnyddio to re-use (*v*)
ailgylchu to recycle (*v*)
ailosod to reset (*v*)
ailsefydlu to re-establish, to reinstate (*v*)
ailstrwythuro to restructure (*v*)
ailystyried to reconsider (*v*)
air word
alaw air, tune, water lily (*nf*)
alawon tunes (*npl*)
Alban Scotland
Albanaidd Scottish (*adj*)
albwm album (*nm*)
alcohol alcohol (*nm*)
all he/she/it can
allaf I can
allai he/she/it could
allan out, outside (*adv*)
allan they can
allanol external, outdoor (*adj*)

allant they can
allbwn output (*nm*)
allbynnau outputs (*npl*)
allech you could
allent they could
allforio to export (*v*)
allor altar (*nf*)
allt wooded slope (*nf*)
alltraeth offshore (*adj*)
alltud exile, deportee (*nm*)
alltud exiled (*adj*)
allu to be able
alluoedd abilities, forces
alluog clever
alluogi to enable
allwch you can
allwedd clef, key (*nf*)
allweddi keys (*npl*)
allweddol key (*adj*)
allwn we can
allyriad emission (*nm*)
allyriadau emissions (*npl*)
allyriannau emissions (*npl*)
allyriant emission (*nm*)
Almaen, yr Germany
Almaeneg German [language] (*nf*)
alw to call
alwad call
alwadau calls
alwedigaeth vocation
alwedigaethol vocational
alwminiwm aluminium (*nm*)
alwodd he/she/it called
am because, since (*conjunction*)
am about, as for, at, for, on, to (*prep*)
amaeth agriculture (*nm*)
amaethu to cultivate (*v*)
amaethwr farmer (*nm*)
amaethwyr farmers (*npl*)
amaethyddiaeth agriculture (*nf*)
amaethyddol agricultural (*adj*)
amatur amateur (*nm*)

amatur amateur (*adj*)
amau to doubt, to suspect (*v*)
ambell occasional, some (*adj*)
ambiwlans ambulance (*nm*)
amcan intention, notion (*nm*)
amcangyfrif estimate (*nm*)
amcangyfrif to estimate (*v*)
amcangyfrifedig estimated (*adj*)
amcangyfrifir is/are/will be estimated (*v*)
amcangyfrifon estimates (*npl*)
amcangyfrifwyd was/were estimated (*v*)
amcanion aims (*npl*)
amcanu to aim, to estimate, to intend (*v*)
amdanaf about me (*prep*)
amdanat about you (*prep*)
amdani about her (*prep*)
amdano about him (*prep*)
amdanoch about you (*prep*)
amdanom about us (*prep*)
amdanyn about them (*prep*)
amdanynt about them (*prep*)
amddifad destitute, orphaned (*adj*)
amddifadedd deprivation, destitution (*nm*)
amddiffyn to defend, to protect (*v*)
amddiffynfa fortress (*nf*)
amddiffynfeydd fortresses (*npl*)
amddiffyniad defence (*nm*)
amddiffynnol defensive, protective (*adj*)
amddiffynnwr defender (*nm*)
amen amen (*nf*)
Americanaidd American (*adj*)
Americanwr American (*nm*)
Americanwyr Americans (*npl*)
amgaeedig enclosed (*adj*)
amgáu to enclose, to surround (*v*)
amgen alternative, different, other (*adj*)
amgenach better, otherwise (*adj*)
amgueddfa museum (*nf*)
amgueddfeydd museums (*npl*)
amgyffred to comprehend (*v*)
amgyffred comprehension (*nm*)
amgylch about, circumcircle (*nm*)

amgylchedd environment (*nm*)
amgylcheddau environments (*npl*)
amgylcheddol environmental (*adj*)
amgylchfyd environment (*nm*)
amgylchiad circumstance, event (*nm*)
amgylchiadau circumstances (*npl*)
amgylchynol surrounding (*adj*)
amgylchynu to surround (*v*)
amhariad impairment (*nm*)
amharod unprepared, unwilling (*adj*)
amharodrwydd reluctance, (*nm*)
amharu to harm, to impair (*v*)
amhenodol indefinite, indeterminate (*adj*)
amherffaith imperfect (*adj*)
amherthnasol irrelevant (*adj*)
amheuaeth doubt, suspicion (*nf*)
amheuir is/are/will be doubted (*v*)
amheuon doubts (*npl*)
amheus doubtful, dubious, suspicious (*adj*)
amhosib impossible (*adj*)
amhosibl impossible (*adj*)
amhriodol improper, inappropriate (*adj*)
amhrisiadwy invaluable, priceless (*adj*)
aml frequent, many, numerous, often (*adj*)
amlach more often (*adj*)
amlaf most often (*adj*)
amlddisgyblaethol multidisciplinary (*adj*)
amlder abundance, frequency (*nm*)
amledd frequency (*nm*)
amlen envelope (*nf*)
amlgyfrwng multimedia (*adj*)
amlinelliad outline, contour, sketch (*nm*)
amlinellir is/are/will be outlined (*v*)
amlinellol outlined (*adj*)
amlinellu to outline (*v*)
amlinellwyd was/were outlined (*v*)
amlwg famous, obvious, prominent (*adj*)
amlycaf most obvious (*adj*)
amlygiad disclosure, manifestation (*nm*)
amlygrwydd prominence (*nm*)
amlygu to expose, to reveal (*v*)
amlygwyd was/were revealed (*v*)

amnewid to replace, to substitute (*v*)
amod condition (*nm*)
amodau conditions (*npl*)
amodol conditional (*adj*)
amrediad range (*nm*)
amrwd crude, raw (*adj*)
amryfal various (*adj*)
amryliw motley, variegated (*adj*)
amryw sundry, various (*adj*)
amryw diversity, variety (*nm*)
amrywiad variation (*nm*)
amrywiadau variations (*npl*)
amrywiaeth miscellany, variety (*nf*)
amrywiaethau varieties (*npl*)
amrywio to differ, to vary (*v*)
amrywiol variable, various (*adj*)
amser tense, time (*nm*)
amserau times (*npl*)
amseriad tempo, timing (*nm*)
amserlen timetable (*nf*)
amserlenni timetables (*npl*)
amseroedd times (*npl*)
amserol timely (*adj*)
amseru to time (*v*)
amsugno to absorb (*v*)
amwynder amenity (*nm*)
amwys ambiguous (*adj*)
amynedd patience (*nm*)
amyneddgar patient (*adj*)
anabl disabled (*adj*)
anabledd disability (*nm*)
anableddau disabilities (*npl*)
anad in preference to, rather than (*prep*)
anaddas inapplicable, unsuitable (*adj*)
anadl breath (*adj*)
anadlu to breathe, to respire (*v*)
anaf injury, lesion (*nm*)
anafiadau injuries (*npl*)
anafu to hurt, to injure (*v*)
anafwyd was/were hurt (*v*)
anallu inability (*nm*)
analog analogue (*adj*)

anaml infrequent, rare, sparse (*adj*)
anarferol unusual (*adj*)
anawsterau difficulties (*npl*)
aned he/she/it was born
anelir is/are/will be aimed (*v*)
anelu to aim, to draw (*v*)
anerchiad address, greeting (*nm*)
anfantais detriment, disadvantage (*nf*)
anfanteision disadvantages (*npl*)
anfarwol immortal, unforgettable (*adj*)
anfasnachol uncommercial (*adj*)
anferth gargantuan, huge, vast (*adj*)
anferthol huge (*adj*)
anffafriol unfavourable (*adj*)
anffodus hapless, unfortunate (*adj*)
anffurfiol informal (*adj*)
anfoddhaol unsatisfactory (*adj*)
anfodlon discontented, unwilling (*adj*)
anfodlonrwydd discontent, displeasure (*nm*)
anfon to accompany, to send (*v*)
anfoneb invoice (*nf*)
anfonebau invoices (*npl*)
anfonir is/are/will be sent (*v*)
anfonodd he/she/it sent (*v*)
anfonwch you send (*v*)
anfonwyd was/were sent (*v*)
anfwriadol unintentional (*adj*)
angau death (*nm*)
angel angel (*nm*)
angen need (*nm*)
angenrheidiol necessary (*adj*)
angenrheidrwydd necessity (*nm*)
angerdd force, passion (*nm*)
angerddol intense (*adj*)
anghenion necessities (*npl*)
anghenraid necessity (*nm*)
anghenus needy (*adj*)
angheuol fatal, mortal (*adj*)
anghofio to forget (*v*)
anghydfod disagreement, dissent (*nm*)
anghydfodau dissensions (*npl*)

anghydraddoldeb inequality (*nm*)
anghydraddoldebau inequalities (*npl*)
anghyfannedd desolate, uninhabited (*adj*)
anghyfartal unequal (*adj*)
anghyfarwydd unaccustomed (to), unfamiliar, unused (to) (*adj*)
anghyfforddus uncomfortable (*adj*)
anghyffredin uncommon (*adj*)
anghyfiawnder injustice (*nm*)
anghyflawn incomplete; transitive (*adj*)
anghyfleuster inconvenience (*nm*)
anghyfleustra inconvenience (*nm*)
anghyfreithlon illegal, illegitimate, unlawful (*adj*)
anghyfyngedig unrestricted (*adj*)
anghymdeithasol unsociable (*adj*)
anghysbell remote (*adj*)
anghyson fickle, inconsistent (*adj*)
anghysondeb anomaly, inconsistency (*nm*)
anghysonderau anomalies (*npl*)
anghytundeb disagreement (*nm*)
anghytuno to disagree (*v*)
anghywir incorrect, wrong (*adj*)
angladd funeral (*nm*)
angladdau funerals (*npl*)
Anglicanaidd Anglican (*adj*)
angylion angels (*npl*)
anhapus unhappy (*adj*)
anhawster difficulty (*nm*)
anheddau dwellings, settlements (*npl*)
anheddiad settlement (*nm*)
anheddu to settle (*v*)
anhepgor indispensable (*adj*)
anhrefn anarchy, confusion (*nf*)
anhwyldeb indisposition, sickness (*nm*)
anhwylder indisposition (*nm*)
anhwylderau illnesses (*npl*)
anhygoel incredible, unbelievable (*adj*)
anhysbys unknown (*adj*)
anial desolate (*adj*)
anial desert, wilderness (*nm*)
anialwch desert, wilderness (*nm*)

anian characteristic, nature, temperament (*nf*)
anifail animal, beast (*nm*)
anifail anwes pet (*nm*) See comment under *anwes*
anifeiliaid animals (*npl*)
animeiddio to animate (*v*)
annedd dwelling (*nf*)
annerbyniol inadmissible, unacceptable (*adj*)
annerch to address (*v*)
annhebyg unlike, unlikely (*adj*)
annhebygol far-fetched, improbable, unlikely (*adj*)
annheg unfair (*adj*)
annibyniaeth independence (*nf*)
annibynnol independent, Congregationalist, Independent (*adj*)
annibynwyr independents (*npl*)
annifyr disagreeable, miserable, unpleasant (*adj*)
annigonol inadequate, insufficient (*adj*)
annisgwyl unexpected, unforeseen (*adj*)
annog to exhort, to urge (*v*)
annomestig non-domestic (*adj*)
annuwiol ungodly (*adj*)
annwyd a cold (*nm*)
annwyl dear (*adj*)
annymunol undesirable, unpleasant (*adj*)
anobaith despair (*nm*)
anochel inescapable, inevitable (*adj*)
anodd difficult, hard, tricky (*adj*)
anoddach harder (*adj*)
anogaeth exhortation (*nf*)
anogir is/are/will be urged (*v*)
anorfod inevitable, invincible (*adj*)
anos more difficult (*adj*)
anrheg gift, present (*nf*)
anrhegion gifts (*npl*)
anrhydedd honour (*nm*)
anrhydeddu to honour (*v*)
anrhydeddus honorary, honourable (*adj*)

ansawdd condition, quality, state (*nm*)
ansefydlog unstable, unsettled (*adj*)
ansicr doubtful, uncertain (*adj*)
ansicrwydd doubt, uncertainty (*nm*)
ansoddair adjective (*nm*)
ansoddeiriau adjectives (*npl*)
ansoddol qualitative (*adj*)
anstatudol non-statutory (*adj*)
anterth peak, prime, zenith (*nm*)
anti auntie (*nf*)
antur adventure, venture (*nf*)
anturiaeth adventure (*nf*)
anturiaethau adventures (*npl*)
anuniongyrchol indirect (*adj*)
anwastad fickle, uneven (*adj*)
anweddus indecent, unbecoming, unseemly (*adj*)
anweithredol inactive, inoperative (*adj*)
anweledig invisible (*adj*)
anwes fondness (*nm*)
anwiredd falsehood, untruth (*nm*)
anwybodaeth ignorance (*nf*)
anwybyddu to ignore, to snub (*v*)
anwyd he/she/it was born (*v*)
ap son of
apêl appeal (*nf*)
apeliad appeal (*nm*)
apeliadau appeals (*npl*)
apelio to appeal, to attract (*v*)
apeliwr appellant (*nm*)
apelydd appellant (*nm*)
apwyntiad appointment (*nm*)
apwyntiadau appointments (*npl*)
ar about (you), at, on, upon (*prep*)
âr tilth (*nm*)
Arabaidd Arabian (*adj*)
aradr plough, (the) Plough (*nm*)
araf slow (*adj*)
arafach slower (*adj*)
arafu to slow, to slow (down) (*v*)
araith speech, oration (*nf*)
arall other (*adj*)

arallgyfeirio to diversify (v)
arbed to salvage, to save (v)
arbedion savings (npl)
arbenigedd expertise, specialism, speciality (nm)
arbenigo to specialize (v)
arbenigol specialized (adj)
arbenigwr expert, specialist (nm)
arbenigwyr specialists (npl)
arbennig distinctive, marvellous, special, splendid, wonderful (adj)
arbrawf experiment (nm)
arbrofi to experiment (v)
arbrofion experiments (npl)
arbrofol experimental (adj)
arch ark, coffin, the Ark of the Covenant (nf)
arch he/she/it asks (v)
archaeoleg archaeology (nf)
archaeolegol archaeological (adj)
archdderwydd archdruid (nm)
archddiacon archdeacon (nm)
archeb order (nf)
archebion orders (npl)
archebu to order (v)
archesgob archbishop (nm)
archfarchnad supermarket (nf)
archfarchnadoedd supermarkets (npl)
archif archive (nf)
archifau archives (npl)
archifdy archive office (nm)
archifol archival (adj)
archwiliad audit, investigation, survey (nm)
archwiliadau investigations (npl)
archwiliedig audited (adj)
archwilio to audit, to inspect (v)
archwiliwr auditor, examiner (nm)
archwiliwyd was/were examined (v)
archwilwyr auditors (npl)
archwilydd auditor (nm)
ardal district (nf)
ardaloedd areas (npl)
ardd garden

arddangos to exhibit, to reveal (v)
arddangosfa exhibition (nf)
arddangosfeydd exhibitions (npl)
arddangosiadau exhibitions (npl)
arddegau teens (npl)
arddel to accept, to acknowledge (v)
ardderchog excellent (adj)
arddull style (nf)
arddulliau styles (npl)
ardrethol rateable (adj)
ardrethu to tax (v)
ardystiad attestation, endorsement (nm)
ardystiedig attested (adj)
ardystio to attest, to certify, to endorse (v)
aredig to plough (v)
aren kidney (nf)
arennau kidneys (npl)
arestio to arrest (v)
arf tool, weapon (nm)
arfaeth God's design, purpose (nf)
arfaethedig intended, proposed (adj)
arfarniad evaluation (nm)
arfarnu to evaluate (v)
arfau arms, weapons (npl)
arfer custom, habit (nm)
arfer to be accustomed (to), to get used to, to use (v)
arferadwy accustomed, usual (adj)
arferai he/she/it used to (v)
arferiad custom (nm)
arferion customs (npl)
arferol usual (adj)
arfog armed (adj)
arfor coastal (adj)
arfordir coast (nm)
arfordirol coastal (adj)
argae dam, embankment (nm)
argaeledd availability (nm)
arglwydd lord, peer [of the realm], the Lord (nm)
arglwyddes lady (nf)
arglwyddi lords (npl)

arglwyddiaeth lordship (*nf*)
argraff impression (*nf*)
argraffadwy impressionable (*adj*)
argraffiad edition, imprint (*nm*)
argraffiadau impressions (*npl*)
argraffu to impress, to impress upon, to print (*v*)
argraffwr printer [person] (*nm*)
argraffwyd was/were printed (*v*)
argraffydd printer [machine] (*nm*)
argyfwng crisis, emergency (*nm*)
argyfyngau crises, emergencies (*npl*)
argyhoeddedig convinced (*adj*)
argyhoeddi to convince (*v*)
argyhoeddiad conviction (*nm*)
argymell to recommend, to urge (*v*)
argymhelliad exhortation, recommendation (*nm*)
argymhellion recommendations (*npl*)
argymhellir is/are/will be recommended (*v*)
argymhellodd he/she/it recommended (*v*)
argymhellwyd he/she/it was recommended (*v*)
arholi to examine (*v*)
arholiad examination (*nm*)
arholiadau examinations (*npl*)
arholwr examiner (*nm*)
arholwyr examiners (*npl*)
arholydd examiner (*nm*)
arhosiad stay (*nm*)
arhosodd he/she/it stayed (*v*)
arial spirit, verve, vigour (*nm*)
arian silver (*nm*)
arian money (*nm*)
arian silver (*adj*)
Ariannin, yr Argentina
ariannol financial, monetary (*adj*)
ariannu to finance, to fund, to silver (*v*)
ariannwyd he/she/it was financed (*v*)
ariennir is/are/will be financed (*v*)
arlein online (*advb*)

ar-lein online, on-line (*adj*)
arlliw shade, trace, vestige (*nm*)
arllwys to pour (*v*)
arloesedd innovation (*nm*)
arloesi to innovate, to pioneer (*v*)
arloesol innovative, pioneering (*adj*)
arlunio to draw, to paint (*v*)
arlunwyr artists (*npl*)
arlunydd artist (*nm*)
arlwyo to cater, to prepare (*v*)
arlywydd president (*nm*)
arna' on me (*prep*)
arnaf on me (*prep*)
arnat on you (*prep*)
arni on her (*prep*)
arno on him (*prep*)
arnoch on you (*prep*)
arnom on us (*prep*)
arnon on them (*prep*)
arnyn on them (*prep*)
arnynt on them (*prep*)
arogl smell (*nm*)
arolwg survey (*nm*)
arolygiad inspection (*nm*)
arolygiadau inspections (*npl*)
arolygiaeth inspectorate, supervision (*nf*)
arolygol supervisory (*adj*)
arolygon inspections (*npl*)
arolygu to supervise, to superintend (*v*)
arolygwr inspector, supervisor (*nm*)
arolygwyd was/were inspected (*v*)
arolygwyr inspectors (*npl*)
arolygydd inspector, superintendent, supervisor (*nm*)
aros to remain, to stay, to stop, to wait, to wait (for) (*v*)
arswyd terror (*nm*)
arswydus fearful, horrific, terrible (*adj*)
arsylw observation (*nm*)
arsylwadau observations (*npl*)
arsylwi to observe (*v*)
arteffact artefact (*nm*)

arteffactau artefacts (*npl*)

arth bear (*nf*)

arthritis arthritis (*nm*)

artiffisial artificial (*adj*)

artist artist (*nm*)

artistiaid artists (*npl*)

artistig artistic (*adj*)

aruthrol immense, terrific, tremendous (*adj*)

arw rough

arwain to conduct, to lead (*v*)

arweiniad guidance, leadership (*nm*)

arweiniodd he/she/it led (*v*)

arweiniol introductory, leading (*adj*)

arweinwyr leaders (*npl*)

arweinydd conductor, leader (*nm*)

arweinyddiaeth leadership (*nf*)

arweinyddion conductors (*npl*)

arwerthiant auction (*nm*)

arwr hero (*nm*)

arwres heroine (*nf*)

arwydd portent, sign, symbol (*nm*)

arwyddion signs (*npl*)

arwyddo to sign, to signify (*v*)

arwyddocâd significance (*nm*)

arwyddocaol significant (*adj*)

arwyddwyd was/were signed (*v*)

arwyneb face, surface (*nm*)

arwynebau surfaces (*npl*)

arwynebedd area, surface (*nm*)

arwynebol superficial (*adj*)

arwyr heroes (*npl*)

AS MP, MS (*nm*)

ASau MPs, MSs (*npl*)

asbestos asbestos (*nm*)

ased asset (*nm*)

asedau assets (*npl*)

asedion assets (*npl*)

aseiniad assignment (*nm*)

aseiniadau assignments (*npl*)

asesiad assessment (*nm*)

asesiadau assignments (*npl*)

asesir is/are/will be assessed (*v*)

asesu to assess (*v*)

aseswr assessor (*nm*)

aseswyd was/were assessed

aseswyr assessors (*npl*)

asesydd assessor (*nm*)

asgell fin, flank, wing (*nf*)

asgwrn bone (*nm*)

Asiaidd Asian (*adj*)

asiant agent (*nm*)

asiantaeth agency (*nf*)

asiantaethau agencies (*npl*)

asiantau agents (*npl*)

asid acid (*nm*)

asidau acids (*npl*)

astud diligent, intense (*adj*)

astudiaeth study (*nf*)

astudiaethau studies (*npl*)

astudio to study (*v*)

astudir is/are/will be studied (*v*)

astudiwyd was/were studied (*v*)

asyn ass (*nm*)

at for, for [the purpose of], to, towards, (up) to (*prep*)

ataf to me (*prep*)

atafaelu to distrain, to sequester (*v*)

atal to keep back, to prevent, to staunch (*v*)

atal impediment, stammer (*nm*)

ataliol preventative, repressive (*adj*)

atalnodi to punctuate (*v*)

atat to you (*prep*)

atborth feedback (*nm*)

ateb to answer, to reply (*v*)

ateb answer, reply, solution (*nm*)

atebion answers (*npl*)

atebodd he/she/it answered (*v*)

atebol accountable, responsible (*adj*)

atebolrwydd responsibility, accountability (*nm*)

atebwch you answer (*v*)

atebwyr respondents (*npl*)

atebydd respondent (*nm*)

ategol ancillary, corroborative (*adj*)
ategu to attach, to confirm, to support (*v*)
atgof reminiscence (*nm*)
atgoffa to remind (*v*)
atgofion reminiscences (*npl*)
atgyfnerthu to reinforce, to strengthen (*v*)
atgyfodiad resurrection, Resurrection (*nm*)
atgynhyrchu to reproduce (*v*)
atgynhyrchwyd was/were reproduced (*v*)
atgyweiriad repair (*nm*)
atgyweiriadau repairs (*npl*)
atgyweirio to repair, to restore (*v*)
athrawes [female] teacher (*nf*)
athrawiaeth doctrine (*nf*)
athrawon teachers (*npl*)
athro professor, [male] teacher (*nm*)
athrofa academy, college (*nf*)
athroniaeth philosophy (*nf*)
athronyddol philosophical (*adj*)
athrylith genius (*nf*)
ati to her (*prep*)
atlas atlas (*nm*)
atmosffer atmosphere (*nm*)
ato to him (*prep*)
atoch to you (*prep*)
atodiad appendix, supplement (*nm*)
atodiadau supplements (*npl*)
atodlen schedule (*nf*)
atodol additional, supplementary (*adj*)
atom atom (*nm*)
atom to us (*prep*)
atomau atoms (*npl*)
atyn to them (*prep*)
atyniad attraction (*nm*)
atyniadau attractions (*npl*)
atyniadol attractive, engaging (*adj*)
atynt to them (*prep*)
au false
aur gold (*nm*)
aur golden (*adj*)
awch keenness, relish, sharpness (*nm*)
awdit audit (*nm*)

awdl poem (*nf*)
awdur author (*nm*)
awdurdod authority (*nm*)
awdurdodaeth jurisdiction (*nf*)
awdurdodau authorities (*npl*)
awdurdodedig authorized (*adj*)
awdurdodi to authorize (*v*)
awdurdodiad authorization (*nm*)
awdurdodir is/are/will be authorized (*v*)
awdurdodol authoritative (*adj*)
awdurdodwyd was/were authorized (*v*)
awdures authoress (*nf*)
awduron authors (*npl*)
awel breeze (*nf*)
awen muse (*nf*)
awen rein (*nf*)
awenau reins (*npl*)
awgrym suggestion (*nm*)
awgryma he/she/it will suggest (*v*)
awgrymiadau suggestions (*npl*)
awgrymir is/are/will be suggested (*v*)
awgrymodd he/she/it suggested (*v*)
awgrymu to intimate, to suggest (*v*)
awgrymwyd was/were suggested (*v*)
awn we shall go (*v*)
awn let's go (*v*)
awr hour, time (*nf*)
Awst August (*nm*)
Awstralasia Australasia
Awstralia Australia
Awstria Austria
awtistiaeth autism (*nf*)
awtomatig automatic (*adj*)
awydd desire (*nm*)
awyddus eager (*adj*)
awyr air, sky (*nf*)
awyren aeroplane (*nf*)
awyrennau aeroplanes (*npl*)
awyrgylch atmosphere (*nm*)
awyrlu air force (*nm*)
awyru to air, to ventilate (*v*)
a.y.b. etc. (*abbr*)

B

a word printed in blue means that the root form of that word begins with **p**, e.g. **babell** root **pabell**

ba what, which
baban baby (*nm*)
babanod babies (*npl*)
babell tent
babi baby (*nm*)
babi poppy
bach hinge, hook (*nm*)
bach dear, small (*adj*)
bach nook (*nf*)
bachgen boy (*nm*)
bachyn hook (*nm*)
baco tobacco (*nm*)
bacteria bacteria (*npl*)
bae bay (*nm*)
bae wage
baech were you to (*v*)
baent were they to (*v*)
baent paint
bag bag (*nm*)
bagiau bags (*npl*)
baglu to stumble, to trip (*v*)
bai blame, fault (*nm*)
bai were he/she to (*v*)
baich burden, load (*nm*)
balans balance (*nm*)
balch pleased, proud, vain (*adj*)
balchder pleasure, pride (*nm*)
ban place, region, summit (*nf*)
banc bank [money; slope] (*nm*)
banciau banks (*npl*)
bancio to bank (*v*)
band band [group; strip] (*nm*)
bandiau bands (*npl*)

banel panel
baner flag, pennant (*nf*)
baneri flags (*npl*)
bannau peaks (*npl*)
bant away, off (*adv*)
bant depression, dip, valley
bapur paper
bapurau papers
bar bar (*nm*)
bâr pair
bara bread (*nm*)
bara to last
baragraff paragraph
baragraffau paragraphs
baratoi to prepare
baratowyd was/were prepared
barau pairs
barc park
barch respect
barchu to respect
barchus respectable
barcio to park
barcud kite (*nm*)
bardd poet (*nm*)
barddas poetics (*nf*)
barddol bardic, poetic (*adj*)
barddoniaeth poetry (*nf*)
barddonol poetic(al) (*adj*)
bargen bargain (*nf*)
barhad continuation
barhaodd he/she/it continued
barhaol continuous
barhau continue

23

barhaus continuous
bariau bars (*npl*)
barn judgement, opinion (*nf*)
barnau judgements (*npl*)
barnu to judge, to think, to try (*v*)
barnwr judge (*nm*)
barnwriaeth judiciary (*nf*)
barnwrol judicial (*adj*)
barnwyr judges (*npl*)
barod ready
barodd he/she/it lasted
barti party
bartïon parties
bartner partner
bartneriaeth partnership
bartneriaethau partnerships
bartneriaid partners
bas bass (*adj*)
basa(i) he/she/it would (*v*)
basbort passport
bas dwbl double-bass (*nm*)
basged basket (*nf*)
basio to pass
baswn I would (*v*)
bath minted (*adj*)
bàth bath (*nm*)
bathodyn badge (*nm*)
batri battery (*nm*)
batrwm pattern
batrymau patterns
baw dirt, excrement (*nm*)
bawb everyone
bawd big toe, thumb (*nf*)
bawn were I to (*v*)
Beca Rebecca
bechan little (*adj/f*)
bechgyn boys (*npl*)
bechod sin
bechodau sins
becyn package
becynnau packages
bedair four

bedd grave (*nm*)
beddau graves (*npl*)
bedol horseshoe
bedw birch (*npl*)
bedwar four
bedwaredd fourth
bedwerydd fourth
bedydd baptism (*nm*)
bedyddio to baptize, to christen (*v*)
Bedyddiwr Baptist (*nm*)
Bedyddwyr Baptists (*npl*)
Beibl Bible, Scripture (*nm*)
Beiblaidd Biblical, Scriptural (*adj*)
beic bicycle, bike (*nm*)
beichiau burdens (*npl*)
beichiog pregnant (*adj*)
beichiogi to become pregnant, to cause to be pregnant, to conceive (*v*)
beichiogrwydd pregnancy (*nm*)
beiciau bicycles (*npl*)
beicio to cycle (*v*)
beidio to stop
beili bailiff (*nm*)
beili bailey, farmyard (*nm*)
beilot pilot
beintio to paint
beirdd poets (*npl*)
beiriannau machines
beiriant machine
beirniad adjudicator, critic (*nm*)
beirniadaeth adjudication, criticism (*nf*)
beirniadol critical (*adj*)
beirniadu to adjudicate, to criticize (*v*)
beirniaid adjudicators (*npl*)
bêl ball
bêl-droed football
belen ball
bell far
bellach further
bellaf furthest
belled as far
bellter distance

ben head
benaethiaid heads
benawdau headlines
bencadlys headquarters
bencampwriaeth championship
bendant definite
benderfyniad decision
benderfyniadau decisions
benderfynodd he/she/it decided
benderfynol determined
benderfynu to decide
benderfynwyd was/were decided
bendigedig blessed, fantastic, lovely (*adj*)
bendith blessing, grace (*nf*)
bendithion blessings (*npl*)
bennaeth head
bennaf primarily
bennill verse
bennir is/are specified
bennod chapter
bennu to specify
bennwyd was/were specified
benodedig specified
benodi to appoint
benodiad appontment
benodiadau appointments
benodir is appointed
benodol specific
benodwyd was/were appointed
bensaernïaeth architecture
bensiwn pension
bensiynwyr pensioners
benthyca to borrow, to lend (*v*)
benthyciad issue, loan (*nm*)
benthyciadau loans (*npl*)
benthyg to borrow (*v*)
bentref village
bentrefi villages
benwythnos weekend
benyw female, woman (*nf*)
benyw female (*adj*)
benywaidd feminine (*adj*)

benywod females, women (*npl*)
ber short (*adj/f*)
berchen owner
berchennog owner
berchenogion owners
bererindod pilgrimage
berf verb (*nf*)
berfau verbs (*npl*)
berffaith perfect
berfformiad performance
berfformiadau performances
berfformio to perform
beri to cause
bernir is/are/will be judged (*v*)
berson parson; person
bersonau parsons; persons
bersonél personnel
bersonol personal
bersonoliaeth personality
berswadio persuade
berthnasau relations
berthnasol relevant
berthyn to belong
berthynai he/she/it belonged
berthynas relationship
berw boiling, turmoil (*nm*)
berw boiled, boiling (*adj*)
berwi to boil (*v*)
berygl danger
beryglon dangers
beryglu to endanger
beryglus dangerous
beth what
bethau things
betio to bet (*v*)
betrol petrol
betys beet (*npl*)
beudy cowshed (*nm*)
beunydd every day (*adv*)
beunyddiol daily, everyday (*adj*)
bibell pipe
bibellau pipes

bid be that *(v)*
big beak
bil bill [of charges;legislative] *(nm)*
biliau bills [of charges;legislative] *(npl)*
biliwn billion *(nm)*
bin bin *(nm)*
bioamrywiaeth biodiversity *(nf)*
bioleg biology *(nf)*
biolegol biological *(adj)*
bisgedi biscuits *(npl)*
biwrocratiaeth bureaucracy *(nf)*
bla plague
blaen front, point, tip *(nm)*
blaen front *(adj)*
blaenaf foremost *(adj)*
blaenau fronts *(npl)*
blaendal deposit *(nm)*
blaenddalen title page *(nf)*
blaengar progressive, innovative,
    prominent *(adj)*
blaenllaw conspicuous, progressive,
    prominent *(adj)*
blaenoriaeth precedence, priority *(nf)*
blaenoriaethau priorities *(npl)*
blaenoriaethu to prioritise *(v)*
blaenorol foregoing, previous *(adj)*
blaid party
blaned planet
blanhigion plants
blanhigyn plant
blannu to plant
blant children
blas taste *(nm)*
blas mansion
blastig plastic
blasu to taste *(v)*
blasus tasty *(adj)*
blawd flour, meal *(nm)*
ble where *(adv)*
bleidiau parties
bleidlais vote
bleidleisiau votes

bleidleisio to vote
blentyn child
blêr untidy *(adj)*
bleser pleasure
blew hair *(npl)*
blewyn blade of grass, hair, whisker *(nm)*
blin cross, sorry, troubled, troublesome
    (adj)
blinder fatigue, tiredness *(nm)*
blinedig tired, tiring *(adj)*
blino to tire, to trouble *(v)*
bloc block *(nm)*
blociau blocks *(npl)*
blodau flowers *(npl)*
blodeuo to flourish, to flower *(v)*
blodyn flower *(nm)*
bloeddio to shout, to yell *(v)*
blwch box *(nm)*
blwm lead [metal]
blwydd year(s) old *(nf)*
blwyddlyfr yearbook *(nm)*
blwyddyn year *(nf)*
blwyf parish
blychau boxes *(npl)*
blygu to bend, to fold
blynedd years *(npl)*
blynyddoedd years *(npl)*
blynyddol annual, yearly *(adj)*
bo he/she/it may be *(v)*
bob every
bob baked
bobl people
bobloedd peoples
boblogaeth population
boblogaidd popular
boced pocket
boch cheek [face] *(nf)*
boch you may be *(v)*
bocs box, tin can *(nm)*
bocsys boxes *(npl)*
bod to be, to matter *(v)*
bod being, existence *(nm)*

bodau beings (*npl*)
bodd consent, favour, pleasure (*nm*)
boddau pleasure(s) (*npl*)
boddhad gratification, satisfaction (*nm*)
boddhaol satisfactory (*adj*)
boddi to drown, to swamp (*v*)
bodlon content, satisfied, willing (*adj*)
bodloni to acquiesce, to satisfy (*v*)
bodlonrwydd satisfaction (*nm*)
bodolaeth existence (*nf*)
bodolai he/she/it would exist (*v*)
bodoli to exist (*v*)
boed let it be (*v*)
boen pain
boeni to worry
boenus painful
boeth hot
boi boy (*nm*)
bois boys (*npl*)
bol stomach (*nm*)
bolisi policy
bolisïau policies
bom bomb (*nm*)
bôn base, stem (*nm*)
bond bond (*nm*)
bondiau bonds (*npl*)
bonedd gentry, nobility (*nm*)
boneddigion gentlemen (*npl*)
bonheddig courteous, gentle, noble (*adj*)
bont bridge
bonws bonus (*nm*)
bopeth everything
bord table (*nf*)
bore a.m., morning (*nm*)
bore early (*adj*)
boreau mornings (*npl*)
borfa grass
bori to browse, to graze
borth porch, port
bosibiliadau possibilities
bosibilrwydd possibility
bosibl possible

bositif positive
bost boast (*nf*)
bost post
bostio to boast (*v*)
bostio to post
botel bottle
botensial potential
botwm button (*nm*)
botymau buttons (*npl*)
braf ample, fine (*adj*)
braich arm; spoke (*nf*)
braidd hardly, rather, scarcely (*adv*)
braidd congregation, flock
brain crows (*npl*)
braint privilege (*nf*)
brân crow (*nf*)
bras coarse, fat, general, large, rich (*adj*)
bras bunting (bird) (*nm*)
brasgamu to lope, to stride (*v*)
braslun sketch (*nm*)
braster fat, fat (of the land), richness (*nm*)
brau brittle, fragile (*adj*)
braw fright (*nm*)
brawd brother, friend, friar (*nm*)
brawddeg sentence (*nf*)
brawddegau sentences (*npl*)
brawf proof, test
brawychus terrible (*adj*)
brechdan sandwich, slice of bread and butter (*nf*)
brechdanau sandwiches (*npl*)
brechiad inoculation, vaccination (*nm*)
brechu to inoculate, to vaccinate (*v*)
brecwast breakfast (*nm*)
bregeth sermon
bregethu to preach
bregus brittle, flimsy (*adj*)
breichiau arms (*npl*)
breifat private
breinio to bless, to favour (*v*)
bren wood, wooden
brenhines queen, queen-bee (*nf*)

brenhiniaeth realm, sovereignty (*nf*)
brenhinoedd kings (*npl*)
brenhinol regal, royal (*adj*)
brenin king (*nm*)
bres brass, money
bresennol present
bresenoldeb presence
brest chest (*nf*)
breswyl residential
breswylwyr residents
breswylydd dweller, resident
breuddwyd daydream, dream (*nf*)
breuddwydio to daydream, to dream (*v*)
breuddwydion dreams (*npl*)
bri honour, respect (*nm*)
briciau bricks (*npl*)
brics bricks (*npl*)
bricsen brick (*nf*)
brîd breed (*nm*)
bridd soil
bridio to breed (*v*)
brif main
brifddinas capital city
brîff brief (*nm*)
briffio to brief (*v*)
briffordd main road
brifo to hurt (*v*)
brifwyl Eisteddfod
brifysgol university
brifysgolion universities
brig peak, top (*nm*)
brigâd brigade (*nf*)
brigau twigs (*npl*)
brin scarce
brinder scarcity
brint print
brintio to print
briod husband, married, wife
briodas wedding
briodasol wedding
briodi to marry
briodol appropriate

briodoli to attribute
briodweddau characteristics
bris price
brisiau prices
brisio to price, to value
brith abundant, dubious, mottled, numerous, shady, speckled, (*adj*)
brithyll trout (*nm*)
briw cut, sore, wound (*nm*)
bro region, vale (*nf*)
broblem problem
broblemau problems
brocer broker (*nm*)
brocer poker
brodor native (*nm*)
brodorion natives (*npl*)
brodorol indigenous (*adj*)
brodyr brothers (*npl*)
broffesiynol professional
broffil profile
brofi to experience, to prove
brofiad experience
brofiadau experiences
brofiadol experienced
brofion tests
brofwyd was/were experienced, proved
bron breast [also of hill], heart (*nf*)
bron almost, nearly (*adv*)
bronnau breasts (*npl*)
broses process
brosesau processes
brosesu to process
brosiect project
brosiectau projects
brotest protest
brown brown (*adj*)
broydd areas, vales (*npl*)
brwd enthusiastic, heated (*adj*)
brwdfrydedd enthusiasm (*nm*)
brwdfrydig fervent (*adj*)
brwnt cruel, dirty, grubby, nasty, smutty (*adj*)

Brwsel Brussels
brwsh brush (*nm*)
brwydr battle (*nf*)
brwydrau battles (*npl*)
brwydro to fight (*v*)
brwyn rushes (*npl*)
Brycheiniog Brecon(shire)
bryd aim, intent (*nm*)
bryd meal
brydau meals
bryddest poem
bryder concern
bryderon worries
bryderus concerned
brydferth beautiful
brydferthwch beauty
brydiau times
brydles lease
brydlon punctual
bryn hill (*nm*)
bryngaer hillfort (*nf*)
brynhawn afternoon
bryniau hills (*npl*)
brynu to buy
brynwyd was/were purchased
brynwyr buyers
brys haste, urgency (*nm*)
Bryste Bristol
bu he/she/it was (*v*)
buan fast, swift (*adj*)
buasai he/she/it would have (*v*)
buaswn I would have (*v*)
buches herd (*nf*)
buchod cows (*npl*)
budd benefit (*nm*)
budd-dal benefit (*nm*)
budd-daliadau benefits (*npl*)
budd-ddeiliad stakeholder (*nm*)
budd-ddeiliaid stakeholders (*npl*)
buddiannau interests, welfare (*npl*)
buddiant interest (*nm*)
buddiol beneficial (*adj*)

buddiolwr beneficiary (*nm*)
buddiolwyr beneficiaries (*npl*)
buddion benefits (*npl*)
buddsoddi to invest (*v*)
buddsoddiad investment (*nm*)
buddsoddiadau investments (*npl*)
buddsoddwr investor (*nm*)
buddsoddwyr investors (*npl*)
buddugol victorious (*adj*)
buddugoliaeth victory (*nf*)
budr dirty, filthy, smutty (*adj*)
bugail pastor, shepherd (*nm*)
bugeiliol pastoral (*adj*)
bum five
bûm I was (*v*)
bumed fifth
bump five
bunnau pounds
bunnoedd pounds
bunt pound
buoch you have been (*v*)
buodd he/she/it has been (*v*)
buom we have been (*v*)
buont they have been (*v*)
bur pure
busnes business (*nm*)
busnesau businesses (*npl*)
buwch cow (*nf*)
bwerau powers
bwlch gap, pass (*nm*)
bwlio to bully (*v*)
bwll pit, pool
bwnc subject
bwrdd board, deck, plank, table (*nm*)
bwrdeistref borough, municipality (*nf*)
bwriad intention (*nm*)
bwriadau intentions (*npl*)
bwriadol intentional (*adj*)
bwriadu to intend (*v*)
bwriadwn we are intending (*v*)
bwriadwyd was/were intended (*v*)
bwriedir is intended (*v*)

bwrlwm bubble, bubbling (*nm*)
bwrpas purpose
bwrpasau purposes
bwrpasol purpously
bwrw to cast, to drop, to give birth to, to hit, to rain, to snow, to throw (*v*)
bws bus, omnibus (*nm*)
bwthyn cottage (*nm*)
bwy who, whom
bwyd food (*nm*)
bwydlen menu (*nf*)
bwydo to feed (*v*)
bwydydd foodstuffs (*npl*)
bwyllgor committee
bwyllgorau committees
bwynt point
bwyntiau points
bwys importance, pound
bwysau pounds, weight
bwysicach more important
bwysicaf most important
bwysig important
bwysigrwydd importance
bwyslais emphasis
bwysleisio to emphasise
bwyso to weigh
bwyta to eat (*v*)
bwytai he/she/it ate (*v*)
bwyty café, restaurant (*nm*)
bwyty you eat, you will eat (*v*)
bychan junior, little, small, unimportant (*adj*)
bychan little one (*nm*)
byd earth, globe, non-Christians, planet, world (*nm*)
bydd he/she/it will (*v*)
bydda I shall, I will (*v*)
byddaf I shall, I will (*v*)
byddai he/she/it would (*v*)
byddan they will (*v*)
byddant they will (*v*)
byddar deaf (*adj*)

bydde he/she/it would (*v*)
byddech you would (*v*)
bydded let there be (*v*)
byddem we would (*v*)
bydden they would (*v*)
byddent they would (*v*)
byddi you will (*v*)
byddid it would (*v*)
byddin army (*nf*)
byddo he/she/it might (*v*)
byddwch you will (*v*)
byddwn we shall, we will (*v*)
byd-eang global, universal, worldwide (*adj*)
bydol worldly (*adj*)
bydwragedd midwives (*npl*)
bydwraig midwife (*nf*)
bydwreigiaeth midwifery (*nf*)
bydysawd universe (*nm*)
bygwth to threaten (*v*)
bygythiad menace, threat (*nm*)
bygythiadau threats (*npl*)
bygythiol menacing (*adj*)
bylchau gaps (*npl*)
byllau pits, pools
bymtheg fifteen
bymthegfed fifteenth
bynciau subjects
bynnag ~ever [e.g. *beth bynnag* whatever] (*pronoun*)
byr short (*adj*)
byrddau boards, tables (*npl*)
byrder brevity, shortness (*nm*)
byrion short (*adj/pl*)
byrrach shorter (*adj*)
bys finger, latch, toe (*nm*)
bysedd fingers (*npl*)
bysellfwrdd keyboard (*nm*)
bysgod fish
bysgodfeydd fishery (*nf*)
bysgota to fish
bysgotwyr fishermen
bysiau buses (*npl*)

bysus buses (*npl*)
byth always, even, ever, never, still (*adv*)
bythefnos fortnight
bythynnod cottages (*npl*)
bytiau snippets
byw to live (*v*)
byw alive, live, lively (*adj*)

byw the living, the quick (*nm*)
byw live, living (*adj*)
bywiog lively, vivacious (*adj*)
bywoliaeth benefice, livelihood, living (*nf*)
bywyd life, lifetime, verve (*nm*)
bywydau lives (*npl*)

C

a word starting with **ch** printed in blue means that the root form of that word begins with **c**, e.g. **chadarn** root **cadarn**

Ch stands as a letter in its own right in Welsh. In a Welsh dictionary, unlike this list, words starting with, or containing 'ch' would commence after those containing **c**.

c p. (penny)
caban cabin (*nm*)
cabinet cabinet (*nm*)
cadair chair; udder (*nf*)
cadarn firm, strong (*adj*)
cadarnhad confirmation (*nm*)
cadarnhaodd he/she/it confirmed (*v*)
cadarnhaol affirmative, positive (*adj*)
cadarnhau to confirm, to ratify (*v*)
cadarnhawyd was/were confirmed (*v*)
cadeiriau chairs (*npl*)
cadeirio to chair (*v*)
cadeiriol chaired (*adj*)
cadeirlan cathedral (*nf*)
cadeirydd chairperson (*nm*)
cadeiryddiaeth chairmanship (*nf*)
cadeiryddion chairpersons (*npl*)
cadi sissy (*nm*)
cadw to keep, to observe, to save (*v*)
cadw reserved (*adj*)
cadwch you keep (*v*)
cadwedig saved (*adj*)
cadwraeth conservation (*nf*)
cadwraethol conservational (*adj*)
cadwyd was/were kept (*v*)
cadwyn chain (*nf*)
cadwyni chains (*npl*)

cae enclosure, field (*nm*)
cae he/she/it closes (*v*)
caead lid, shutter (*nm*)
caead to close (*v*)
caeau fields (*npl*)
caeedig closed (*adj*)
cael to allow, to discover, to have (*v*)
caer castle, fort, rampart (*nf*)
Caerdydd Cardiff
caeth addicted, captive, confined (*adj*)
caethiwed addiction, captivity (*nm*)
caf I have/I will have (*v*)
caffael to acquire (*v*)
caffaeliad acquisition (*nm*)
caffe café (*nm*)
caffi café (*nm*)
cafodd he/she/it had (*v*)
câi he/she/it would have (*v*)
caiff he/she/it will have (*v*)
cain fine, stylish (*adj*)
cainc air, branch, knot, strand (*nf*)
cais application, attempt, effort, quest, request; try (rugby) (*nm*)
cais he/she/it tries (*v*)
cal penis (*nf*)
calch lime, quicklime (*nm*)
calchfaen limestone (*nm*)
caled difficult, hard, severe (*adj*)
caledi adversity, hardship (*nm*)
caledwedd hardware (*nm*)
calendr calendar (*nm*)
Calfinaidd Calvinistic (*adj*)
call sane, sensible, smart, wise (*adj*)

calon centre, core, heart, spirit (*nf*)
calonnau hearts (*npl*)
calonogol encouraging, heartening (*adj*)
cam footfall, footprint, stage, step (*nm*)
cam wrong (*adj*)
cam bent, crooked, incorrect (*adj*)
camarweiniol misleading (*adj*)
camau steps (*npl*)
camddefnyddio to abuse, to misuse (*v*)
cam-drin to abuse, to ill-treat (*v*)
camdriniaeth abuse, ill-treatment (*nf*)
camera camera (*nm*)
camerâu cameras (*npl*)
camgymeriad mistake (*nm*)
camgymeriadau mistakes (*npl*)
camlas canal, channel (*nf*)
camlesi canals (*npl*)
camp feat, achievement, sport (*nf*)
camp lawn grand slam (*nf*)
campau feats, achievements, sports (*npl*)
campws campus (*nm*)
camu to pace, to step (*v*)
camu to bend, to distort (*v*)
camweinyddu to maladminister (*v*)
camymddwyn to misbehave (*v*)
can hundred
cân lyric, poem, song (*nf*)
cân he/she/it sings (*v*)
cancr canker (*nm*)
caneuon songs (*npl*)
canfod to discern, to perceive (*v*)
canfu he/she/it discovered, perceived (*v*)
canfuwyd was/were discovered, perceived (*v*)
canfyddiad perception (*nm*)
canfyddiadau perceptions (*npl*)
cangen bough, branch (*nf*)
canghellor chancellor (*nm*)
canghennau branches (*npl*)
canhwyllau candles (*npl*)
caniatâ he/she/it allows, permits (*v*)
caniatâd permission (*nm*)

caniataol granted (*adj*)
caniatáu to grant, to permit (*v*)
caniateir is/are/will be allowed, permitted (*v*)
canllaw guideline, handrail (*nm*)
canllawiau guidelines (*npl*)
canlyn to court, to go out with [romantically], to follow (*v*)
canlyniad conclusion, consequence, result (*nm*)
canlyniadau results (*npl*)
canlyniadol resultant (*adj*)
canlynol following (*adj*)
canmlwyddiant centenary (*nm*)
canmol to laud, to praise; to pat (*v*)
canmoliaeth praise (*nf*)
cannoedd hundreds (*npl*)
cannwyll candle (*nf*)
canodd he/she/it sang (*v*)
canol centre, middle, midriff, waist (*nm*)
canol mid, middle (*adj*)
canolbarth midlands (*nm*)
canolbwynt essence, focus (*nm*)
canolbwyntio to concentrate (*v*)
canoldir inland region, Mediterranean (*nm*)
canolfan centre (*nf*)
canolfannau centres (*npl*)
canoli to centralize, to mediate (*v*)
canolig mediocre, middling, moderate (*adj*)
canoloesol medieval (*adj*)
canolog basic, central (*adj*)
canolwr centre, intermediary, mediator, middleman (*nm*)
canon canon [church] (*nm*)
canon cannon [gun] (*nm*)
canran per cent, percentage (*nf*)
canrannau percentages (*npl*)
canrif century (*nf*)
canrifoedd centuries (*npl*)
canser cancer (*nm*)
canslo to cancel (*v*)
cant hundred, hundredweight (*nm*)

cantorion singers (*npl*)
canu to sing, to ring, to play (*v*)
canu poem, (the) singing (*nm*)
canwr player, singer (*nm*)
canwyd was/were sung (*v*)
canys because, since (*conjunction*)
cap cap (*nm*)
capel chapel (*nm*)
capeli chapels (*npl*)
capten captain (*nm*)
car car (*nm*)
câr kinsman, relative (*nm*)
carafán caravan (*nf*)
carafannau caravans (*npl*)
carbon carbon (*nm*)
carchar jail, prison (*nm*)
carchardai prisons (*npl*)
carcharor captive, prisoner (*nm*)
carcharorion prisoners (*npl*)
cardiau cards (*npl*)
caredig kind (*adj*)
caredigrwydd kindness (*nm*)
carfan beam, faction, rail (*nf*)
cariad love (*nm*)
cariad dear, love, lover, sweetheart (*nm*)
cariadon lovers (*npl*)
cario to bear, to carry (*v*)
carol carol (*nf*)
carolau carols (*npl*)
carped carpet (*nm*)
carreg pip, stone; testicle (*nf*)
carthffosiaeth drainage, sewerage (*nf*)
carthion excrement (*npl*)
cartref home (*nm*)
cartrefi homes (*npl*)
cartrefol at home, homely (*adj*)
caru to love (*v*)
cas hateful, nasty (*adj*)
cas case (*nm*)
cas he/she/it had (*v*)
casgliad abscess, collection, conclusion, gathering (*nm*)

casgliadau collections, conclusions (*npl*)
casglu to collect, to conclude, to congregate, to fester, to gather (*v*)
casglwyd was/were collected (*v*)
Casnewydd Newport
cast cast, prank, trick; caste (*nm*)
castell castle, rook [chess] (*nm*)
catalog catalogue (*nm*)
categori category (*nm*)
categorïau categories (*npl*)
cath cat (*nf*)
cathod cats (*npl*)
Catholig Roman Catholic (*adj*)
Catholigion Roman Catholics (*npl*)
cau to close, to fasten, to shut (*v*)
cau hollow (*adj*)
cawell basket, creel, hamper (*nm*)
cawl broth, soup, mess (*nm*)
cawn reeds, stubble (*npl*)
cawn we have, we will have (*v*)
cawod shower; mildew, rash (*nf*)
cawr giant (*nm*)
caws cheese (*nm*)
cawsai he/she/it had (*v*)
cawsant they had (*v*)
cawsoch you had (*v*)
cawsom we had (*v*)
cawson they had (*v*)
cebl cable (*nm*)
ceblau cables (*npl*)
cedwir is/are/will be kept (*v*)
cedyrn strong (*adj/pl*)
cefais I had (*v*)
ceffyl horse (*nm*)
ceffylau horses (*npl*)
cefn back, rear, reverse, ridge (*nm*)
cefnau backs (*npl*)
cefndir background, setting (*nm*)
cefndiroedd backgrounds (*npl*)
cefnog wealthy, well-off, well-to-do (*adj*)
cefnogaeth backing, support (*nf*)

cefnogi to encourage, to second, to support (v)
cefnogir is/are/will be supported (v)
cefnogol encouraging, supportive (adj)
cefnogwr supporter (nm)
cefnogwyr supporters (npl)
cefnu to desert, to withdraw (v)
ceg mouth (nm)
cegin kitchen (nf)
cei you have, you will have (v)
cei quay (nm)
ceid was/were to be found, had (v)
ceidwad keeper (nm)
ceidwadol conservative (adj)
ceidwadwr conservative (nm)
ceidwadwyr conservatives (npl)
ceiliog cockerel (nm)
ceiniog penny (nf)
ceir is to be found, had (v)
ceirch oats (npl)
ceirw deer (npl)
ceisiadau requests (npl)
ceisio to attempt, to seek, to try (v)
ceisiodd he/she/it attempted (v)
ceisiwch you attempt (v)
ceiswyr seekers (npl)
ceisydd applicant (npl)
celf art (nf)
celfi furniture, implements, tools (npl)
celfydd skilful (adj)
celfyddyd art (nf)
celfyddydau arts (npl)
celfyddydol artistic (adj)
cell cell (nf)
celli copse, grove (nf)
celloedd cells (npl)
Celt Celt (nm)
Celtaidd Celtic (adj)
Celtiaid Celts (npl)
celwydd lie (nm)
celyn holly (npl)
cemeg chemistry (nf)

cemegau chemicals (npl)
cemegol chemical (adj)
cen dandruff, flake, lichen, scale (nm)
cenedl gender; nation (nf)
cenedlaethau generations (npl)
cenedlaethol national, nationalistic (adj)
cenedlaetholdeb nationalism (nm)
cenedligrwydd nationhood (nm)
cenhadaeth mission (nf)
cenhedlaeth generation (nf)
cenhedloedd nations (npl)
cenhedlu to beget, to procreate (v)
cer you go (v)
cerbyd carriage, vehicle (nm)
cerbydau carriages, vehicles (npl)
cerdd music; poem (nf)
cerdded to move on, to walk (v)
cerddi poems (npl)
cerddodd he/she/it walked (v)
cerddor musician (nm)
cerddorfa orchestra (nf)
cerddoriaeth music (nf)
cerddorion musicians (npl)
cerddorol musical (adj)
cerddwr pedestrian, walker (nm)
cerddwyr pedestrians, walkers (npl)
cerdyn card (nm)
cerflun sculpture, statue (nm)
cerrig stones (npl)
cerrynt current (nm)
ces I had, received (v)
cesglir is/are/will be collected (v)
cestyll castles (npl)
cewc estimation, peep (nm)
cewch you have, you will have (v)
chadarn mighty, strong
chadarnhau to confirm
chadeirydd chairman
chadw to keep
chadwraeth conservation
chaeau fields
chael to have

chaer fort
chafodd he/she/it had
chaiff he/she/it has, he/she/it will have
chais request
chalon heart
cham pace, step
chamau steps
chamddefnyddio to misuse
chan to have
chân song
chanfod to perceive
chaniatâd permission
chaniatáu to permit
chaniateir is/are/will be allowed, permitted
chanllawiau guidelines, rails
chanlyniad result
chanlyniadau results
chanol centre, middle
chanolbarth midland
chanolbwyntio centre, focus
chanolfan centre
chanolfannau centres
chanolig middling
chanser cancer
chant hundred
chânt they shall
chanu to sing
chap cap
char car
chardiau cards
chariad love
chartref home
chartrefi homes
chasgliad conclusion
chasgliadau conclusions
chasglu to collect
chastell castle, rook [chess]
chau to close
chawn we have/we will have
chawsant they had
chawsom we had

chdi you (*pronoun*)
chedwir is/are/will be kept
chefais I had
chefn back
chefndir background
chefnogaeth support
chefnogi to support
cheg mouth
cheir is to be had
cheisiadau requests
cheisio to seek
chenedl gender, nation
chenedlaethol national
cherbydau carriages, vehicles
cherdded to walk
cherddi poems
cherddoriaeth music
cherrig stones
chewch you will have
chi you (*pronoun*)
chi dog
chig meat
chithau even you, you on the other hand, you too (*pronoun*)
chladdu to bury
chlefyd disease, fever
chleifion patients
chludiant transport
chludo to carry, to transport
chlybiau clubs
chlywed to hear
chlywodd he/she/it heard
chodi to lift, to raise
chodir is/are/will be raised
chododd he/she/it lifted, raised
choed trees, wood
choedwigaeth forestry
choetiroedd woodlands
chofio to remember
chofnodi to record
chofnodion minutes, records
chofrestru to register

choleg college
cholegau colleges
cholledion losses
cholli to lose
chontractwyr contractors
chopi copy
chopïo to copy
chorff body
chost cost
chrefft craft
chrefydd religion
chrefyddol religious
chreu to create
chriw crew
chronfeydd reserves, reservoirs
chryfhau to strengthen
chryn quite
chwaneg more
chwblhau to complete
chwe six (*num*)
chwech six (*num*)
chweched sixth (*ordinal num*)
chwedegau sixties (*num*)
chwedl fable, story, tale (*nf*)
chwedlau tales (*npl*)
chwedlonol fabulous, legendary, mythical (*adj*)
Chwefror February (*nm*)
chweil (worth) while (*adv*)
chwerthin to laugh (*v*)
chwerthin laugh, laughter (*nm*)
chwerw acrid, bitter (*nm*)
chwestiwn question
chwestiynau questions
chwi you (*pronoun*)
chwifio to brandish, to wave (*v*)
chwilen beetle (*nf*)
chwilfrydedd curiosity (*nm*)
chwiliad search (*nm*)
chwiliadau searches (*npl*)
chwilio to examine, to search (*v*)
chwiliwch you search, you will search (*v*)

chwilod beetles (*npl*)
chwilota to rummage, to search (*v*)
chwim fleet, nimble, swift (*adj*)
chwiorydd sisters (*npl*)
chwisiau quizzes
chwistrellu to inject, to spray, to squirt (*v*)
chwith amiss, awkward, left, offended, sad, strange (*adj*)
chwith the left (*nm*)
chwithau even you, you on the other hand, you too (*pronoun*)
chwithig clumsy, strange (*adj*)
chwm valley
chwmni company
chwmnïau companies
chwmpas compass
chwrdd meeting, service
chwrs course
chwsmeriaid customers
chwyddiant distension, inflation (*nm*)
chwyddo to become puffed up, to swell, to zoom (*v*)
chwyldro revolution (*nm*)
chwyldroadol revolutionary (*nm*)
chwyn weeds (*npl*)
chwynion complaints
chwyrn heated, vigorous (*npl*)
chwys perspiration, sweat (*nm*)
chwythu to blow, to blow up, to puff (*v*)
chychwyn to start
chyd together
chyda with
chydag with
chydlynu to coordinate
chydnabod to acknowledge
chydsyniad agreement
chydweithio to cooperate
chydweithrediad cooperation
chydymffurfio to conform
chyfanrwydd entirety
chyfansoddi to compose
chyfansoddiad composition

chyfanswm total
chyfarfod meeting
chyfarfodydd meetings
chyfarpar equipment
chyfartaledd average, proportion
chyfarwyddiadau directions
chyfarwyddwr director
chyfarwyddyd direction, instruction
chyfathrebu to communicate
chyfeillion friends
chyfeiriad address, direction
chyfeiriadau addresses, directions
chyfeirio to direct
chyfer for, headlong
chyffro excitement
chyffrous exciting
chyffuriau drugs
chyfiawnder justice
chyfiawnhau to justify
chyfieithu to translate
chyflawni to complete
chyfle opportunity
chyflenwi to supply
chyflenwyr suppliers
chyfleoedd opportunities
chyfleu to convey
chyfleus convenient
chyfleusterau conveniences, facilities
chyflog wage
chyflogaeth employment
chyflogau wages
chyflogi to employ
chyflogwyr employers
chyflwr condition
chyflwyniad presentation
chyflwyno to present
chyflwynwyd was/were presented
chyfnewid to exchange
chyfnod period
chyfnodau periods
chyfoes contemporary
chyfoeth wealth

chyfradd rate
chyfraddau rates
chyfraith law
chyfran share
chyfraniad contribution
chyfraniadau contributions
chyfrannu to contribute
chyfreithiwr lawyer
chyfres series
chyfrif account
chyfrifoldeb responsibility
chyfrifoldebau duties, responsibilities
chyfrifon accounts
chyfryngau media
chyfyngiadau restrictions
chyfyngu to restrict
chyhoeddi to publish
chyhoeddiadau publication
chyhoeddus public
chyhoeddusrwydd publicity
chyhoeddwyd was/were published
chylch circle
chylchgronau magazines
chyllid finance
chyllido to finance
chymaint as much
chymdeithas society
chymdeithasau societies
chymdeithasol social
chymeradwyo to recommend
chymeriad character
chymeriadau characters
chymerodd he/she/it took
chymerwyd was/were taken
chymharu to compare
chymhelliant motivation, motive
chymhleth complex
chymhwyso to adjust
chymhwyster qualifications
chymorth help, support
chymryd to take, to hold
chymuned community

chymunedau communities
chymunedol community
chymwysterau qualifications
chyn before
chynefinoedd habitats
chynghorau councils
chynghori to advise
chynghorwyr advisers, councillors
chynghorydd advisor, councillor
chyngor advice, council
chynhaliaeth support, sustenance
chynhaliwyd was/were held, supported
chynhelir is/are/will be held
chynhwysfawr comprehensive
chynhwysir is/are/will be contained
chynhyrchion products
chynhyrchu to produce
chynigion attempts, proposals
chynllun plan
chynlluniau plans
chynllunio to plan
chynnal to support
chynnig proposal
chynnwys contains, content
chynnydd increase
chynnyrch produce, product
chynorthwyo to support
chynrychiolaeth representation
chynrychiolydd representative
chynulliad assembly, group
chynyddu to increase
chyrff bodies
chyrhaeddiad reach
chyrraedd to arrive
chyrsiau courses
chysgu to sleep
chyson constant
chysondeb consistency
chyswllt contact
chysylltiad link
chysylltiadau contacts
chysylltu to link, to contact

chytundeb agreement, contract
chytundebau agreements, contracts
chytuno to agree
chytunwyd was/were agreed
chywir correct
chywirdeb accuracy
ci dog (*nm*)
cic kick (*nf*)
cicio to kick (*v*)
cig meat (*nf*)
cil corner, eclipse, nook, retreat, waning (*nm*)
cilio to ebb, to languish, to pass, to recede, to retreat, to shrink, to wane (*v*)
cilometr kilometre (*nm*)
cinio dinner, lunch (*nm*)
cip glimpse (*nm*)
cipio to snatch, to take, to win (*v*)
cipolwg glance, glimpse (*nm*)
cist chest, coffin (*nf*)
ciwbig cubic, cubical (*adj*)
claddfa cemetery, graveyard (*nf*)
claddu to bury, to inter (*v*)
claddwyd was/were buried (*v*)
claf ill, sick (*adj*)
claf invalid, patient (*nm*)
clai clay (*nm*)
clas cloister (*nm*)
clasurol classic, classical (*adj*)
clawdd ditch, dyke, gutter, hedge (*nm*)
clawr board, cover, lid, surface (*nm*)
clebran to chatter, to gossip (*v*)
clecs gossip (*npl*)
cleddyf cleat, sword (*nm*)
clefyd disease, illness, infection (*nm*)
clefydau diseases (*npl*)
cleient client (*nm*)
cleientau clients (*npl*)
cleientiaid clients (*npl*)
cleifion patients (*npl*)
clerc clerk (*nm*)
clicio to click (*v*)

cliciwch you click (v)

clinic clinic (nm)

clinigau clinics (npl)

clinigol clinical (adj)

clir clear (adj)

cliriach clearer (adj)

clirio to clear (v)

clo lock, lock-forward (nm)

cloc clock, speedometer (nm)

cloch bell, bubble, o'clock (nf)

clod credit, praise (nm)

cloddiau hedges (npl)

cloddio to burrow, to dig, to excavate, to quarry (v)

clogwyn boulder, cliff, precipice (nm)

clogwyni cliffs (npl)

cloi to conclude, to end, to lock (v)

clos close, farmyard; trousers, breeches (nm)

cludiant transport (nm)

cludir is/are/will be carried, transported (v)

cludo to carry, to convey, to transport (v)

clust ear (nf)

clustiau ears (npl)

clustnodi to earmark (v)

clwb club (nm)

clwstwr cluster (nm)

clwy': **clwyf** disease, sore, wound (nm)

clybiau clubs (npl)

clychau bells (npl)

clymu to bind, to knit, to knot, to tie (v)

clystyrau clusters (npl)

clyw earshot, hearing (nm)

clyw you hear, you will hear (v)

clyw he/she/it hears, will hear (v)

clywais I heard (v)

clywch you hear, you will hear (v)

clywed to hear (v)

clywedol auditory, aural (adj)

clywodd he/she/it heard (v)

cm cm (abbr)

cnau nuts (npl)

cnawd flesh (nm)

cnewyllol nuclear (adj)

cnewyllyn core, heart, kernel, nucleus (nm)

cnoi to bite, to chew (v)

cnwd covering, crop, shock (nm)

cnydau crops (npl)

còb cob, lad, wag (nm)

coch (the colour) red (nm)

coch auburn, ginger, poor, red, ropy (adj)

cochion red(s) (adj/pl)

cocos cockles; cogs (npl)

cod bag, husk, pod, pouch (nf)

cod you get up (v)

cod code (nm)

codau codes (npl)

codi to build, to get up, to grow, to lift (v)

codiad erection, hillock, raise, rise (nm)

codir is/are/will be raised (v)

cododd he/she/it lifted, raised (v)

codwyd was/were lifted, raised (v)

coed trees (npl)

coeden tree (nf)

coediog sylvan, wooded (adj)

coedwig forest, wood (nf)

coedwigaeth forestry (nf)

coedwigoedd forests (npl)

coes leg (nf)

coes handle, leg, stalk, stem (nm)

coesau legs (npl)

coetir woodland (nm)

coetiroedd woodlands (npl)

cof memory (nm)

cofeb memorial (nf)

coffa memorial, remembrance (nm)

coffi coffee (nm)

cofia you remember, you will remember (v)

cofiadwy memorable (adj)

cofiaf I remember, I will remember (v)

cofio to recall, to remember (v)

cofiwch you remember, you will remember (v)

cofnod memorandum, minute, record (nm)

cofnodi to minute, to note, to record, to register (*v*)

cofnodion minutes, records (*npl*)

cofnodir is/are/will be recorded (*v*)

cofnodwyd was/were recorded (*v*)

cofrestr register (*nf*)

cofrestra he/she/it records, will record (*v*)

cofrestrau registers (*npl*)

cofrestredig registered (*adj*)

cofrestrfa registry (*nf*)

cofrestriad registration (*nm*)

cofrestriadau registrations (*npl*)

cofrestru to enrol, to register (*v*)

cofrestrwyd was/were registered (*v*)

cofrestrydd registrar (*nm*)

coginio to cook (*v*)

colect collect [prayer] (*nm*)

coleg college (*nm*)

colegau colleges (*npl*)

coler band, collar (*nf*)

coll loss (*nm*)

coll lost, missing (*adj*)

collddail deciduous (*adj*)

colled insanity, loss (*nf*)

colledion losses (*npl*)

colli to lose, to mislay, to miss, to spill (*v*)

collir is/are/will be lost (*v*)

collodd he/she/it lost (*v*)

collwyd was/were lost (*v*)

colofn column, pillar (*nf*)

colofnau columns (*npl*)

comedi comedy (*nf*)

comin common (*nm*)

comisiwn commission (*nm*)

comisiynu to commission (*v*)

comisiynwr commissioner (*nm*)

comisiynwyd was/were commissioned (*v*)

comisiynwyr commissioners (*npl*)

comisiynydd commissioner (*nm*)

condemnio to condemn (*v*)

confensiwn convention (*nm*)

confensiynau conventions (*npl*)

confensiynol conventional (*adj*)

consenswo consensus (*nm*)

consortiwm consortium (*nm*)

contract contract (*nm*)

contractau contracts (*npl*)

contractio to contract (*v*)

contractiwr contractor (*nm*)

contractwr contractor (*nm*)

contractwyr contractors (*npl*)

copa crown, pate (*nf*)

copa peak, summit (*nm*)

copi copy (*nm*)

copïau copies (*npl*)

copïo to copy, to imitate (*v*)

copïwch you copy, you will copy (*v*)

copr copper (*nm*)

côr chancel, choir, crib, pew, stall (*nm*)

corau choirs (*npl*)

corddi to churn, to seethe, to stir (*v*)

corff body, corpse, group, (heavenly) body, trunk (*nm*)

corfforaeth corporation (*nf*)

corfforaethol corporate (*adj*)

corfforol bodily, physical (*adj*)

coridor corridor (*nm*)

coridorau corridors (*npl*)

corn antler, callus, chimney, corn, drinking-horn, handle, hooter, horn, stethoscop (*nm*)

corn absolute, complete (*adj*)

cornel corner, corner (kick) (*nf*)

coron crown, garland, sovereign (*nf*)

coronaidd coronary (*adj*)

cors bog, marsh, morass, swamp (*nf*)

corsydd bogs (*npl*)

cosb penalty, punishment (*nf*)

cosbau punishments (*npl*)

cosbi to penalize, to punish (*v*)

cost cost (*nf*)

costau costs (*npl*)

costio to cost (*v*)

costus dear, expensive (*adj*)

cot coat, coating (*nf*)
cot beating (*nf*)
cotwm cotton (*nm*)
craff discerning, observant, shrewd, smart (*adj*)
craffu to observe closely, to pore, to scrutinize (*v*)
crafu to peel, to scrape, to scratch (*v*)
cragen shell (*nf*)
crai crude, raw, rude (*adj*)
craidd centre, crux, essence (*nm*)
craig boulder, crag, rock (*nf*)
crand grand, smart (*adj*)
cras aired, baked, coarse, dry, harsh, rough, strident, toasted (*adj*)
creadigaeth creation, procreation (*nf*)
creadigol created, creative (*adj*)
creadur creature (*nm*)
creaduriaid creatures (*npl*)
cred belief, Christendom, trust (*nf*)
credaf I believe/I will believe (*v*)
credai he/she/it would believe (*v*)
credir is/are/will be believed (*v*)
credo credo, creed (*nf*)
credoau creeds (*npl*)
credu to believe (*v*)
credwch you believe, you will believe (*v*)
credwn we believe, we will believe (*v*)
credyd credit (*nm*)
credydau credits (*npl*)
credydwr creditor (*nm*)
credydwyr creditors (*npl*)
cref strong (*adj/f*)
crefft craft, trade (*nf*)
crefftau crafts (*npl*)
crefftwr craftsman (*nm*)
crefftwyr craftsmen (*npl*)
crefydd religion (*nf*)
crefyddol religious (*adj*)
cregyn shells (*npl*)
creiddiol central, essential (*adj*)
creigiau rocks (*npl*)

creigiog craggy, rocky (*adj*)
creodd he/she/it created (*v*)
creu to create, to make (*v*)
creulon brutal, cruel, heartless (*adj*)
creulondeb brutality, cruelty (*nm*)
crëwyd was/were created (*v*)
crib comb, crest, ridge (*nm*)
criced cricket (*nm*)
crio to cry (*v*)
Crist Christ
Cristion Christian (*nm*)
Cristnogaeth Christianity (*nf*)
Cristnogion Christians (*npl*)
Cristnogol Christian (*adj*)
critigol critical (*adj*)
criw crew, gang (*nm*)
croen film, hide, peel, rind, skin (*nm*)
croes cross, crucifix (*nf*)
croes adverse, cross, perverse (*adj*)
croesawodd he/she/it welcomed (*v*)
croesawu to welcome (*v*)
croesawyd was/were welcomed (*v*)
croesfan crossing (*nf*)
croesi to cross, to traverse, to delete (*v*)
croeso hospitality, welcome (*nm*)
crogi to hang (*v*)
cromfach bracket, parenthesis (*nf*)
cromfachau brackets (*npl*)
cron circular, round (*adj/f*)
cronedig accumulated (*adj*)
cronfa dam, fund, reservoir (*nf*)
cronfeydd funds, reservoirs (*npl*)
cronig chronic (*adj*)
cronni to amass, to collect (*v*)
croth uterus, womb (*nf*)
croyw fresh, pure, unleavened (*adj*)
crwn circular, entire, rotund, round (*adj*)
crwner coroner (*nm*)
crwydro to digress, to roam, to stray, to wander (*v*)
crybwyll to mention, to refer to (*v*)
crybwyllir is/are/will be mentioned (*v*)

crybwyllwyd was/were mentioned (*v*)

cryf brawny, healthy, loud, powerful, ripe, strong, tough (*adj*)

cryfach stronger (*adj*)

cryfaf strongest (*adj*)

cryfder might, power, strength (*nm*)

cryfderau strengths (*npl*)

cryfhau to convalesce, to grow powerful, to strengthen (*v*)

cryfion strong (*adj/pl*)

cryn fair, pretty, tolerable (*adj*)

crynhoad assembly, compendium, digest, gathering, summary, summing up (*nm*)

crynhoi to accumulate, to assemble, to fester, to muster, to summarize (*v*)

cryno compact, concise, tidy (*adj*)

crynoadau compendia (*npl*)

crynodeb abstract, résumé, summary (*nm*)

crynodiad concentration (*nm*)

crynswth entirety, gross, whole (*nm*)

crynu to shake, to shiver, to tremble (*v*)

crys shirt (*nm*)

crysau shirts (*npl*)

cu beloved, dear (*adj*)

cudd concealed, covert, hidden, secret (*adj*)

cuddio to conceal, to hide, to obscure (*v*)

cul narrow, narrow-minded (*adj*)

curo to beat, to defeat, to knock, to throb (*v*)

cwbl everything (*nm*)

cwbl complete, entire, total (*adj*)

cwblhau to complete, to finish (*v*)

cwblhawyd was/were completed (*v*)

cwblhewch you complete, you will complete (*v*)

cwch boat, hive (*nm*)

cwest inquest (*nm*)

cwestiwn question (*nm*)

cwestiynau questions (*npl*)

cwis quiz (*nm*)

cwisiau quizzes (*npl*)

cwlwm bunch, cluster, knot, tangle (*nm*)

cwm coomb, glen (*nm*)

cwmni companions, company (*nm*)

cwmnïau companies (*npl*)

cwmpas ambit, register, scope; pair of compasses (*nm*)

cwmpasu to encompass (*v*)

cwmwl cloud (*nm*)

cŵn dogs (*npl*)

cwningen rabbit (*nf*)

cwningod rabbits (*npl*)

cwnstabl constable (*nm*)

cwota quota (*nm*)

cwpan capsule, chalice, cup (*nm*)

cwpled couplet (*nm*)

cwpwl: cwpl couple (*nm*)

cwpwrdd cupboard (*nm*)

cwr corner, edge, outskirts (*nm*)

cwrdd meeting, service (*nm*)

cwrdd to meet, to touch (*v*)

cwricwlaidd curricular (*adj*)

cwricwlwm curriculum (*nm*)

cwrs chase; course (*nm*)

cwrs coarse (*adj*)

cwrt court, courtyard, mansion (*nm*)

cwrtais courteous (*adj*)

cwrw ale, beer (*nm*)

cwsg sleep (*nm*)

cwsmer customer (*nm*)

cwsmeriaid customers (*npl*)

cwt cot, hut, shanty; tail;-cut (*nm*)

cwtogi to contract, to shorten, to shrink (*v*)

cwymp collapse, descent, fall, slump, surrender (*nm*)

cwympo to fall, to slope down (*v*)

cwyn accusation, complaint (*nf*)

cwynion complaints (*npl*)

cwyno to complain (*v*)

cwynodd he/she/it complained (*v*)

cychod boats (*npl*)

cychwyn to begin, to start (*v*)

cychwynnodd he/she/it started (*v*)

cychwynnol initial (*adj*)

cychwynnwyd was/were started (*v*)
cydau bags (*npl*)
cydbwysedd balance, equilibrium (*nm*)
cydbwyso to balance, to weigh (*v*)
cyd-destun context (*nm*)
cyd-destunau contexts (*npl*)
cyd-fynd to agree (*v*)
cydgysylltu to coordinate (*v*)
cydio to hold fast, to join, to seize (*v*)
cydlynol cohesive (*adj*)
cydlynu to cohere, to coordinate (*v*)
cydlynydd coordinator (*nm*)
cydnabod to acknowledge, to show appreciation (*v*)
cydnabod acquaintance (*nm*)
cydnabuwyd was/were acknowledged (*v*)
cydnabyddedig acknowledged, recognized (*adj*)
cydnabyddiaeth acknowledgement, appreciation, recognition (*nf*)
cydnabyddir is/are/will be acknowledged (*v*)
cydnaws compatible, congenial (*adj*)
cydol the whole (*nm*)
cydradd equal (*adj*)
cydraddoldeb equality (*nm*)
cydran component (*nf*)
cydrannau components (*npl*)
cydsyniad agreement, consent (*nm*)
cydsynio to agree, to assent (*v*)
cydweddu to conform (*v*)
cydweithio to collaborate, to cooperate (*v*)
cydweithiwr colleague (*nm*)
cydweithrediad collaboration, co-operation (*nm*)
cydweithredol collaborative, co-operative (*adj*)
cydweithredu to cooperate (*v*)
cydweithwyr colleagues (*npl*)
cydwybod conscience (*nf*)
cydymdeimlad commiseration, sympathy (*nm*)

cydymdeimlo to commiserate, to sympathize (*v*)
cydymffurfiad compliance (*nm*)
cydymffurfiaeth conformity (*nf*)
cydymffurfio to conform (*v*)
cyf. ltd. (*abbr*)
cyfaddas suitable (*adj*)
cyfaddef to admit, to confess (*v*)
cyfadran faculty (*nf*)
cyfadrannau faculties (*npl*)
cyfagos adjoining, close, contiguous, (not) nearly (*adj*)
cyfaill friend (*nm*)
cyfaint volume (*nm*)
cyfalaf capital [money] (*nm*)
cyfamod covenant (*nm*)
cyfamser meantime, meanwhile (*nm*)
cyfan complete, whole (*adj*)
cyfan total, whole (*nm*)
cyfandir continent (*nm*)
cyfannol holistic, integral, integrated (*adj*)
cyfanrwydd totality, wholeness (*nm*)
cyfansawdd compound (*adj*)
cyfansoddi to compose (*v*)
cyfansoddiad composition, constitution (*nm*)
cyfansoddiadol constitutional (*npl*)
cyfansoddion compounds (*npl*)
cyfansoddol constituent (*npl*)
cyfansoddwr composer (*nm*)
cyfanswm sum, total (*nm*)
cyfansymiau sums, totals (*npl*)
cyfarch address, greeting (*nm*)
cyfarch to greet (*v*)
cyfarfod meeting (*nm*)
cyfarfod to meet (*v*)
cyfarfodydd meetings (*npl*)
cyfarpar apparatus, equipment (*nm*)
cyfartal equal (*adj*)
cyfartaledd average, equality, mean, proportion (*nm*)
cyfartalog average (*adj*)

cyfarwydd familiar (*adj*)
cyfarwydd raconteur, storyteller (*nm*)
cyfarwyddeb directive (*nf*)
cyfarwyddiadau directions (*npl*)
cyfarwyddiaeth directorship (*nf*)
cyfarwyddo to become accustomed to, to direct (*v*)
cyfarwyddwr director (*nm*)
cyfarwyddwraig director (*nf*)
cyfarwyddwyr directors (*npl*)
cyfarwyddyd advice, direction, instruction (*nm*)
cyfateb to correspond, to tally (*v*)
cyfatebol corresponding (*adj*)
cyfathrach intercourse (*nf*)
cyfathrebu to communicate (*v*)
cyfeillgar amicable, friendly (*adj*)
cyfeillgarwch friendliness, friendship (*nm*)
cyfeillion friends (*npl*)
cyfeiriad address, direction, reference (*nm*)
cyfeiriadau addresses, directions (*npl*)
cyfeiriadur directory (*nm*)
cyfeirio to address, to direct, to make for, to refer, to steer (*v*)
cyfeiriodd he/she/it referred (*v*)
cyfeirir is/are/will be referred (*v*)
cyfeiriwyd was/were referred (*v*)
cyfeirlyfr reference book (*nm*)
cyfeirnod grid reference (*nm*)
cyfenw surname (*nm*)
cyfer acre (*nm*)
cyferbyn opposite (*adj*)
cyferbyniad contrast (*nm*)
cyffelyb like, such (*adj*)
cyffiniau bounds, vicinity (*npl*)
cyffordd junction (*nf*)
cyfforddus comfortable (*adj*)
cyffredin common, ordinary (*adj*)
cyffredinol general, universal (*adj*)
cyffro commotion, excitement, stir (*nm*)
cyffroi to agitate, to stir (*v*)
cyffrous agitated, exciting (*adj*)

cyffur drug (*nm*)
cyffuriau drugs (*npl*)
cyffwrdd to touch (*v*)
cyfiawn absolute, just, righteous (*adj*)
cyfiawnder justice, righteousness (*nm*)
cyfiawnhad justification, vindication (*nm*)
cyfiawnhau to justify, to vindicate (*v*)
cyfieithiad translation (*nm*)
cyfieithiadau translations (*npl*)
cyfieithu to translate (*v*)
cyfieithwyr translators (*npl*)
cyfieithydd interpreter, translator (*nm*)
cyflawn complete, entire; intransitive (*adj*)
cyflawni to accomplish, to fulfil (*v*)
cyflawniad accomplishment, achievement (*nm*)
cyflawnir is/are/will be accomplished (*v*)
cyflawnodd he/she/it accomplished (*v*)
cyflawnwyd was/were accomplished (*v*)
cyfle chance, opportunity (*nm*)
cyflenwad complement, supply (*nm*)
cyflenwadau supplies (*npl*)
cyflenwi to supply (*v*)
cyflenwol complementary (*adj*)
cyflenwr supplier (*nm*)
cyflenwydd supplier (*nm*)
cyflenwyr suppliers (*npl*)
cyfleoedd opportunities (*npl*)
cyfleon they conveyed (*v*)
cyfleu to convey (*v*)
cyfleus convenient, handy (*adj*)
cyfleuster convenience (*nm*)
cyfleusterau conveniences (*npl*)
cyfleustra convenience (*nm*)
cyflog hire, pay, salary, wages (*nm*)
cyflogaeth employment (*nf*)
cyflogai he/she/it would employ (*v*)
cyflogau wages (*npl*)
cyflogedig employed, salaried (*adj*)
cyflogeion employees (*npl*)
cyflogi to employ, to engage (*v*)
cyflogwr employer (*nm*)

cyflogwyr employers (*npl*)
cyflogydd employer (*nm*)
cyflwr condition, state (*nm*)
cyflwyniad presentation (*nm*)
cyflwyniadau dedications, presentations (*npl*)
cyflwynir is/are/will be presented (*v*)
cyflwyno to introduce, to present, to submit (*v*)
cyflwynodd he/she/it presented (*v*)
cyflwynwr presenter (*nm*)
cyflwynwyd was/were presented (*v*)
cyflwynwyr presenters (*npl*)
cyflwynydd presenter (*nm*)
cyflym keen, quick, rapid (*adj*)
cyflymach quicker (*adj*)
cyflymder pace, rapidity, speed, swiftness, velocity (*nm*)
cyflymdra speed (*nm*)
cyflymu to accelerate, to hasten (*v*)
cyflyrau conditions (*npl*)
cyfnewid to exchange, to trade (*v*)
cyfnewidiol changeable, variable (*adj*)
cyfnod era, period (*nm*)
cyfnodau periods, times (*npl*)
cyfnodol periodic (*adj*)
cyfnodolion periodicals (*npl*)
cyfnodolyn periodical (*nm*)
cyfochrog collateral, parallel (*adj*)
cyfoedion contemporaries (*npl*)
cyfoes contemporary (*adj*)
cyfoeth affluence, wealth (*nm*)
cyfoethog rich, wealthy (*adj*)
cyfoethogi to enrich, to make rich (*v*)
cyfradd rate (*nf*)
cyfraddau rates (*npl*)
cyfraith law (*nf*)
cyfran lot, portion, quota, share (*nf*)
cyfranddaliadau shares (*npl*)
cyfraniad contribution (*nm*)
cyfraniadau contributions (*npl*)
cyfrannau shares (*npl*)

cyfrannodd he/she/it contributed (*v*)
cyfrannol contributory (*adj*)
cyfrannu to contribute (*v*)
cyfranogi to partake of, to participate (*v*)
cyfranogiad participation (*nm*)
cyfranogwr participator (*nm*)
cyfranogwyr participators (*npl*)
cyfranwyr contributors (*npl*)
cyfredol concurrent, current (*adj*)
cyfreithiau laws (*npl*)
cyfreithiol judicial, legal (*adj*)
cyfreithiwr lawyer, solicitor (*nm*)
cyfreithlon lawful, legitimate (*adj*)
cyfreithwyr lawyers (*npl*)
cyfres list, serial, series (*nf*)
cyfresi series (*npl*)
cyfri to count (*v*)
cyfrif account (*nm*)
cyfrif to add, to be of worth, to calculate, to count (*v*)
cyfrifeg accountancy (*nf*)
cyfrifiad calculation, census (*nm*)
cyfrifiadau censuses (*npl*)
cyfrifiadur computer (*nm*)
cyfrifiadurol computer (*adj*)
cyfrifiaduron computers (*npl*)
cyfrifir is/are/will be counted (*v*)
cyfrifo to calculate (*v*)
cyfrifol responsible (*adj*)
cyfrifoldeb onus, responsibility (*nm*)
cyfrifoldebau responsibilities (*npl*)
cyfrifon accounts (*npl*)
cyfrinach secret (*nf*)
cyfrinachedd confidentiality (*nm*)
cyfrinachol confidential, secret (*adj*)
cyfrinair password (*nm*)
cyfrol volume (*nf*)
cyfrolau volumes (*npl*)
cyfrwng medium (*nm*)
cyfrwng-Cymraeg Welsh-medium (*adj*)
cyfryngau media (*npl*)
cyfryw such (*adj*)

cyfun comprehensive, concordant, united (*adj*)
cyfundeb union (*nm*)
cyfundrefn system (*nf*)
cyfundrefnau systems (*npl*)
cyfundrefnol systemic (*adj*)
cyfuniad blend, combination (*nm*)
cyfuniadau combinations (*npl*)
cyfuno to become one, to combine (*v*)
cyfunol combined (*adj*)
cyfweld to interview (*v*)
cyfweliad interview (*nm*)
cyfweliadau interviews (*npl*)
cyfwerth equal, equivalent (*adj*)
cyfyd he/she/it lifts, will lift (*v*)
cyfyng narrow, restricted (*adj*)
cyfyngedig confined, limited (*adj*)
cyfyngiad limit (*nm*)
cyfyngiadau limits (*npl*)
cyfyngir is/are/will be restricted (*v*)
cyfyngu to contract, to limit, to restrict (*v*)
cyfystyr synonymous, tantamount (*adj*)
cyhoedd public (*nm*)
cyhoeddedig published (*adj*)
cyhoeddi to announce, to publish (*v*)
cyhoeddiad announcement, publication (*nm*)
cyhoeddiadau announcements, publications (*npl*)
cyhoeddir is/are/will be announced (*v*)
cyhoeddodd he/she/it announced (*v*)
cyhoeddus public (*adj*)
cyhoeddusrwydd prominence, publicity (*nm*)
cyhoeddwr announcer, publisher (*nm*)
cyhoeddwyd was/were published (*v*)
cyhoeddwyr publishers (*npl*)
cyhuddiad accusation, charge (*nm*)
cyhuddiadau accusations (*npl*)
cyhuddo to accuse (*v*)
cyhyd as long as, so long as (*adj*)
cyhyr muscle (*nm*)

cyhyrau muscles (*npl*)
cyhyryn muscle (*nm*)
cylch circle, cycle, group, hoop, orbit, zone (*nm*)
cylchdaith circuit, orbit, tour (*nf*)
cylchdro rotation (*nm*)
cylched circuit (*nf*)
cylchgrawn journal, magazine, periodical (*nm*)
cylchgronau magazines (*npl*)
cylchlythyr circular, newsletter (*nm*)
cylchoedd circles (*npl*)
cylchrediad circulation (*nm*)
cyllell knife (*nf*)
cyllid income, revenue (*nm*)
cyllideb budget (*nf*)
cyllidebau budgets (*npl*)
cyllidir is/are/will be financed (*v*)
cyllido to finance (*v*)
cyllidol financial, fiscal (*adj*)
cyllyll knives (*npl*)
cymaint as many, as much, so much (*adj*)
cymal clause, joint (*nm*)
cymalau joints (*npl*)
Cymanwlad Commonwealth (*nf*)
cymar companion, mate, peer (*nm*)
cymariaethau comparisons (*npl*)
cymdeithas company, organisation, society (*nf*)
cymdeithasau societies (*npl*)
cymdeithasol sociable, social (*adj*)
cymdeithasu to socialize (*v*)
cymdogaeth neighbourhood (*nf*)
cymdogion neighbours (*npl*)
cymedr arithmetic mean (*nm*)
cymedrig mean (*adj*)
cymedrol abstemious, indifferent, medium, moderate, temperate (*adj*)
cymell to drive, to incite, to urge (*v*)
cymer confluence (*nm*)
cymer you take! (*v*)
cymeradwy acceptable, approved (*adj*)

cymeradwyaeth applause, approval, ovation (*nf*)
cymeradwyir is/are/will be approved (*v*)
cymeradwyo to applaud, to approve, to recommend (*v*)
cymeradwywyd was/were recommended (*v*)
cymeriad character (*nm*)
cymeriadau characters (*npl*)
cymerir is/are/will be taken (*v*)
cymerodd he/she/it took (*v*)
cymerwch you take, you will take (*v*)
cymerwyd was/were taken (*v*)
cymesur symmetrical, proportionate (*adj*)
cymhareb ratio (*nf*)
cymhariaeth comparison, simile (*nf*)
cymharol comparative, moderate (*adj*)
cymharu to compare, to liken (*v*)
cymharwch you compare, you will compare (*v*)
cymhelliad impulse, incentive, motive, urging (*nm*)
cymhelliant motivation (*nm*)
cymhellion motives (*npl*)
cymhleth complicated, elaborate (*adj*)
cymhleth complex [mental] (*nm*)
cymhlethdod complexity (*nm*)
cymhorthdal grant, subsidy (*nm*)
cymhorthion aids (*npl*)
cymhwysedd competence (*nm*)
cymhwysiad adjustment, application (*nm*)
cymhwysir is/are/will be adapted, adjusted (*v*)
cymhwyso to adapt, to adjust (*v*)
cymhwyster aptitude, competence, qualification, suitability (*nm*)
cymoedd valleys (*npl*)
cymorth aid (*nm*)
cymorthdaliadau grants, subsidies (*npl*)
Cymraeg Welsh language (*nf*)
Cymraes Welshwoman (*nf*)
Cymreictod Welshness (*nm*)

Cymreig Welsh (*adj*)
Cymro Welshman (*nm*)
Cymru Wales (*nf*)
cymryd to take, to hold (*v*)
cymun communion, Eucharist (*nm*)
cymuned community (*nf*)
cymunedau communities (*npl*)
cymunedol community (*adj*)
cymwys appropriate, suitable (*adj*)
cymwysedig applied, qualified (*adj*)
cymwysiadau applications (*npl*)
cymwysterau qualifications (*npl*)
cymydog neighbour (*nm*)
cymylau clouds (*npl*)
cymysg mixed (*adj*)
cymysgedd concoction, mixture (*nm*)
cymysgu to confuse, to mix (*v*)
cyn before, previous to (*prep*)
cyn as, so (*adv*)
cynadleddau conferences (*npl*)
cynaeafu to harvest (*v*)
cynaladwyedd sustainability (*nm*)
cynaliadwy supportable, sustainable (*adj*)
cyndyn obstinate, reticent, stubborn (*adj*)
cynefin accustomed, familiar (*adj*)
cynefin habitat, haunt (*nm*)
cynefinoedd habitats (*npl*)
cynffon tail, appendage (*nf*)
cynfyfyrwyr ex-students (*npl*)
cyngerdd concert (*nm*)
cynghanedd harmony (*nf*)
cyngherddau concerts (*npl*)
cynghorau councils (*npl*)
cynghori to advise, to counsel (*v*)
cynghorir is/are/will be advised (*v*)
cynghorwr adviser, counsellor (*nm*)
cynghorwyr councillors (*npl*)
cynghorydd councillor (*nm*)
cynghrair alliance, confederation, league (*nf*)
cyngor advice, counsel (*nm*)
cyngor council, senate (*nm*)

cynhadledd conference (*nf*)
cynhaeaf autumn, harvest (*nm*)
cynhaliaeth maintenance, subsistence, support, sustenance, upkeep (*nf*)
cynhaliodd he/she/it supported (*v*)
cynhaliol supporting (*adj*)
cynhaliwr supporter, upholder (*nf*)
cynhaliwyd was/were supported (*v*)
cynhalwyr supporters, upholders (*npl*)
cynhanesyddol prehistoric (*adj*)
cynharach earlier (*adj*)
cynharaf earliest (*adj*)
cynhelir is/are/will be held (*v*)
cynhenid inherent, innate (*adj*)
cynhesu to warm (*v*)
cynhwysedd capacity (*nm*)
cynhwysfawr capacious, comprehensive (*adj*)
cynhwysion ingredients (*npl*)
cynhwysir is/are/will be included (*v*)
cynhwysol inclusive (*adj*)
cynhwyswyd was/were included (*v*)
cynhwysydd container (*nm*)
cynhyrchiad production (*nm*)
cynhyrchiant production (*nm*)
cynhyrchiol productive, prolific (*adj*)
cynhyrchion products (*npl*)
cynhyrchir is/are/will be produced (*v*)
cynhyrchodd he/she/it produced (*v*)
cynhyrchu to bring forth, to produce, to yield (*v*)
cynhyrchwyd was/were produced (*v*)
cynhyrchwyr producers (*npl*)
cynhyrchydd generator, producer (*nm*)
cyni hardship, straits (*nm*)
cynifer as many, even, so many (*adj*)
cynigiad motion, proposal (*nm*)
cynigion proposals (*npl*)
cynigir is/are/will be proposed (*v*)
cynigiwyd was/were proposed (*v*)
cynilion savings (*npl*)
cynilo to save (*v*)

cynllun plan, plot, scheme (*nm*)
cynlluniau plans (*npl*)
cynllunio to design, to plan (*v*)
cynlluniwyd was/were planned (*v*)
cynnal to maintain, to support, to sustain (*v*)
cynnar early (*adj*)
cynnau to light, to switch on (the light) (*v*)
cynnes affectionate, warm (*adj*)
cynnig offer, proposal (*nm*)
cynnig to aim, to apply, to attempt, to offer, to propose, to try (for) (*v*)
cynnil frugal, spare, sparing, subtle (*adj*)
cynnwrf agitation, commotion (*nm*)
cynnwys content(s) (*nm*)
cynnwys to consist, to include (*v*)
cynnydd development, gain, growth, increase, progress, waxing (*nm*)
cynnyrch crops, output, produce (*nm*)
cynorthwyo to assist, to help (*v*)
cynorthwyol auxiliary, supporting (*adj*)
cynorthwywr assistant, helper (*nm*)
cynorthwywyr assistants (*npl*)
cynorthwyydd assistant (*nm*)
cynradd primary (*adj*)
cynrychiolaeth representation (*nf*)
cynrychioli to represent (*v*)
cynrychiolydd representative (*nm*)
cynt quicker (*adj*)
cynt before, formerly (*adv*)
cynta': cyntaf first (*num*)
cynta first, swiftest (*adj*)
cynted as soon as (*adj*)
cyntedd porch, vestibule (*nm*)
cyntefig primitive (*adj*)
cynulleidfa audience, congregation (*nf*)
cynulleidfaoedd audiences (*npl*)
cynulliad assembly, gathering (*nm*)
cynullydd convener (*nm*)
cynwysedig included, inclusive (*adj*)
cynyddodd he/she/it increased (*v*)
cynyddol increasing, progressive (*adj*)

cynyddu to augment, to increase *(v)*
cyraeddiadau attainments *(npl)*
cyrch attack *(nm)*
cyrchfan destination *(nf)*
cyrchu to gather (together), to make for *(v)*
cyrff bodies *(npl)*
cyrhaeddiad attainment, comprehension, reach *(nm)*
cyrhaeddodd he/she/it reached *(v)*
cyrion fringes *(npl)*
cyrn horns *(npl)*
cyrraedd to attain, to reach *(v)*
cyrsiau courses *(npl)*
cysegredig holy, sacred *(adj)*
cysgod shadow, shelter *(nm)*
cysgodion shadows *(npl)*
cysgodol shadow, shady, sheltered *(adj)*
cysgu to sleep *(v)*
cyson consistent, constant, regular *(adj)*
cysondeb consistency, regularity *(nm)*
cysoni to reconcile *(v)*
cystadlaethau competitions *(npl)*
cystadleuaeth competition *(nf)*
cystadleuol competitive *(adj)*
cystadleuwr competitor, rival *(nm)*
cystadleuwyr competitors *(npl)*
cystadlu to compete, to vie *(v)*
cystal as good as *(adj)*
cystal equally, may as well *(adv)*
cysur comfort, consolation, solace *(nm)*
cysurus comfortable *(adj)*
cyswllt connection, link *(nm)*
cysyllta he/she/it will contact *(v)*
cysylltau contacts, links *(npl)*
cysyllter should be connected, linked *(v)*

cysylltiad connection, contact, liaison, linking *(nm)*
cysylltiadau contacts *(npl)*
cysylltiedig connected *(adj)*
cysylltiol associated, linked *(adj)*
cysylltir is/are/will be connected, linked *(v)*
cysylltu to connect, to join, to link *(v)*
cysylltwch you (will) contact, link *(v)*
cysyniad concept *(nm)*
cysyniadau concepts *(npl)*
cytbwys balanced, unbiased *(adj)*
cythraul demon, devil, fiend *(nm)*
cythreuliaid demons *(npl)*
cytsain consonance, consonant *(nm)*
cytseiniaid consonants *(npl)*
cytûn agreeing, in accordance, in agreement, of one mind *(adj)*
cytundeb agreement, contract, pact, settlement *(nm)*
cytundebau agreements, contracts *(npl)*
cytundebol contractual *(adj)*
cytunir is/are/will be agreed *(v)*
cytuno to agree, to correspond, to strike a bargain, to suit *(v)*
cytunodd he/she/it agreed *(v)*
cytunwyd was/were agreed *(v)*
cyw chick, young animal *(nm)*
cywair key, register, tone *(nm)*
cywaith project *(nm)*
cywilydd disgrace, shame *(nm)*
cywion chicks *(npl)*
cywir correct, faithful, honest, true *(adj)*
cywirdeb accuracy, correctness, truth *(nm)*
cywiro to correct *(v)*
cywydd poem *(nm)*

D

a word starting with **d** printed in blue means that the root form of that word begins with **t**, e.g. **dad** root **tad**

a word starting with **dd** printed in blue means that the root form of that word begins with **d**, e.g. **ddafad** root **dafad**

Dd stands as a letter in its own right in Welsh. In a Welsh dictionary, unlike this list, words containing '**dd**' would commence after those containing **d:**

adweithio to react

adwerthu to retail

adwy breach, gap

addas suitable, worthy

addasiad adaptation, modification

addasiadau modifications

da good, well *(adj)*

da the good *(nm)*

da cattle, goods, possessions *(npl)*

da pat, stroke *(nm)*

dacw there, there (he/she/it) is, there they are *(adv)*

dad father

dadansoddi to analyse *(v)*

dadansoddiad analysis, synopsis *(nm)*

dadansoddiadau analyses *(npl)*

dadansoddol analytical *(adj)*

dadau fathers

dadeni renaissance, revival *(nm)*

dadgofrestru to de-register *(v)*

dadl argument, debate *(nf)*

dadlau to argue, to debate *(v)*

dadlennu to disclose, to reveal *(v)*

dadleuol controversial, debatable *(adj)*

dadleuon arguments *(npl)*

dadlwytho to unload *(v)*

dadlwythwch you unload *(v)*

daear earth, lair, land, soil *(nf)*

daeareg geology *(nf)*

daearegol geological *(adj)*

daearol earthly, terrestrial *(adj)*

daearyddiaeth geography *(nf)*

daearyddol geographical *(adj)*

daenu to spread

daer earnest, insistent

daeth he/she/it came *(v)*

daethant they came *(v)*

daethom we came *(v)*

daethpwyd was/were brought *(v)*

dafad sheep *(nf)*

dafaden wart *(nf)*

dafarn pub

daflen sheet

daflenni sheets

daflu to throw

dafod tongue

dafodiaith dialect

dagrau tears *(npl)*

dai houses

daid grandfather

dail leaves *(npl)*

daioni goodness *(nm)*

dair three

daith journey

dal to capture, to catch, to continue, to hold, to persevere, to support *(v)*

dal tall

dâl payment
daladwy payable
dalaith province, state
dalcen forehead
daleithiau provinces, states
dalen page, sheet
dalent talent
dalfa catch; gaol, prison (*nf*)
dalgylch catchment area (*nm*)
dalgylchoedd catchment areas (*npl*)
daliad belief, opinion; catch, (*nm*)
daliad payment
daliadau convictions (*npl*)
daliadau payments
daliodd he/she/it held (*v*)
dall blind (*adj*)
dallt to understand (*v*)
dalu to pay
dalwyd was/were paid
damaid bit
damcaniaeth hypothesis, theory (*nf*)
damcaniaethau hypotheses (*npl*)
damcaniaethol hypothetical, theoretical (*adj*)
damwain accident, mishap (*nf*)
damweiniau accidents (*npl*)
damweiniol accidental, inadverdent (*adj*)
dan under
dân fire
danau fires
danfon to accompany, to send (*v*)
dangos to demonstrate, to show (*v*)
dangosir is/are/will be shown (*v*)
dangosodd he/she/it showed (*v*)
dangoswch you show (*v*)
dangoswyd was/were shown (*v*)
dangosydd indicator (*nm*)
dangosyddion indicators (*npl*)
dani under (her)
danio to fire
dannedd teeth (*npl*)
dano under (him)

danseilio to undermine
dant tooth (*nm*)
danwydd fuel
danynt under (them) (*prep*)
danysgrifio to subscribe
dâp tape
darbwyllo to convince, to persuade (*v*)
darddiad source
darfod to cease, to come to pass, to die, to happen (*v*)
darfu he/she/it did (*v*)
darganfod to discover (*v*)
darganfuwyd was/were discovered (*v*)
darganfyddiad discovery, find (*nm*)
darganfyddiadau discoveries (*npl*)
darged target
dargedau targets
dargedu to target
darlith lecture (*nf*)
darlithio to lecture (*v*)
darlithoedd lectures (*npl*)
darlithwyr lecturers (*npl*)
darlithydd lecturer (*nm*)
darllediad broadcast (*nm*)
darllediadau broadcasts (*npl*)
darlledu to broadcast (*v*)
darlledwr broadcaster (*nm*)
darllen to read (*v*)
darllenadwy legible, readable (*adj*)
darlleniad reading (*nm*)
darlleniadau readings (*npl*)
darllenwch you read (*v*)
darllenwr reader (*nm*)
darllenwyr readers (*npl*)
darllenydd reader (*nm*)
darlun illustration, picture, portrait (*nm*)
darluniau pictures (*npl*)
darlunio to depict, to draw, to illustrate, to portray (*v*)
darn part, piece, portion (*nm*)
darnau pieces (*npl*)
daro to strike

darogan to foretell, to predict (*v*)

darostyngedig humble, subject to, subjugated (*adj*)

darpar designate, elect, intended, prospective (*adj*)

darpariaeth preparation, provision (*nf*)

darpariaethau preparations (*npl*)

darparodd he/she/it prepared (*v*)

darparu to prepare, to provide (*v*)

darparwr provider (*nm*)

darparwyd was/were prepared (*v*)

darparwyr providers (*npl*)

darparydd provider (*nm*)

darperir is/are/will be prepared, provided (*v*)

darren knoll, rock

daru he/she/it did (*v*)

dasg task

dasgau tasks

data data (*npl*)

datblygedig developed (*adj*)

datblygiad development (*nm*)

datblygiadau developments (*npl*)

datblygir is/are/will be developed (*v*)

datblygodd he/she/it developed (*v*)

datblygu to develop (*v*)

datblygwr developer (*nm*)

datblygwyd was/were developed (*v*)

datblygwyr developers (*npl*)

datgan to announce, to declare, to proclaim (*v*)

datganiad proclamation, pronouncement, recital, statement (*nm*)

datganiadau announcements (*npl*)

datganodd he/she/it announced (*v*)

datganoledig decentralised (*adj*)

datganoli to decentralize, to devolve (*v*)

datgeliad disclosure (*nm*)

datgeliadau disclosures (*npl*)

datgelu to divulge, to reveal (*v*)

datguddio to manifest, to reveal, to uncover (*v*)

dathliad celebration (*nm*)

dathliadau celebrations (*npl*)

dathlu to celebrate (*v*)

datrys to solve, to unravel, to untangle (*v*)

datrysiad solution (*nm*)

datws potatoes

dau both, couple, two (*num/m*)

daw he/she/it comes (*v*)

dawel quiet

dawelwch quiet

dawn flair, knack, talent (*nf*)

dawns dance (*nf*)

dawnsio to dance (*v*)

dawnsiwr dancer (*nm*)

dawnswyr dancers (*npl*)

dawnus gifted, skilful (*adj*)

dda good

ddadansoddi to analyse

ddadansoddiad analysis

ddadl debate

ddadlau to argue, to debate

ddadleuon arguments

ddadlwytho to unload

ddaear earth

ddaearyddiaeth geography

ddaearyddol geographical

ddaeth he/she/it came

ddaethant they came

ddafad sheep

ddagrau tears

ddail leaves

ddaioni goodness

ddal to catch, to hold

ddalen page, sheet

ddalfa catch, gaol, prison

ddaliad conviction, view

ddaliadau opinions, views

ddall blind

ddamcaniaeth theory

ddamwain accident

ddamweiniau accidents

ddamweiniol accidental

ddanfon to send
ddangos to show
ddangosir is/are/will be shown
ddangosodd he/she/it showed
ddangoswyd was/were shown
ddangosyddion indicators
ddannedd teeth
ddarfod to cease, to expire
ddarganfod to discover
ddarganfuwyd was/were discovered
ddarganfyddiadau discoveries
ddarlith lecture
ddarlithoedd lectures
ddarlithydd lecturer
ddarlledu to broadcast
ddarllen to read
ddarllenadwy legible, readable
ddarllenwyr readers
ddarlun picture
ddarluniau pictures
ddarlunio to illustrate
ddarn part
ddarnau parts
ddarostyngedig subservient
ddarpar prospective
ddarpariaeth provision
ddarpariaethau preparations
ddarparu to prepare, to provide
ddarparwr provider
ddarparwyd was/were prepared, provided
ddarparwyr providers
ddarperir is/are/will be prepared
ddaru he/she/it happened
ddata data
ddatblygiad development
ddatblygiadau developments
ddatblygir is/are/will be developed
ddatblygodd he/she/it developed
ddatblygu to develop
ddatblygwyd was/were developed
ddatgan to state
ddatganiad statement

ddatganiadau statements
ddatganoli to decentalize
ddatgelu to reveal
ddathlu to celebrate
ddatrys to solve
ddau two
ddaw he/she/it comes
ddawn ability
ddawns dance
ddawnsio to dance
dde right, south
ddeall to understand
ddealladwy intelligible
ddealltwriaeth understanding
ddeallus intelligent, wise
ddechrau to start
ddechreuodd he/she/it started
ddechreuwyd was/were started
ddeddf law
ddeddfau laws
ddeddfwriaeth legislation
ddedfryd sentence
ddedfrydu to sentence
ddedwydd happy
ddefaid sheep
ddeffro to wake
ddefnydd material, use
ddefnyddiau materials
ddefnyddid would be used
ddefnyddio to use
ddefnyddiodd he/she/it used
ddefnyddiol useful
ddefnyddir is/are/will be used
ddefnyddiwr user
ddefnyddiwyd was/were used
ddefnyddwyr users
ddeg ten
ddegawd decade
ddeheuol southerly
ddehongli to interpret
ddeialog dialogue
ddeilen leaf

ddeiliad holder, occupant
ddeiliaid holders, occupants
ddeillio to derive from
ddeilliodd he/she/it derived from
ddeintyddion dentists
ddeintyddol dental
ddeiseb petition
ddelfrydol ideal
ddelio to deal
ddelir is/are/will be dealt
ddelw idol, image
ddelwedd image
ddelweddau images
ddemocrataidd democratic
ddeng ten
ddengys he/she/it shows
ddeniadol attractive
ddenu to attract
dderbyn to accept
dderbyniadau receipts, receptions
dderbyniodd he/she/it received
dderbyniol acceptable
dderbyniwyd was/were accepted
dderbynnir is/are/will be accepted
dderwen oak tree
ddesg desk
ddethol select
ddetholiad selection
ddeuddeg twelve
ddeuddegfed twelfth
ddeugain forty
ddeunaw eighteen
ddeunawfed eighteenth
ddeunydd material
ddeunyddiau materials
ddewis choice
ddewisiadau choices
ddewisir is/are/will be chosen
ddewislen menu
ddewisodd he/she/it chose
ddewisol discretionary, select
ddewiswyd was/were chosen

ddewr brave
ddial revenge
ddiamau certain
ddiamod unconditional
ddianc to escape, to flee
ddiangen unnecessary
ddiau doubtless
ddiben purpose
ddibenion
ddibwys unimportant
ddibynadwy dependable
ddibyniaeth dependancy
ddibynnol dependant
ddibynnu to depend
ddichon perhaps
ddi-dâl unpaid
ddiddordeb interest
ddiddordebau interests
ddiddorol interesting
ddiddymu to annul, to repeal
ddi-dor unbroken
ddidrafferth effortless
ddiduedd objective, unbiased
ddidynnwyd was/were subtracted
ddieithr strange
ddieithriad without exception
ddifetha to spoil
ddiffiniad definition
ddiffinio to define
ddiffinnir is defined
ddiffodd to extinguish, to put out
ddiffuant sincere
ddiffyg absence, lack
ddiffygiol lacking
ddiffygion defects
ddiflannu to disappear
ddiflas dull
ddifreintiedig underprivileged
ddifri serious
ddifrif serious
ddifrifol grave, serious
ddifrod damage

ddifrodi to destroy
ddifyr entertaining, interesting
ddig angry
ddigalon disheartened
ddigartref homeless
ddigidol digital
ddigon enough
ddigonol sufficient
ddigwydd to happen
ddigwyddiad event
ddigwyddiadau events
ddigwyddodd he/she/it happened
ddileu to delete
ddillad clothes
ddilyn to follow
ddilyniant sequence
ddilynir is/are/will be followed
ddilynodd he/she/it followed
ddilynol following
ddilynwyr followers
ddilys authentic
ddilysu to authenticate
ddim not, nothing, zero
ddinas city
ddinasoedd cities
ddinasyddion citizens
ddinesig civic
ddinesydd citizen
ddinistrio to destroy
ddiniwed harmless
ddiod drink
ddioddef to suffer
ddioddefodd he/she/it suffered
ddioddefwyr sufferers, victims
ddiodydd drinks
ddiog lazy
ddiogel safe
ddiogelu to preserve, to protect
ddiogelwch safety
ddiolch thanks
ddiolchgar grateful
ddirfawr enormous

ddirgelwch mystery
ddirprwy deputy
ddirprwyo to deputize
ddirwy fine
ddirwyn to wind up
ddirywiad decline
ddisg disc, disk
ddisglair bright
ddisgrifiad description
ddisgrifiadau descriptions
ddisgrifio to describe
ddisgrifir is/are/will be described
ddisgrifiwyd was/were described
ddisgwyl to expect, to look
ddisgwyliadau expectations
ddisgwyliedig expected
ddisgwylir is/are/will be expected
ddisgybl pupil
ddisgyblaeth discipline
ddisgyblaethau disciplines
ddisgyblion pupils
ddisgyblu to discipline
ddisgyn to fall, to land
ddisodli to displace, to supplant
ddistaw quiet
ddiswyddiad dismissal
ddiswyddo to dismiss
ddi-waith unemployed
ddiwallu to satisfy
ddiwedd end
ddiweddar late
ddiweddaraf latest
ddiweddaru to up-date
ddiweithdra unemployment
ddiwethaf last
ddiwrnod day
ddiwrnodau days
ddiwyd diligent
ddiwydiannau industries
ddiwydiannol industrial
ddiwydiant industry
ddiwygiadau revivals (religious)

ddiwygiedig revised
ddiwygio to revise
ddiwylliannau cultures
ddiwylliannol cultural
ddiwylliant culture
ddiymdroi without delay
ddiystyru to ignore
ddod to come
ddodi to lay, to put
ddodrefn furniture
ddoe yesterday
ddoeth wise
ddoethineb wisdom
ddofn deep
ddogfen document
ddogfennaeth documentation
ddogfennau documents
ddogfennol documentary
ddolen link
ddoniau skills
ddoniol amusing, funny
ddosbarth class, form
ddosbarthiad classification, distribution
ddosbarthiadau classes
ddosbarthu to distribute
ddosbarthwyd was/were distributed
ddraenen thorn
ddrafft draft; draught
ddraig dragon
ddrama dramas, play
ddramatig dramatic
ddringo to climb
ddrud costly, dear
ddrwg bad, wicked
ddrws door
ddrysau doors
ddryslyd muddled
ddryswch confusion
ddu black
ddull manner
ddulliau methods
ddur steel

dduw god
dduwiau gods
ddwbl double
ddweud to say
ddwfn deep
ddwfr water
ddwy two
ddwyieithog bilingual
ddwylaw hands
ddwylo hands
ddwyn to steal
ddwyrain east
ddwyreiniol eastern
ddwys intense
ddwywaith twice
ddychmygu to imagine
ddychryn to frighten
ddychwelodd he/she/it returned
ddychwelyd to return
ddychymyg imagination
ddydd day
ddyddiad date
ddyddiadau dates
ddyddiau days
ddyddiol daily
ddyfais device
ddyfal diligent
ddyfalu to guess
ddyfarniad verdict
ddyfarnu to pronounce, to referee
ddyfarnwyd was/were adjudged
ddyfeisio to devise
ddyfernir is/are/will be adjudged
ddyffryn vale
ddyfnach deeper
ddyfnder depth
ddyfod to come
ddyfodiad arrival
ddyfodol future
ddyfroedd waters
ddyfyniadau quotations
ddyfynnir is/are/will be quoted

ddyfynnu to quote
ddygwyd was/were taken
ddylai he/she/it should
ddylanwad influence
ddylanwadau influences
ddylanwadu to influence
ddyled debt
ddyledion debts
ddyledus indebted
ddyletswydd duty
ddyletswyddau duties
ddylunio to design
ddylwn I should
ddymchwel to overturn
ddymuniad desire
ddymuno to desire, to wish
ddymunol pleasant
ddyn man
ddynes woman
ddynion men
ddynodi to indicate
ddynodir is/are/will be indicated
ddynodwyd was/were indicated
ddynol human
ddynoliaeth mankind
ddyrannu to allocate
ddysg learning
ddysgir is/are/will be learned
ddysgl dish
ddysgodd he/she/it learned
ddysgu to learn, to teach
ddysgwyd was/were learned
ddysgwyr learners
ddywed he/she/it says
ddywedais I said
ddywedasant they said
ddywediad saying
ddywedir is/are/will be said
ddywedodd he/she/it said
ddywedwyd was/were said
ddywedyd to say
de south (*nm*)

de right (*nf*)
de tea
deall intellect, understanding (*nm*)
deall to understand (*v*)
dealladwy intelligible, understandable (*adj*)
deallol intellectual (*adj*)
dealltwriaeth agreement, understanding (*nm*)
deallus intelligent, wise (*adj*)
deallusol intellectual (*adj*)
deallusrwydd intelligence (*nm*)
debycach more like
debyd debit (*nm*)
debyg like
debygol likely
decach fairer
dechneg technique
dechnegau techniques
dechnegol technical
dechnoleg technology
dechnolegau technologies
dechrau beginning, start (*nm*)
dechrau to begin, to start (*v*)
dechreuad beginning (*nm*)
dechreuais I started (*v*)
dechreuodd he/she/it started (*v*)
dechreuol initial, original (*adj*)
dechreuwch you start (*v*)
dechreuwyd was/were started (*v*)
deddf act, law, statute (*nf*)
deddfau laws (*npl*)
deddfwriaeth legislation (*nf*)
deddfwriaethol legislative (*adj*)
de-ddwyrain south-east (*nm*)
dedfryd judgement, sentence, verdict (*nf*)
dedfrydau sentences (*npl*)
dedfrydu to sentence (*v*)
dedwydd blessed, happy (*adj*)
defaid sheep (*npl*)
deffro to awake, to rouse, to wake (*v*)
defnydd material, textile, usage, use (*nm*)
defnyddiau materials (*npl*)

defnyddid would be used (*v*)

defnyddio to make use of, to use, to utilize (*v*)

defnyddiodd he/she/it used (*v*)

defnyddiol helpful, useful (*adj*)

defnyddir is/are/will be used (*v*)

defnyddiwch you use (*v*)

defnyddiwr consumer, user (*nm*)

defnyddiwyd was/were used (*v*)

defnyddwyr consumers, users (*npl*)

defod ceremony, custom, rite (*nf*)

defodau customes, rites (*npl*)

deg ten (*num*)

deg fair, fine

degau tens (*npl*)

degawd decade (*nm*)

degawdau decades (*npl*)

degwch beauty, fairness

degwm tithe (*nm*)

deheubarth southern part (*nm*)

deheuol southern (*adj*)

dehongli to interpret (*v*)

dehongliad interpretation (*nm*)

dehongliadau interpretations (*npl*)

deialog dialogue (*nm*)

deiet diet (*nm*)

deigryn tear (*nm*)

deilen leaf (*nf*)

deiliad holder, householder, occupant, tenant (*nm*)

deiliaid occupants (*npl*)

deillio to derive, to stem from (*v*)

deilliodd he/she/it derived (*v*)

deillion blind (people) (*npl*)

deialog dialogue (*nm*)

deilwng deserving

deimlad feeling

deimladau feelings

deimlo to feel

deintydd dentist (*nm*)

deintyddion dentists (*npl*)

deintyddol dental (*adj*)

deipio to type

deirgwaith threefold, three times

deiseb petition (*nf*)

deithiau journeys

deithio to travel

deithiol peripatetic, travelling

deithwyr passengers, travellers

deitl title

deitlau titles

del pretty (*adj*)

deledu television

delerau terms

delfrydol ideal, idealistic (*adj*)

delio to deal (*v*)

delir is/are/will be payed

delta delta (*nm*)

delw effigy, idol, image, statue (*nf*)

delwedd image (*nm*)

delweddau images (*npl*)

delyn harp

deml temple

democrat democrat (*nm*)

democrataidd democratic (*adj*)

democratiaeth democracy (*nf*)

democratiaid democrats (*npl*)

demtasiwn temptation

denant tenant

denantiaeth tenancy

denantiaid tenants

denau thin

dendro to tender

deng ten

dengys he/she/it shows (*v*)

deniadol alluring, attractive, inviting (*adj*)

denu to attract, to draw, to entice (*v*)

deon dean (*nm*)

de-orllewin south-west (*nm*)

derbyn to accept, to admit, to receive (*v*)

derbyniad reception (*nm*)

derbyniadau receipts (*npl*)

derbyniodd he/she/it received (*v*)

derbyniol acceptable (*adj*)

derbyniwyd was/were received *(v)*
derbynnir is/are/will be received *(v)*
derbynnydd receiver *(nm)*
derbynnydd receptor *(nm)*
derfyn end
derfynau limits
derfynol final
derfynu to end, to terminate
derm term
dermau terms
derw oaks *(npl)*
derwen oak *(nf)*
desg desk *(nf)*
destament testament
destun subject
destunau subjects
dethol choice, select *(adj)*
dethol to choose, to select *(v)*
detholiad selection *(nm)*
deuai he/she/it would come *(v)*
deuant they come/they will come *(v)*
deud to tell *(v)*
deuddeg twelve *(num)*
deuddegfed twelfth *(num)*
deuddeng twelve
deugain forty *(num)*
deulawr two storey *(adj)*
deulu family
deuluoedd families
deuluol domestic
deunaw eighteen *(num)*
deunawfed eighteenth *(num)*
deunydd material, matter, stuff *(nm)*
deunyddiau materials *(npl)*
deuocsid dioxide *(nm)*
deuol dual *(adj)*
deuwch you come *(v)*
dew fat
dewch you come! *(v)*
dewis choice, selection *(nm)*
dewis to choose *(v)*
dewis chosen, optional, select *(adj)*

dewisiadau choices, options *(npl)*
dewisir is/are/will be chosen *(v)*
dewislen menu *(nf)*
dewisodd he/she/it chose *(v)*
dewisol choice, discretionary, select *(adj)*
dewiswch you choose *(v)*
dewiswyd was/were chosen *(v)*
dewr brave, valiant *(adj)*
dewrder bravery, courage, pluck *(nm)*
deyrnas kingdom
deyrnged tribute
di you
diafol demon, devil *(nm)*
diagnosis diagnosis *(nm)*
diagnostig diagnostic *(adj)*
diagram diagram *(nm)*
diagramau diagrams *(npl)*
dial reprisal, revenge, vengeance *(nm)*
dial to avenge, to wreak vengeance *(v)*
diamau certain, doubtless *(adj)*
diamod unconditional, unqualified *(adj)*
dianc to escape, to flee *(v)*
diangen unnecessary *(adj)*
diau certain, sure, undoubted *(adj)*
diawl bloody hell!, devil *(nm)*
diben aim, purpose *(nm)*
dibenion aims *(npl)*
dibwys trivial, unimportant *(adj)*
dibynadwy dependable, reliable, trustworthy *(adj)*
dibynadwyaeth dependability *(nf)*
dibyniaeth dependence, reliance *(nm)*
dibynnol dependent; subjunctive *(adj)*
dibynnu to depend, to rely upon *(v)*
dichon perhaps *(adv)*
dichonoldeb feasibility, potentiality *(nm)*
dicter anger, wrath *(nm)*
di-dâl unpaid *(adj)*
diddanu to amuse, to entertain *(v)*
diddordeb interest *(nm)*
diddordebau interests *(npl)*
diddorol interesting *(adj)*

diddymu to abolish, to annul, to repeal, to rescind (v)

didoli to separate, to sort (v)

di-dor incessant, unbroken, uninterrupted (nm)

didrafferth easy, trouble-free (adj)

diduedd impartial, unbiased (adj)

didynnu to deduct, to subtract (v)

didynnwyd was/were deducted, subtracted (v)

dieithr alien, foreign, strange, uncommon, (adj)

dieithriad without exception (adj)

difa to consume, to destroy, to ravage (v)

difaru to regret (v)

difaterwch apathy, indifference, nonchalance (nm)

diferu to drip, to trickle (v)

difetha to destroy, to spoil (v)

diffaith barren, desert, desolate, paralysed, rotten, worthless (adj)

diffiniad definition (nm)

diffiniadau definitions (npl)

diffiniedig defined (adj)

diffinio to define (v)

diffinnir is/are/will be defined (v)

diffodd to extinguish, to go out, to put out, to turn off (v)

diffuant genuine, sincere (adj)

diffyg defect, deficiency, eclipse, lack, shortcoming, shortfall (adj)

diffygiol defective, deficient, imperfect (adj)

diffygion shortcomings (npl)

diffynnydd defendant (nm)

diflannodd he/she/it disappeared (v)

diflannu to disappear, to vanish (v)

diflas boring, depressing, distasteful, dull (adj)

difreintiedig underprivileged (adj)

difri serious (adj)

difrif earnest, serious (adj)

difrifol earnest, grave, serious (adj)

difrifoldeb earnestness, seriousness (nm)

difrod damage, devastation (nm)

difrodi to destroy, to devastate (v)

difyr agreeable, entertaining, pleasant (adj)

dig anger, indignation (nm)

dig angry, indignant, irate (adj)

digalon depressed, despondent, disheartened (adj)

digartref homeless (adj)

digido to digitize (v)

digidol digital (adj)

digon ample, enough, plenty (nm)

digonedd abundance, plenty (nm)

digonol adequate, ample, sufficient (adj)

digwydd to happen (v)

digwydd hardly (adv)

digwydd action (nm)

digwyddiad event (nm)

digwyddiadau events (npl)

digwyddiadur events diary (nm)

digwyddodd he/she/it (v)

di-Gymraeg non-Welsh-speaking (adj)

diheintio to disinfect (v)

dileu to abolish, to delete (v)

dilëwyd was/were deleted (v)

dillad bedclothes, clothes, garments (npl)

dilyn to follow, to grasp, to imitate, to pursue, to result, to study (v)

dilyniant progression, sequence (nm)

dilynir is/are/will be (v)

dilynodd he/she/it (v)

dilynol following, subsequent (adj)

dilynwch you follow (v)

dilynwr follower (nm)

dilynwyr followers (npl)

dilys authentic, genuine, valid (adj)

dilysrwydd genuineness, validity (nm)

dilysu to authenticate, to validate (v)

dim anything, nil, none, nothing, nought, something, zero (nm)

dîm team

dimai halfpenny (nf)

dimau teams
dimensiwn dimension (*nm*)
din arse
dinas city (*nf*)
dinasoedd (*npl*)
dinasyddiaeth citizenship (*nf*)
dinasyddion citizens (*npl*)
dinesig civic, municipal, urban (*adj*)
dinesydd citizen, inhabitant (*nm*)
dinistr destruction, havoc, ruin (*nm*)
dinistrio to annihilate, to destroy, to ruin (*v*)
dinistriol destructive, ruinous (*adj*)
diniwed blameless, harmless, innocent, naive (*adj*)
diod drink, liquor (*nf*)
dioddef to endure, to suffer, to tolerate (*v*)
dioddefaint suffering (*nm*)
dioddefodd he/she/it suffered (*v*)
dioddefwr sufferer, victim (*nm*)
dioddefwyr sufferers (*npl*)
diodydd drinks (*npl*)
diog idle, lazy (*nm*)
diogel certain, safe, substantial, sure (*nm*)
diogelir is/are/will be protected (*v*)
diogelu to assure, to ensure, to preserve, to protect (*v*)
diogelwch safety, security (*nm*)
diolch gratitude, thanks (*nm*)
diolch to thank (*v*)
diolchgar grateful, thankful (*adj*)
diolchodd he/she/it thanked (*v*)
dip dip (*nm*)
dip tip
dipio to dip (*v*)
diploma diploma (*nm*)
dipyn a bit
dir land
dirfawr enormous, immense (*adj*)
dirgel mysterious, secret (*adj*)
dirgel secret (*nm*)
dirgelwch mystery, (*nm*)

diriaethol concrete, tangible (*adj*)
diriogaeth territory
dirnad to comprehend, to fathom, to understand (*v*)
diroedd land (s)
dirprwy deputy, surrogate (*nm*)
dirprwy deputy (*adj*)
dirprwyedig deputized (*adj*)
dirprwyo to commission, to deputize for (*v*)
dirwedd landscape, relief
dirwy fine (*nf*)
dirwyn to coil, to wind up (*v*)
dirwyon fines (*npl*)
dirymu to annul, to revoke (*v*)
dirywiad decadence, decline, degeneration, deterioration (*nm*)
dirywio to degrade, to deteriorate (*v*)
disg disc, disk (*nm*)
disglair bright, brilliant, dazzling (*adj*)
disgleirio to shine, to sparkle (*v*)
disgownt discount (*nm*)
disgresiwn discretion (*nm*)
disgrifiad description (*nm*)
disgrifiadau descriptions (*npl*)
disgrifio to describe (*v*)
disgrifiodd he/she/it described (*v*)
disgrifir is/are/will be described (*v*)
disgrifiwch you describe (*v*)
disgrifiwyd was/were described (*v*)
disgwyl to appear, to await, to expect, to look, to look for (*v*)
disgwyliad expectation (*nm*)
disgwyliadau expectations (*npl*)
disgwylid would be expected (*v*)
disgwyliedig anticipated, expected (*adj*)
disgwylir is/are/will be expected (*v*)
disgwyliwn we expect/we will expect (*v*)
disgybl disciple, pupil (*nm*)
disgyblaeth discipline (*nf*)
disgyblaethau disciplines (*npl*)
disgyblion pupils (*npl*)
disgyblu to discipline (*v*)

disgyn to descend from, to dismount, to fall, to flow, to land (*v*)

disgyrchiant gravity (*nm*)

disodli to displace, to supplant (*v*)

distaw calm, peaceful, quiet, silent, soft (*adj*)

distawrwydd silence, stillness (*nm*)

diswyddiad dismissal, sack (*nm*)

diswyddo to dismiss, to sack (*v*)

dithau yourself

di-waith redundant, unemployed (*adj*)

diwallu to satisfy (*v*)

diwedd end (*nm*)

diweddar late, recent (*adj*)

diweddara latest (*adj*)

diweddarach latest (*adj*)

diweddaraf latest (*adj*)

diweddariad revision, update (*nm*)

diweddaru to modernize, to up-date (*v*)

diweddarwyd was/were updated (*v*)

diweddglo conclusion, finale (*nm*)

diweddu to end, to finish (*v*)

diweithdra unemployment (*nm*)

diwethaf last (*adj*)

diwinyddiaeth theology (*nf*)

diwinyddol theological (*adj*)

diwrnod day (*nm*)

diwrnodau days (*npl*)

diwtoriaid tutors

diwyd assiduous, diligent (*adj*)

diwydiannau industries (*npl*)

diwydiannol industrial (*adj*)

diwydiant industry (*nm*)

diwyg appearance, format (*nm*)

diwygiad reform, revival (*nm*)

diwygiadau reforms, revivals [religious] (*npl*)

diwygiedig amended, revised (*adj*)

diwygio to amend, to reform, to revise (*v*)

diwygiwyd was/were amended, reformed (*v*)

diwylliannau cultures (*npl*)

diwylliannol cultural (*adj*)

diwylliant culture (*nm*)

diymdroi immediate, without delay (*adj*)

diystyru to disregard, to ignore (*v*)

dlawd poor

dlodi poverty

dlos pretty

do yes (*adv*)

doctor doctor (*nm*)

docyn ticket

docynnau tickets

dod to become, to come (*v*)

dodi to plant, to put (*v*)

dodrefn furniture (*npl*)

dodwy to lay (*v*)

doe yesterday (*adv*)

doedd he/she/it was not (*v*)

doeddwn I was not (*v*)

does there is not (*v*)

doeth discreet, wise (*adj*)

doethineb sagacity, wisdom (*nm*)

dofednod poultry (*npl*)

dofn deep (*adj/f*)

dogfen document (*nf*)

dogfennaeth documentation (*nf*)

dogfennau documents (*npl*)

dogfennol documentary (*adj*)

doi you/*you* will come (*v*)

dôl dale, meadow (*nf*)

dôl dole (*nm*)

dolen connection, handle, link, loop (*nf*)

dolennau handles, links, loops (*npl*)

dolenni links (*npl*)

Dolig Xmas (*nm*)

doll tax, toll

dolur anguish, hurt, sickness, sore, sorrow, wound (*nm*)

dolydd meadows (*npl*)

dom manure

domen dump, dunghill

domestig domestic (*adj*)

don wave

dôn tune

doniau abilities, gifts (*npl*)
doniol amusing, humorous (*adj*)
donnau waves
dop top
dor belly, midriff
dorf crowd
doriad break, cut
dorri to break
dorrodd he/she/it broke
dos go! (*v*)
dos dose (*nf*)
dosbarth class, district, division, form (*nm*)
dosbarthiad classification, distribution (*nm*)
dosbarthiadau classes (*npl*)
dosbarthu to arrange, to classify, to deliver, to distribute (*v*)
dosbarthwyd was/were distributed (*v*)
dosberthir is/are/will be distributed (*v*)
dost sore, unwell
dost toast
dowch come! (*v*)
down we come, we will come, we are coming (*v*)
Dr doctor (*nm*)
dra extremely, very
drachefn again
draddodi to commit, to deliver
draddodiad tradition
draddodiadau traditions
draddodiadol traditional
draean a third
draed feet
draenen thorn-tree (*nf*)
draeniad drainage (*nm*)
draenio to drain (*v*)
draeth beach
draethau beaches
draethawd dissertation, essay
drafferth difficulty
drafferthion difficulties
draffig traffic
drafft draft (*nm*)

drafftio to draft (*v*)
drafnidiaeth traffic
drafod to discuss
drafodaeth discussion
drafodaethau discussions
drafodion proceedings, transactions
drafodir is/are/will be discussed
drafodwyd was/were discussed
dragwyddol eternal
dragywydd eternal
draig dragon (*nf*)
drais rape, violence
drama drama, play (*nf*)
dramatig dramatic (*adj*)
dramâu dramas, plays (*npl*)
dramgwydd hindrance
dramodwr dramatist, playwright (*nm*)
dramodydd dramatist, playwright (*nm*)
dramor overseas
drannoeth next day
dras kin, pedigree
draul wear
draw there, yonder (*adv*)
drawiadol striking
draws cross
drawsnewid to transform
dre town
drech superior
drechu to defeat
dref town
drefi towns
drefn order
drefniadaeth organisation
drefniadau arrangements
drefniant arrangement
drefnir is/are/will be arranged
drefnu to arrange
drefnus orderly
drefnwyd was/were arranged
drefol urban
dreftadaeth heritage
dreigiau dragons (*npl*)

dreigl passage
drenau trains
dreth tax
drethadwy taxable
drethi rates, taxes
drethu to tax
dreuliau expenses
dreulio to spend
dreuliodd he/she/it spent
dri three
dribiwnlys tribunal
drigolion inhabitants
drin to treat
drindod trinity
dringo to climb, to scale (v)
driniaeth treatment
driniaethau treatments
drio to try
drist sad
dristwch sadness
dro time, turn, walk
drodd he/she/it turned
droed feet
droedfeddi feet
droeon twists
droi to turn
drol cart
drom heavy
dros for, over
drosedd crime
droseddau crimes
droseddol criminal
droseddu to commit an offence
droseddwyr criminals, culprits
drosglwyddiad transference
drosglwyddir is/are/will be transferred
drosglwyddo to transfer
drosglwyddwyd was/were transferred
drosi to convert, to translate
drosoch for (you), over (you)
drosodd for (him/it), over (him/it)
drosom for (us), over (us)

drothwy threshold
drowyd was/were turned
druan poor thing
drud costly, dear, valuable (adj)
drueni pity
druenus piteous
drugaredd mercy
drugarog merciful
drwch thickness
drwchus thick
drwg evil, harm (nm)
drwg bad, counterfeit, evil, nasty, naughty, rotten, wicked (adj)
drwm heavy
drwodd through
drws door, door to door, doorway, gap, opening (nm)
drwsio to mend
drwyadl thorough
drwydded licence
drwyddedau licences
drwyddedu to licence
drwyn nose
drych image, looking-glass, mirror (nm)
drychineb disaster
drydan electricity
drydedd third
drydydd third
drygioni evil, mischief, naughtiness, wickedness (nm)
dryloyw transparent
drylwyr thorough
drysau doors (npl)
dryslyd confused, muddled, tangled (adj)
drysor treasure
drysorau treasures
drysu to become knotted, to bewilder, to confuse, to entangle (v)
dryswch bewilderment, confusion, muddle, perplexity (nm)
drywydd track
du black, dark, dirty (adj)

dudalen page
dudalennau pages
duedd tendency
dueddiadau tendencies
dueddol inclined, liable
dug duke (*nm*)
dug he/she/it took (*v*)
dull manner, method, style (*nm*)
dulliau methods (*npl*)
duon black (*adj/pl*)
dur steel (*nm*)
duw god (*nm*)
duwiau gods (*npl*)
duwiol devout, godly, pious (*adj*)
dwad to come (*v*)
dwbl double (*adj*)
dwbl double (*nm*)
dweud to assert, to claim, to mention, to say, to tell (*v*)
dwf growth
dwfn deep, difficult to understand, profound (*adj*)
dwfn the depths (*nm*)
dwfr water (*nm*)
dwll hole
dwp silly
dwr crowd, heap
dŵr water (*nm*)
dwristiaeth tourism
dwristiaid tourists
dwsin dozen (*nm*)
dwt neat, tidy
dwy two (*num/f*)
dwyfol divine, sacred (*adj*)
dwyieithog bilingual (*adj*)
dwyieithrwydd bilingualism (*nm*)
dwyll deceit
dwyllo to deceive
dwylo hands (*npl*)
dwyn to bear, to bear (fruit), to bring, to carry, to give birth to, to make, to steal (*v*)

dwyrain east (*nm*)
dwyreiniol easterly, eastern, oriental (*adj*)
dwys concentrated, intense, profound, serious (*adj*)
dwysedd density (*nm*)
dwywaith double, twice (*adv*)
dy thine, thy, you, your (*pronoun*)
dybiaeth presumption
dybio to presume
dyblu to double, to repeat (*v*)
dyblygu to duplicate (*v*)
dybryd atrocious, dire, monstrous (*adj*)
dychmygol fictitious, imaginary, imaginative (*adj*)
dychmygu to fancy, to imagine, to picture (*v*)
dychmygus imaginative, inventive (*adj*)
dychmygwch you imagine (*v*)
dychryn fright, scare, terror (*nm*)
dychryn to dread, to frighten, to terrify (*v*)
dychrynllyd awful, dreadful, terrible (*adj*)
dychwelodd he/she/it returned (*v*)
dychwelwch you return (*v*)
dychwelyd to return, to revert (*v*)
dychymyg fancy, imagination (*nm*)
dydd day (*nm*)
dyddiad date (*nm*)
dyddiadau dates (*npl*)
dyddiadur diary (*nm*)
dyddiaduron diaries (*npl*)
dyddiau days (*npl*)
dyddiedig dated (*adj*)
dyddio to date, to dawn (*v*)
dyddiol daily (*adj*)
dyddlyfr diary (*nm*)
dydi (*he, she, it*) is not (*v*)
dydw I am not (*v*)
dydy he/she/it is not (*v*)
dydyn we are not (*v*)
dyfais device, gadget, invention (*nf*)
dyfal diligent, painstaking, persistent (*adj*)
dyfalu to guess, to work out (*v*)

dyfarniad adjudication, verdict (*nm*)

dyfarniadau verdicts (*npl*)

dyfarnu to adjudicate, to award, to pronounce, to referee, to umpire (*v*)

dyfarnwr referee, umpire (*nm*)

dyfarnwyd was/were adjudged, pronounced (*v*)

dyfeisgar ingenious, inventive, resourceful (*adj*)

dyfeisiau devices (*npl*)

dyfeisio to devise, to invent (*v*)

dyfernir is/are/will be adjudged (*v*)

dyffryn vale, valley (*nm*)

dyffrynnoedd vales, valleys (*npl*)

dyfi you grow

dyfiant growth

dyfnach deeper (*adj*)

dyfnder depth, intensity, profundity, seriousness (*nm*)

dyfnion deep (*adj/pl*)

dyfod to come (*v*)

dyfodiad arrival, coming (*nm*)

dyfodol future (*nm*)

dyfrgi otter (*nm*)

dyfrgwn otters (*npl*)

dyfrhau to irrigate, to water (*v*)

dyfroedd waters (*npl*)

dyfu to grow

dyfyniad extract, quotation (*nm*)

dyfyniadau quotations (*npl*)

dyfynnir is/are/will be quoted (*v*)

dyfynnu to cite, to quote (*v*)

dygwyd was/were brought, taken (*v*)

dygymod to accept, to be reconciled to, to put up with (*v*)

dyhead aspiration, longing, yearning (*nm*)

dyheadau aspirations (*npl*)

dyheu to aspire, to long for, to yearn (*v*)

dylai he/she/it should (*v*)

dylanwad influence (*nm*)

dylanwadau influences (*npl*)

dylanwadol influential (*adj*)

dylanwadu to hold sway, to influence (*v*)

dylech you should (*v*)

dyled debt (*nf*)

dyledion debts (*npl*)

dyledus due, indebted, outstanding, owing (*adj*)

dyledwr debtor (*nm*)

dyledwyr debtors (*npl*)

dylem we should (*v*)

dylen they should (*v*)

dylent they should (*v*)

dyletswydd devotion, duty (*nf*)

dyletswyddau duties (*npl*)

dylid you should (*v*)

dyllau holes

dyluniad design (*nm*)

dyluniadau designs (*npl*)

dylunio to design (*v*)

dyluniwyd was/were designed (*v*)

dylwn I should (*v*)

dyma here is, this is, these are (*adv*)

dymchwel to demolish, to overthrow, to overturn (*v*)

dymheredd temperature

dymhorol seasonal

dymor season, term

dymunant they wish/they will wish (*v*)

dymuniad desire, wish (*nm*)

dymuniadau desires, wishes (*npl*)

dymuno to desire, to wish (*v*)

dymunol agreeable, delightful, pleasant (*adj*)

dymunwch you wish (*v*)

dymunwn we wish/we will wish (*v*)

dyn man, mortal (*nm*)

dyna that is, those are, there (*adv*)

dyner tender

dynes female, woman (*nf*)

dyngarol humane, humanitarian, philanthropic (*adj*)

dynged fate

dyngedfennol crucial, fateful

dyniaethau humanities (*npl*)
dynion men (*npl*)
dynn tight
dynnir is/are/will be drawn, pulled
dynnodd he/she/it drew, pulled
dynnu to draw, to pull
dynnwyd was/were drawn, pulled
dynodedig designated (*adj*)
dynodi to denote, to indicate (*v*)
dynodir is/are/will be denoted (*v*)
dynodwyd was/were denoted (*v*)
dynol human, manly, mortal (*adj*)
dynoliaeth humaneness, humanity, mankind (*nf*)
dynwared to copy, to imitate, to mimic (*v*)
dyraniad allocation (*nm*)
dyraniadau allocations (*nml*)
dyrannu to allocate, to dissect, to share out (*v*)
dyrchafiad preferment, promotion (*nm*)
dyrchafu to elevate, to lift, to promote (*v*)
dyrfa crowd
dyrys complicated, entangled, intricate, perplexing (*adj*)
dysg learning (*nf*)
dysgeidiaeth doctrine, teaching (*nf*)
dysgir is/are/will be taught (*v*)
dysgl dish, platter (*nf*)

dysgodd he/she/it learned, taught (*v*)
dysgu to learn, to memorize, to teach (*v*)
dysgwr learner (*nm*)
dysgwyd was/were learned, was/were taught (*v*)
dysgwyr learners (*npl*)
dyst witness
dystiolaeth evidence
dystion witnesses
dystysgrif certificate
dystysgrifau certificates
dyw is not (*v*)
dywed he/she/it says (*v*)
dywedai he/she/it said (*v*)
dywedais I said (*v*)
dywedasant they said (*v*)
dyweder (*let it be*) said! (*v*)
dywediad saying (*nm*)
dywedir is/are/will be said (*v*)
dywedodd he/she/it said (*v*)
dywedwch you say (*v*)
dywedwyd was/were said (*v*)
dywedyd to say (*v*)
dywod sand
dywydd weather
dywyll dark
dywysoges princess
dywysogion princes

E

a word starting with **e** printed in blue means that the root form of that word begins with **g**, e.g. **eiriau** root **geiriau**

---

eang broad, extensive, wide (*adj*)
ebe quoth, said (*v*)
e-bost electronic mail, e-mail (*nm*)
e-bostia you e-mail (*v*)
e-bostio to e-mail (*v*)
e-bostiwch you e-mail (*v*)
ebr he/*she*) said (*v*)
Ebrill April (*nm*)
echdyniad extraction (*nm*)
echdyniadau extractions (*npl*)
echdynnu to extract (*v*)
echdynwyr extractors (*npl*)
ecoleg ecology (*nf*)
ecolegol ecological (*adj*)
economaidd economic (*adj*)
economeg economics (*nf*)
economi economy (*nm*)
ecosystem ecosystem (*nf*)
ecosystemau ecosystems (*npl*)
edau cotton, thread, yarn (*nf*)
e-ddysgu e-learning (*nm*)
edmygedd admiration (*nm*)
edmygu to admire, to esteem (*v*)
edrych to look (*v*)
edrychai he/she/it would look (*v*)
edrychodd he/she/it (*v*)
edrychwch you look (*v*)
edrychwn we look/we will look (*v*)
ef he, him, it (*pronoun*)
efail smithy
efallai maybe, perhaps, possibly (*adv*)
e-fasnach e-trading (*nf*)
efe he, him (*pronoun*)

efelychu to emulate, to imitate (*v*)
efengyl Gospel, gospel truth (*nf*)
efengylaidd evangelical (*adj*)
effaith effect (*nf*)
effeithiau effects (*npl*)
effeithio to affect (*v*)
effeithiodd he/she/it affected (*v*)
effeithiol effective, efficient (*adj*)
effeithiolrwydd effectiveness, efficacy (*nm*)
effeithir is/are/will be affected (*v*)
effeithiwyd was/were affected (*v*)
effeithlon efficient (*adj*)
effeithlonrwydd efficiency (*nm*)
effro alert, awake, vigilant (*adj*)
efo together with, with (*prep*)
e-fusnes e-business (*nm*)
efydd brass, bronze (*nm*)
efydd brassy (*adj*)
e-gardiau e-cards (*npl*)
egin shoots (*npl*)
eglur clear, distinct, plain (*adj*)
eglurdeb clarity, clearness (*nm*)
eglurder clarity (*nm*)
eglurhad explanation (*nm*)
egluro to clarify, to explain (*v*)
eglurodd he/she/it explained (*v*)
eglurwch you explain (*v*)
eglwys church (*nf*)
eglwysi churches (*npl*)
eglwysig ecclesiastical (*adj*)
egni energy, might (*nm*)
egnïol energetic, strenuous, vigorous (*adj*)

egwyddor principle, rudiments (*npl*)
egwyddorion principles (*npl*)
egwyl break, intermission, interval (*nf*)
ehangach wider (*adj*)
ehangaf widest (*adj*)
ehangder breadth, expanse, stretch (*nm*)
ehangiad extension (*nm*)
ehangu to broaden, to expand, to extend (*v*)
ei her, him, his, it, its (*pronoun*)
ei you go/you will go (*v*)
eich you, your (*pronoun*)
eicon icon (*nm*)
Eidal, yr Italy
Eidalaidd Italian (*adj*)
Eidaleg Italian (language) (*nf*)
eiddgar ardent, enthusiastic, zealous (*adj*)
eiddo possessions, property (*nm*)
eidion bullock (*nm*)
Eifftiad Egyptian (*adj*)
Eifftiaid Egyptians (*npl*)
eigion bottom, depths, the deep (*nm*)
eilaidd secondary (*adj*)
eiliad moment, second (*nf*)
eiliadau seconds (*npl*)
eilradd secondary, second-rate (*adj*)
eilwaith again, second time (*adv*)
ein our, us (*pronoun*)
Eingl Angles (*npl*)
einioes life, lifetime (*nf*)
eir he/she/it goes, will go (*v*)
eira snow (*nm*)
eirfa vocabulary
eiriau words
eiriolaeth advocacy, intercession (*nf*)
eironig ironic (*adj*)
eisiau destitution, lack, need, want (*nm*)
eisoes already (*adv*)
eistedd to seat, to sit (*v*)
eisteddai he/she/it would sit (*v*)
eisteddfod competitive meeting (*nf*)
eisteddfodau (*npl*)
eisteddfodol (*adj*)

eisteddodd he/she/it sat (*v*)
eitem item (*nf*)
eitemau items (*npl*)
eithaf extreme, highest, quite, superlative, ultimate, utmost (*adj*)
eithaf extremity, limit (*nm*)
eithafol excessive, extreme (*adj*)
eithin furze, gorse, whin (*npl*)
eithr but, save that (*conj*)
eithriad exception (*nf*)
eithriadau exceptions (*npl*)
eithriadol exceptional, outstanding (*adj*)
eithriedig excluded (*adj*)
eithrio to exclude, to exempt (*v*)
electroneg electronics (*nf*)
electronig electronic (*adj*)
eleni this year (*adv*)
elfen aptitude, element, factor (*nf*)
elfennau elements (*npl*)
elfennol elementary, rudimentary (*adj*)
eli balm, ointment (*nm*)
eliffant elephant (*nm*)
elifiant effluence (*nm*)
elli you can, you will be able
ellid could be able (*v*)
ellir he/she/it can/will be able
ellwch you are able, you will be able, you could
elusen alms, charity (*nf*)
elusennau charities (*npl*)
elusennol charitable (*adj*)
elw gain, proceeds, profit (*nm*)
elwa to benefit, to profit (*v*)
elwid would be called
elwir is/are/will be called
elyn enemy
elynion enemies
em gem
emosiwn emotion (*nm*)
emosiynau emotions (*npl*)
emosiynol emotional (*adj*)
emyn hymn (*nm*)

emynau hymns (*npl*)

enaid soul (*nm*)

enau mouth

enbyd grievous, perilous (*adj*)

endid entity (*nm*)

enedigaeth birth

enedigol native

eneidiau souls (*npl*)

eneth girl

enetig genetic

enfawr colossal, enormous, immense (*adj*)

enghraifft example (*nf*)

enghreifftiau examples (*npl*)

enghreifftiol illustrative (*adj*)

englyn verse (*nm*)

englynion verses (*npl*)

eni to be born

enillion earnings, spoils, winnings (*npl*)

enillir is/are/will be won (*v*)

enillodd he/she/it won (*v*)

enillwr winner (*nm*)

enillwyd was/were won (*v*)

enillwyr winners (*npl*)

enillydd winner (*nm*)

ennill to earn, to obtain, to win (*v*)

ennyd while (*nm*)

ennyn to awaken, to ignite, to light (*v*)

entrepreneur entrepreneur (*nm*)

entrepreneuraidd entrepreneurial (*adj*)

entrepreneuriaeth entrepreneurship (*nf*)

entrepreneuriaid entrepreneurs (*npl*)

enw name, noun, reputation (*nm*)

enwad denomination (*nm*)

enwadau denominations (*npl*)

enwau names, nouns (*npl*)

enwebedig nominated (*adj*)

enwebiad nomination (*nm*)

enwebiadau nominations (*npl*)

enwebu to nominate(*v*)

enwebwyd was/were nominated (*v*)

enwedig especially, particularly (*adj*)

enwi to call, to name (*v*)

enwir is/are/will be named (*v*)

enwocaf most famous

enwog celebrated, famous (*adj*)

enwogion celebrities (*npl*)

enwogrwydd fame, renown (*nm*)

enwyd was/were named (*v*)

eog salmon (*nm*)

eogiaid salmon (*npl*)

epistol epistle (*nm*)

er despite, for, since (*prep*)

eraill others (*adj*)

erbyn after, against, by, come to, in time for, opposed to, versus (*prep*)

erbyn by the time (*conj*)

erchyll dreadful, hideous, horrible (*adj*)

erfyn instrument, tool (*nm*)

erfyn to beg, to entreat, to implore (*v*)

ergyd blast, blow, shot (*nf*)

erioed ever, never, (not) at all (*adv*)

erledigaeth persecution (*nf*)

erlid to hound, to persecute (*v*)

erlyn to prosecute, to sue (*v*)

erlyniad prosecution (*nm*)

ers since (*prep*)

erthygl article, clause (*nf*)

erthyglau articles (*npl*)

erw acre (*nf*)

erwau acres (*npl*)

erydiad erosion (*nm*)

erydu to erode (*v*)

eryr eagle (*nm*)

eryr herpes, shingles (*nm*)

erys he/she/it stays (*v*)

es I went (*v*)

esblygiad evolution (*nm*)

esblygu to evolve (*v*)

esboniad commentary, explanation (*nm*)

esboniadau commentaries, explanations (*npl*)

esboniadol explanatory (*adj*)

esbonio to explain (*v*)

esboniodd he/she/it explained (*v*)

esboniwch you explain (*v*)

esgeuluso to disregard, to neglect, to shirk (*v*)

esgeulustod carelessness, negligence (*nm*)

esgid boot, shoe (*nf*)

esgidiau shoes (*npl*)

esgob bishop (*nm*)

esgobaeth bishopric, diocese (*nf*)

esgobion bishop (*npl*)

esgor to give birth (*v*)

esgus excuse, pretext (*nm*)

esgyn to ascend, to mount, to rise

esgyrn bones (*npl*)

esiampl example (*nf*)

esiamplau examples (*npl*)

esmwyth easy, glib, quiet, smooth (*adj*)

esthetig aesthetic (*adj*)

estron alien, foreign (*adj*)

estyn to extend, to hand, to stretch (*v*)

estynedig extended (*adj*)

estyniad extension (*nm*)

estyniadau extensions (*npl*)

estynnodd he/she/it handed, reached (*v*)

ethnig ethnic (*adj*)

ethol to elect (*v*)

etholaeth constituency, electorate, ward (*nf*)

etholaethau constituencies (*npl*)

etholedig elect (*adj*)

etholiad election (*nm*)

etholiadau elections (*npl*)

etholiadol electoral (*adj*)

etholwr constituent, elector, voter (*nm*)

etholwyd was/were elected (*v*)

etholwyr electors (*npl*)

ethos ethos (*nm*)

etifedd heir, inheritor (*nm*)

etifeddiaeth inheritance (*nf*)

etifeddu to inherit (*v*)

eto still, yet (*conjunction*)

eto again, ditto, yet (*adv*)

eu their, them (*pronoun*)

euog guilty (*adj*)

euogfarn conviction (*nf*)

euogfarnau convictions (*npl*)

euogrwydd guilt (*nm*)

euraid golden [of gold] (*adj*)

euraidd golden [like gold] (*adj*)

euthum I went (*v*)

ewch you go (*v*)

ewro euro (*nm*)

Ewrop Europe

Ewropeaidd European (*adj*)

ewyllys will (determination) (*nm*)

ewyllys last will and testament, will (*nf*)

ewyn foam, froth, lather, scum (*nm*)

ewythr uncle (*nm*)

F

a word starting with **f** printed in blue means that the root form of that word begins either with a **b***, e.g. ***fabanod** root **babanod** or with an **m**, e.g. **fab** root **mab**

Ff stands as a letter in its own right in Welsh. In a Welsh dictionary, unlike this list, words starting with, or containing '**ff**' would commence after those containing **f**

ficer vicar
Fictoraidd Victorian
fy my
ffa beans, broad beans
ffacs fax (facsimile)
ffactor factor:

fab son
*fabanod babies
fabwysiadu to adopt
fabwysiadwyd was/were adopted
*fach little, small
*fachgen boy
*fae bay
faen stone
faenor manor
faer mayor
faes field
faethu to nurture
*fag bag
fagu to nurse, to rear
fagwyd was/were nursed, reared
*fai fault
Fai May
*faich burden
fain narrow, slim
fainc bench
faint much, size

faith long
*falch glad, proud
*falchder pride
falle perhaps (*adv*)
falu to grind
fam mother
famau mothers
fam-gu grandmother
fan van (*nf*)
fân small, tiny
*fanc bank
*fanciau banks
*fand band
fandaliaeth vandalism (*nf*)
*fandiau bands
*faner flag
fangre place, premises
fannau places
*fannau peaks
fantais advantage
fanteisio to take advantage
fanteisiol advantageous
fanteision advantages
fantell cloak
fantol balance
fantolen balance sheet
fanwl detailed
fanylach more detailed
fanylder detail
fanyleb specification
fanylebau specifications
fanylion details
fap map

fapiau maps
fapio to map
far bar
*fara bread
farc mark
farchnad market
farchnadoedd markets
farchnata to market, to trade
farciau marks
farcio mark
*fardd bard, poet
*farddoniaeth poetry
*fargen bargen
*farn nuisance, opinion
*farnu to judge
*farnwr judge
*farnwriaeth judiciary
farw dead (ones), die
farwolaeth death
farwolaethau deaths
*fas bass
*fasged basket
fasnach trade
fasnachol commercial
fasnachu to trade
fasnachwyr traders
*faswn bassoon
fater matter
faterion matters
*fath bath
fath sort
fathau sorts
fawr big
fe {introduces a statement}
    fe'ch you
    fe'i he, him, it, she
    fe'u they
fe he, him, it (pronoun)
fecanyddol mechanical
*fechan little
*fechgyn boys
fedal medal

*fedd grave
fedd he/she/it owns
feddal soft
feddalwedd software
feddiannu to possess
feddiant possession
feddu to possess
feddwl to think
feddyg doctor
feddygfa surgery
feddyginiaeth cure, treatment
feddygol medical
feddygon doctors
feddyliau thoughts
feddyliol mental
fedr ability
fedrai he/she/it would be able
fedrau skills
fedru to be able
fedrus capable
fedrwch you can
fedrwn we are able, we will be able
feddwl mind
fei (come to) light (nm)
feibion sons
*feic bike
*feichiog pregnant
feini slabs, stones
*feirdd bards, poets
*feirniadaeth criticism
*feirniadol critical
*feirniadu to adjudge, to adjudicate, to criticize
*feirniaid adjudicators, critics
feistr master
feithrin to nurture
feithrinfa nursery
fel as, like, similar (prep)
fel as, how (adv)
fêl honey
felen yellow
felin mill

felly so, such, therefore, thus (*adv*)

felyn yellow

felys sweet

*****fendigedig** excellent, great

*****fendith** blessing

fenter venture

*****fenthyca** to borrow, to lend

*****fenthyciad** loan

*****fenthyciadau** loans

*****fenthyg** borrowed

fentrau ventures

fentro to dare, to venture

fenyw woman

fenywod women

*****fer** short

ferch girl

ferched girls

*****ferf** verb

fersiwn version (*nm*)

fersiynau versions (*npl*)

fertigol vertical (*adj*)

*****ferwi** to boil

festri vestry (*nf*)

fesul by

fesur to measure

fesurau measurements

fetel metal

fethiannau failures

fethiant failure

fethodd he/she/it failed

fethodoleg methodology

fethu to fail

fetrig metric

*****feunyddiol** daily

fewnforio to import

fewnfudwyr immigrants

fewnol internal

feysydd fields

ffa beans, broad beans (*npl*)

ffacs fax (facsimile) (*nm*)

ffactor factor (*Maths*) (*nm*)

ffactor factor (*nf*)

ffactorau factors (*npl*)

ffafr favour (*nf*)

ffafrio to favour, to prefer (*v*)

ffafriol favourable, preferential (*adj*)

ffair fair, market (*nf*)

ffaith fact (*nf*)

ffanatic fanatic (*nm*)

ffanatig fanatic (*nm*)

ffansi fancy (*nf*)

ffarm farm (*nf*)

ffarmwr farmer (*nm*)

ffarwelio to bid farewell (*v*)

ffasiwn fashion, vogue (*nf*)

ffasiwn sort, such (*adj*)

ffasiynol fashionable (*adj*)

ffatri factory (*nf*)

ffatrïoedd factories (*npl*)

ffawd destiny, fate, fortune (*nf*)

ffederal federal (*adj*)

ffederasiwn federation (*nm*)

ffefryn favourite, pet (*nm*)

ffefrynnau favourites (*npl*)

ffeil file (*nf*)

ffeiliau files (*npl*)

ffeilio to file (*v*)

ffeindio to find (*v*)

ffeiriau fairs (*npl*)

ffeithiau facts (*npl*)

ffeithiol factual, non-fiction (*adj*)

ffenest: ffenestr window (*nf*)

ffenestri windows (*npl*)

ffens fence (*nf*)

ffensys fences (*npl*)

fferi ferry (*nf*)

fferm farm (*nf*)

ffermdai farmhouses (*npl*)

ffermdy farmhouse (*nm*)

ffermio to farm (*v*)

ffermwr farmer (*nm*)

ffermwyr farmers (*npl*)

ffermydd farms (*npl*)

fferyllol pharmaceutical (*adj*)

fferyllwyr pharmacists (*npl*)
fferyllydd chemist, pharmacist (*nm*)
ffi fee (*nf*)
ffibr fibre, roughage (*nm*)
ffidl fiddle, violin (*nf*)
ffigur figure (*nm*)
ffigwr figure (*nm*)
ffigyrau figures (*npl*)
ffilm film, movie (*nf*)
ffilmiau films (*npl*)
ffilmio to film (*v*)
ffin border, boundary, frontier (*nf*)
ffiniau borders (*npl*)
ffioedd fees (*npl*)
ffiseg physics (*nf*)
ffisegol physical (*adj*)
ffit cheeky, fit (*adj*)
ffit fit [suitable] (*adj*)
ffit fit [attack] (*nf*)
ffitio to fit (*v*)
ffitrwydd fitness, suitability (*nm*)
fflach flash, glint, match (*nf*)
fflam flame (*nf*)
fflamau flames (*npl*)
fflat dull, flat (*adj*)
fflat flat (*nm*)
fflatiau flats (*npl*)
ffliw flu, influenza (*nm*)
ffliw flue (*nf*)
fflyd crowd, fleet, gang (*nf*)
ffo escape, flight (*nm*)
ffoadur fugitive, refugee (*nm*)
ffoaduriaid refugees (*npl*)
ffocws focus (*nm*)
ffocysu to focus (*v*)
ffodus fortunate, lucky (*adj*)
ffoi to flee, to run away (*v*)
ffolder folder (*nf*)
ffolineb folly, foolishness, silliness (*nm*)
ffon rung, stick, walking-stick (*nf*)
ffôn phone, telephone (*nm*)
ffonau telephones (*npl*)

ffonio to phone, to telephone (*v*)
ffoniwch you phone (*v*)
ffont font, fount (*nm*)
ffordd road, route, way (*nf*)
fforddiadwy affordable (*adj*)
fforddio to afford (*v*)
fforest forest (*nf*)
fforestydd forests (*npl*)
fformat format (*nm*)
fformatau formats (*npl*)
fformiwla formula (*nf*)
fformiwlâu formulae (*npl*)
ffortiwn fortune (*nf*)
fforwm forum (*nm*)
fforymau fora, forums (*npl*)
ffos ditch, moat, trenches (*nf*)
ffosydd ditches, trenches (*npl*)
ffotograff photograph (*nm*)
ffotograffaidd photographic (*adj*)
ffotograffau photographs (*npl*)
ffotograffiaeth photography (*nf*)
ffotograffig photographic (*adj*)
ffotograffydd photographer (*nm*)
ffrae quarrel, squabble (*nf*)
ffraeo to quarrel, to squabble (*v*)
ffraeth facetious, witty (*adj*)
ffrâm frame (*nf*)
fframiau frames (*npl*)
fframwaith framework, structure (*nm*)
fframweithiau structures (*npl*)
fframin frame (*nm*)
Ffrangeg French (language) (*nf*)
Ffrengig French (*adj*)
ffres fresh (*adj*)
ffrind friend (*nm*)
ffrindiau friends (*npl*)
ffrio to fry (*v*)
ffroen muzzle, nostril (*nf*)
ffroenau nostrils (*npl*)
ffrog dress, frock (*nf*)
ffrwd brook, stream (*nf*)
ffrwydro to blast, to explode (*v*)

ffrwydron explosives (*npl*)
ffrwydryn detonator, explosive (*nm*)
ffrwyth berry, essence, fruit (*nm*)
ffrwythau fruits (*npl*)
ffrwythlon fertile, fruitful, lush (*adj*)
ffrydiau streams (*npl*)
ffrynt front (*nm*)
ffug counterfeit, fake, false (*adj*)
ffuglen fiction (*nf*)
ffurf form, shape (*nf*)
ffurfafen firmament (*nf*)
ffurfiau forms (*npl*)
ffurfio to form (*v*)
ffurfiol formal (*nf*)
ffurfiwyd was/were formed (*v*)
ffurflen form, pro forma (*nf*)
ffurflenni forms (*npl*)
ffwng fungus (*nm*)
ffwrdd away (*adv*)
ffwrn oven (*nf*)
ffwrnais furnace (*nf*)
ffydd confidence, faith (*nf*)
ffyddiog confident (*adj*)
ffyddlon faithful, loyal, true, trusty (*adj*)
ffyddlondeb faithfulness, fidelity (*nm*)
ffyn sticks (*npl*)
ffynhonnau fountains, springs (*npl*)
ffynhonnell fount, source, spring (*nf*)
ffyniannus prosperous, successful (*adj*)
ffyniant prosperity, success (*nm*)
ffynnon fount, spring, well (*nf*)
ffynnu to flourish, to prosper, to thrive (*v*)
ffynonellau sources, wells (*npl*)
ffyrdd ways (*npl*)
ffyrnig ferocious, fierce (*adj*)
fi I, me (*pronoun*)
ficer vicar (*nm*)
Fictoraidd Victorian (*adj*)
fideo video (*adj*)
fideos (*npl*)
*fil bill
fil thousand

filiwn million
filiynau millions
filltir mile
filltiroedd miles
filoedd thousands
filwr soldier
filwrol military
filwyr soldiers
*fin bin
fin edge
firws virus (*nm*)
firysau viruses (*npl*)
fis month
fisoedd months
fisol monthly
fitamin vitamin (*nm*)
fitaminau vitamins (*npl*)
fiwsig music
*flaenaf foremost
*flaengar prominent
*flaenllaw foremost
*flaenoriaeth priority
*flaenoriaethau priorities
*flaenorol previous
*flas taste
*flasu to taste
*flawd flour
*flin annoyed
*flinedig tired
*flodau flowers
*flwch box
*flwydd year
*flwyddyn year
*flychau boxes
*flynedd years
*flynyddoedd years
*flynyddol annual
fo him (*pronoun*)
*foch cheek
foch pigs
*focs box
*fod to be

*fod that
*fodd satisfaction
fodd means, way
*foddhad satisfaction
*foddhaol satisfactory
*foddi to drown
foddion medicine
fodel model
fodelau models
fodern modern
foderneiddio to modernize
fodiwlau modules
*fodlon satisfied
*fodloni to satisfy
*fodolaeth existence
*fodolai he/she/it would exist
*fodoli to exist
fodrwy ring
fodryb aunt
foel bald, bare
foesol moral
*fol belly, stomach
foltedd voltage (*nm*)
foment moment
*fôn base, root
fonitro monitor
fôr sea
*ford table
fordaith voyage
*fore early
forgais mortgage
forwyn maid, virgin
fory tomorrow (*adv*)
*fotwm button
*fraich arm
*fraint honour
*fras coarse, fat, general
*fraster fat
*frawd brother
*frawddeg sentence
*frawddegau sentences
*frecwast breakfast

*fregus shaky
*freichiau arms
*frenhines queen
*frenhiniaeth kingdom
*frenhinol royal
*frenin king
*frest chest
*freuddwyd dream
*freuddwydion dreams
*fri distinction
*fridio to breed
*frig tip, top
*frigâd brigade
*frith speckled
*fro area, vale
*frodorol native
*frodyr brothers
*fron breast
*frown brown
*frwd keen
*frwdfrydedd enthusiasm
*frwdfrydig enthusiastic
*frwydr battle
*frwydro to battle
fry above, aloft (*adv*)
*fryd mind, sights
*fryn hill
*fryngaer hillfort
*fryniau hills
*frys haste
*fu he/she/it was
*fuan quick
*fuasai he/she/it would have
*fuaswn I would have
*fuches milking herd
fud mute
*fudd benefit
*fudd-daliadau benefits
*fuddiannau assets
*fuddiant benefit
*fuddiol useful
*fuddsoddi to invest

*fuddsoddiad investment
*fuddsoddiadau investments
*fuddugol victorious
*fuddugoliaeth victories
fudiad movement
fudiadau movements
*fun maiden
funud minute
funudau minutes
*fuodd he/she/it has been, was
fur wall
furiau walls
*fusnes business
*fusnesau businsses
*fuwch cow
fwg smoke
*fwlch gap
*fwrdd table
*fwrdeistref borough
*fwriad intention
*fwriadol intentional
*fwriadu to intend
*fwriadwyd was/were intended
*fwriedir is intended
*fwrlwm bubbling
*fwrw to hit, to rain
*fws bus
*fwthyn cottage
fwy bigger, more
fwyaf biggest, greatest
fwyafrif majority
*fwyd food
*fwydlen menu
*fwydo to feed
*fwydydd food, foodstuffs
fwyfwy ever more
fwyn gentle, mineral
fwynau minerals
fwynhad enjoyment
fwynhau to enjoy
*fwyta to eat
fy me, my (*pronoun*)

*fychan small
*fyd world
*fydd he/she/it will
*fydda I will
*fyddaf I will
*fyddai he/she/it would
*fyddan they will
*fyddant they will
*fyddar deaf
*fyddech you would
*fyddem we would
*fydden they would
*fyddent they would
*fyddi you will
*fyddin army
*fyddo he/she/it may, might
*fyddwch you are
*fyddwn we are
*fyd-eang world-wide
fyfyrio to meditate
fyfyriwr student
fyfyrwraig student
fyfyrwyr students
*fygwth to threaten
*fygythiad threat
*fygythiol threatening
*fylchau gaps
fymryn little, touch of
fynd to go
fynedfa entrance
fynediad entrance
fynegai index
fynegi to express
fynegiant expression
fynegir is/are/will be expressed
fynegwyd was/were expressed
fynnai he/she/it would insist
fynnir is/are/will be insisted, insists
fynnu to insist
fynwent cemetery
fynwes breast
fyny up, upwards (*adv*)

fynych frequent
fynychaf most frequently
fynychu to frequent
fynydd mountain
fynyddoedd mountains
*****fyr** short
*****fyrddau** boards, tables
*****fyrder** haste
*****fys** finger

*****fysedd** fingers
*****fysiau** buses
*****fyth** ever, never
*****fyw** to live
*****fywiog** lively
*****fywoliaeth** livelyhood
*****fywyd** life
*****fywydau** lives

G

a word starting with **g** printed in blue means that the root form of that word begins with **g**, e.g. gadair root **cadair**

---

gad he/she/it will leave (v)
gadael to allow, to bequeath, to leave (v)
gadair chair
gadarn firm
gadarnhaol affirmative
gadarnhau to confirm
gadawodd he/she/it left (v)
gadawyd was/were left (v)
gadeiriau chairs
gadeirio to chair
gadeiriol chaired
gadeirlan cathedral
gadeirydd chairman
gadeiryddiaeth chairmanship
gadewch you leave (v)
gadw to keep
gadwraeth conservation
gadwyd was/were left (v)
gadwyd was/were kept
gadwyn chain
gae field
gaeaf winter (nm)
gaeau fields
gael to have
gaer fort
gaeth addicted, captive
gaf I have/I will have (v)
gafael to grasp, to grip, to hold tight (v)
gafael grasp, grip, hold (nf)
gaffael to acquire
gaffaeliad acquisition
gafodd he/she/it had
gâi he/she/it would have

gaiff he/she/it will have
gain fine
gair promise; word (nm)
gais he/she/it seeks
gais try
gal penis
galar grief, mourning (nm)
galaru to grieve, to mourn (v)
galch chalk, lime
galed hard
galendr calendar
gall he/she/it will be able to (v)
gallaf I can/I will be able to (v)
gallai he/she/it would be able to (v)
gallant they can/they will be able to (v)
gallasai he/she/it could have (v)
gallech you could (v)
gallem we could (v)
gallent they could (v)
gallu to be able (v)
gallu ability, power (nm)
galluoedd abilities (npl)
galluog able, clever, gifted (adj)
galluogi to enable (v)
gallwch you can, you may (v)
gallwn we can/we will be able (v)
galon heart
galonogol encouraging
galw call, demand (nm)
galw to call, to name, to visit (v)
galwad call, decision, invitation, summons, visit (nf)
galwadau calls (npl)

81

galwch you call (*v*)
galwedigaeth calling, occupation, profession, vocation (*nf*)
galwedigaethol occupational (*adj*)
galwedigaethol vocational (*adj*)
galwodd he/she/it called (*v*)
galwr caller (*nm*)
galwyd was/were called (*v*)
gam crooked
gamarweiniol misleading
gamau steps
gamddefnyddio misuse
gam-drin to abuse
gamdriniaeth abuse
gamgymeriad mistake
gamgymeriadau mistakes
gamlas canal
gamp feat
gampws campus
gamu to step
gamweinyddu to maladminister
gamymddwyn to misbehave
gan by, from, of (*prep*)
gan because, since (*conj*)
gan hundred
gân song
ganddi *from/of her* (*prep*)
ganddo *from/of him* (*prep*)
ganddyn *from/of them* (*prep*)
ganddynt *from/of them* (*prep*)
ganed was/were born (*v*)
ganeuon songs
ganfod to discover
ganfuwyd was/were discovered
ganfyddiadau discoveries
gang gang (*nm*)
gangen branch
ganghellor chancellor
ganghennau branches
ganiatâd permission
ganiataol granted
ganiatáu to allow, to permit

ganiateir is/are/will be allowed
ganllaw guideline
ganllawiau guidelines
ganlyn to follow
ganlyniad result
ganlyniadau results
ganlynol following
ganmol to praise
ganmoliaeth praise
gannoedd hundreds
gannwyll candle
ganodd he/she/it sang
ganol middle
ganolbwynt centre, focus
ganolbwyntio focus
ganolfan centre
ganolfannau centres
ganolig central
ganoloesol medieval
ganolog central
ganran per cent
ganrif century
ganrifoedd centuries
ganser cancer
ganslo to cancel
gant hundred
gânt they sing/they will sing
ganu to sing
ganwyd was/were sung
gap cap
gapel chapel
gapten captain
gar car
gâr kinsman
garchar prison
garcharor prisoner
garcharorion prisoners
gardd garden (*nf*)
garddio to garden (*v*)
gardiau cards
garedig kind
garedigrwydd kindness

garej garage (*nf*)
garfan beam, faction
gariad love
gario to carry
garreg stone
gartre at home (*adv*)
gartref at home, home (*adv*)
gartrefi homes
gartrefol homely
garu to love
garw harsh, rough, stormy, unrefined (*adj*)
gas nasty
gasgliad collection
gasgliadau collections
gasglu to collect
gasglwyd was/were collected
gastell castle
gât gate (*nf*)
gategori category
gategorïau categories
gath cat
gatiau gates
gau to close
gau hollow (*adj*)
gawl mess, soup
gawn we have/we will have
gawod shower
gaws cheese
gawsai he/she/it had
gawsant they had
gawsoch you had
gawsom we had
gawson they had
gedwir is/are/will be kept
gefais I had
geffyl horse
geffylau horses
gefn back
gefndir background
gefndiroedd settings
gefnogaeth support
gefnogi to support

gefnogir is/are/will be supported
gefnogol supportive
gefnogwyr supporters
geg mouth
gegin kitchen
gei you will have
geid was/were to be had
geidwad keeper, Saviour
geidwadol conservative
geifr goats
geiniog penny
geir he/she/it has, will have
geirfa glossary, vocabulary (*nf*)
geiriad wording (*nm*)
geiriadur dictionary (*nm*)
geiriaduron dictionaries (*npl*)
geiriau words (*npl*)
geiriol oral, verbal (*adj*)
geisiadau requests
geisio to seek
geisiodd he/she/it sought
gelf art
gelfydd artistic
gelfyddyd art
gell cell
gelli you can (*v*)
gelli grove
gellid would be able
gellir is/are/will be able
gelloedd cells
gellwch you can (*v*)
gelwid would be called (*v*)
gelwir is/are/will be called (*v*)
gelyn enemy, foe (*nm*)
gelyn holly
gelynion foes (*npl*)
gem gem, jewel (*nf*)
gêm game, match (*nf*)
gemau gems (*npl*)
gêmau games (*npl*)
gen dandruff, lichen
genau mouth (*nm*)

genedigaeth birth (*nf*)
genedigaethau births (*npl*)
genedigol native (*adj*)
genedl gender, nation
genedlaethau generations
genedlaethol national
generig generic (*adj*)
geneteg genetics (*nf*)
geneth girl, lass (*nf*)
genethod girls (*npl*)
genetig genetic (*adj*)
genhadaeth mission
genhedlaeth generation
genhedloedd nations
geni to give birth (*v*)
gennych *from/of you* (*prep*)
gennyf *from/of me* (*prep*)
gennym *from/of us* (*prep*)
gennyt *from/of you* (*prep*)
ger by, close to (*prep*)
gerbron before, in the presence of (*prep*)
gerbyd carriage, vehicle
gerbydau carriages, vehicles
gerdd music; poem
gerdded to walk
gerddi gardens; poems
gerddorfa orchestra
gerddoriaeth music
gerddorol musical
gerddwyr walkers
gerdyn card
gerllaw beside, close to (*prep*)
gerrig stones
ges I had
gesglir is/are/will be collected
gestyll castles
gewch you will have
gi dog
gic kick
gig meat
gig gig (*nm*)
gilydd together (*pronoun*)

ginio dinner
gipio to snatch
gist chest
gitâr guitar (*nf*)
gladdfa cemetery
gladdu to bury
glaf ill, patient
glan bank, side (*nf*)
glân clean, complete, fair, holy, spotless (*adj*)
glanhau to clean (*v*)
glanio to land (*v*)
glannau banks (*npl*)
glanweithdra cleanliness (*nm*)
glas azure, blue, green, raw, slate-grey, young (*adj*)
glas blue, break of day (*nm*)
glasurol classical
glaswellt grass, pasture (*nm*)
glaswelltir grassland (*nm*)
glaw rain, shower (*nm*)
glawiad rainfall (*nm*)
glawr cover, lid
glefyd disease
glefydau diseases
gleientiaid clients
gleifion patients
gleision blue (s)
glendid beauty; cleanliness (*nm*)
glicio to click
glin knee, lap
glinigol clinical
glir clear
gliriach clearer
glirio to clear
glo coal (*nm*)
glo lock
gloch bell
glod praise
gloddiau hedges
gloddio to dig
glofaol mining (*adj*)
gloi to lock

glos farmyard; trousers
glöwr coal-miner, collier (*nm*)
glowyr colliers (*npl*)
gloyw bright, shining, sparkling (*adj*)
gludiant transport
gludir is/are/will be conveyed
gludo to carry
glust ear
glustiau ears
glustnodi to earmark
glwb club
glwcos glucose (*nm*)
glybiau clubs
glymu to tie
glyn glen, valley (*nm*)
glynu to stick (*v*)
glyw you listen
glywais I heard
glywed to hear
glywodd he/she/it heard
gnau nuts
gnawd flesh
gnwd crop
gnydau crops
go partly, quite, rather (*adv*)
go' memory
gobaith hope (*nm*)
gobeithio to hope (*v*)
gobeithiol hopeful, optimistic (*adj*)
gobeithion hopes (*npl*)
gobeithir is/are/will be hoped (*v*)
gobeithiwn we hope, we will hope (*v*)
goblygiad consequence, implication, ramification (*nm*)
goblygiadau implications (*npl*)
goch red
god you get up
goddef to allow, to endure, to suffer, to tolerate (*v*)
goddefol passive (*adj*)
godi to raise
godiad erection

godidog excellent, magnificent, outstanding, wonderful (*adj*)
godir is/are/will be raised
gododd he/she/it got up, raised
godro to milk (*v*)
godwyd was/were raised
goed trees, wood
goeden tree
goedwig forest
goedwigaeth forestry
goedwigoedd forests
goes handle, leg
goesau legs
goetir woodland
goetiroedd woodlands
gof blacksmith, smith (*nm*)
gofal care (*nm*)
gofalu to care (for), to take care (*v*)
gofalus careful, mindful, painstaking (*adj*)
gofalwch you take care (*v*)
gofalwr caretaker, janitor (*nm*)
gofalwyr carers, caretakers (*npl*)
gofalydd carer (*nm*)
gofeb memorial
gofelir will take care (*v*)
goffa memorial
goffi coffee
gofiadwy memorable
gofid distress, trouble, worry (*nm*)
gofidio to be anxious, to worry (*v*)
gofio to remember
gofnod record
gofnodi to minute, to record
gofnodion minutes, records
gofnodir is/are/will be recorded
gofnodwyd was/were minuted, recorded
gofod space (*nm*)
gofodwr astronaut, cosmonaut (*nm*)
gofodwyr astronauts (*npl*)
gofrestr register
gofrestredig registered
gofrestrfa registry

gofrestru to register
gofrestrwyd was/were registered
gofrestrydd registrar
gofyn call, demand, request (*nm*)
gofyn to ask, to claim, to invite (*v*)
gofyniad requirement (*nm*)
gofynion requirements (*npl*)
gofynnais I asked (*v*)
gofynnir is/are/will be asked (*v*)
gofynnodd he/she/it asked (*v*)
gofynnol interrogative, necessary (*adj*)
gofynnwch you ask (*v*)
gofynnwyd was/were asked (*v*)
gog cuckoo
Gog North Walian (*nm*)
goginio to cook
gogledd north (*nm*)
gogledd-ddwyrain north-east (*nm*)
gogleddol northerly, northern (*adj*)
gogoniant glory, splendour (*nm*)
gogwydd bias, downward trend, slant, tendency (*nm*)
gogyfer facing, opposite (*adj*)
gogyfer for, for the purpose of (*prep*)
gohebiaeth correspondence (*nf*)
gohebu to correspond, to report (*v*)
gohebydd correspondent, journalist, reporter (*nm*)
gohirio to adjourn, to postpone (*v*)
gohiriwyd was/were postponed (*v*)
gol. ed., editor (*abbreviation*)
gôl goal (*nf*)
golau light (*nm*)
golau bright, fair, light (*adj*)
golchi to wash (*v*)
goleg college
golegau colleges
goleuadau lights (*npl*)
goleuni brightness, light (*nm*)
goleuo to enlighten, to light up (*v*)
golff golf (*nm*)
goll lost

golled insanity, loss
golledion losses
golli to lose
gollir is/are/will be lost
gollodd he/she/it lost
gollwng to drop, to leak, to release (*v*)
gollwyd was/were lost (*v*)
gollyngiad dispensation (*nm*)
gollyngiadau dispensations (*npl*)
golofn column
golosg charcoal, coke (*nm*)
golwg eyesight, regard, respect, sight, vision (*nm*)
golwg appearance, look of (*nf*)
golyga he/she/it will entail (*v*)
golygai he/she/it would mean (*v*)
golygfa scene, sight, view (*nf*)
golygfeydd views (*npl*)
golygir is/are/will entail (*v*)
golygu to edit, to intend, to mean (*v*)
golygwyd was/were edited (*v*)
golygydd editor (*nm*)
golygyddion editors (*npl*)
golygyddol editorial (*nm*)
golygyddol editorial (*adj*)
gomisiwn commission
gomisiynu to commission
gomisiynwyd was/were commissioned
gonest frank, honest, true (*adj*)
gonestrwydd honesty (*nm*)
gontract contract
gontractau contracts
gontractwyr contracters
gopi copy
gopïau copies
gopïo to copy
gorau best (*adj*)
gorau (the) best (*nm/f*)
gorbwyso to be overweight (*v*)
gorchfygu to conquer, to defeat, to overcome, to surmount (*v*)
gorchmynion commands (*npl*)

gorchudd covering, lid, veil (*nm*)
gorchuddio to cover, to envelop (*v*)
gorchwyl job, task (*nm*)
gorchwylion tasks (*npl*)
gorchymyn command, decree, order (*nm*)
gorchymyn to command (*v*)
gore best (*adj*)
goresgyn to conquer, to invade, to vanquish (*v*)
goreuon best (*npl*)
gorff body
gorffen to conclude, to end, to finish (*v*)
gorffenedig completed, finished (*adj*)
Gorffennaf July (*nm*)
gorffennol past, past tense (*nm*)
gorfforaeth corporation
gorfforaethol corporate
gorfforol physical
gorffwylledd dementia, insanity (*nm*)
gorffwys to repose, to rest (*v*)
gorffwysfa caesura, resting place (*nf*)
gorfod compulsion, constraint (*nm*)
gorfod to be compelled to, to have to (*v*)
gorfodaeth coercion, duress (*nf*)
gorfodi to compel, to force, to make (*v*)
gorfodol compulsory, obligatory (*adj*)
gorfoledd jubilation, rejoicing (*nm*)
gorgyffwrdd to overlap (*v*)
gorlawn overflowing (*adj*)
gorlifdir floodplain (*nm*)
gorlifo to flood, to inundate, to overflow (*v*)
gorllewin west (*nm*)
gorllewinol westerly, western (*adj*)
gormes oppression, tyranny (*nm*)
gormod excess, much, too many (*nm*)
gormod excessive, too much (*adj*)
gormodedd excess, glut (*nm*)
gormodol excessive, fulsome (*adj*)
gorn absolute, complete
gorn horn, trumpet, antler, callus
gornel corner
gornest bout, contest (*nf*)

goroesi to outlast, to outlive, to survive (*v*)
goron crown
goror border, frontier (*nm*)
gororau frontiers, Marches (*npl*)
gors bog, marsh
gorsaf depot, station (*nf*)
gorsafoedd stations (*npl*)
gorsedd throne (*nf*)
goruchwyliaeth charge, stewardship, supervision (*nf*)
goruchwylio to oversee, to supervise (*v*)
goruchwyliwr overseer, supervisor (*nm*)
gorwedd to lie, to rest (*v*)
gorwel horizon (*nm*)
gorwelion horizons (*npl*)
gosb punishment
gosbi to punish
gosod to arrange, to lay, to let, to plant, to put (*v*)
gosod false, set [in place] (*adj*)
gosodiad assertion, setting, statement (*nm*)
gosodiadau statements (*npl*)
gosodir is/are/will be put (*v*)
gosododd he/she/it put (*v*)
gosodwch you put (*v*)
gosodwyd was/were put (*v*)
gost cost
gostio to cost
gostus expensive
gostwng to bow, to curtsy, to lower, to reduce (*v*)
gostyngiad fall, slump (*nm*)
gostyngiadau reductions (*npl*)
gostyngol reduced (*adj*)
got coat
gradd degree, grade, order (*nf*)
graddau degrees, grades (*npl*)
graddedig graded, graduated (*adj*)
graddedigion graduates (*npl*)
graddfa scale (*nf*)
graddfeydd grades, scales (*npl*)
graddio to grade, to graduate (*v*)

graddol gradual (*adj*)
graean gravel, shingle (*nm*)
graff graph (*nm*)
graffeg graphics (*nf*)
graffiau graphs (*npl*)
graffig graphic (*nf*)
graffiti graffiti (*npl*)
gragen shell
graidd crux
graig rock
gram gram, gramme (*nm*)
gramadeg grammar (*nm*)
gramadegol grammatical (*adj*)
grand grand
grant grant (*nm*)
grantiau grants (*npl*)
gras grace (*nm*)
gras dry, harsh
grawn grain (*npl*)
greadigaeth creation
greadigol creative
greadur creature
greaduriaid creatures
gred belief
gredu to believe
gredyd credit
gredydau credits
gref strong
grefft craft
grefydd religion
grefyddol religious
greigiau rocks
greodd he/she/it created
grêt great (*adj*)
greu to create
greulon cruel
greulondeb cruelty
grëwyd was/were created
grib comb, ridge
grid grid (*nm*)
gridiau grids (*npl*)
grisiau staircase, stairs, steps (*npl*)

griw crew, gang
gro earth, gravel, shingle (*nm*)
Groeg Greek (*nf*)
groen skin
groes cross
groesawu to welcome
groesfan crossing
groesi to cross
groeso welcome
gron round
gronfa fund
gronfeydd funds
gronyn grain, particle, seed of corn (*nm*)
gronynnau grains, particles (*npl*)
groth womb
grug heather (*nm*)
grwn round
grŵp group (*nm*)
grwpiau groups (*npl*)
grwpio to group (*v*)
grwydro to wander
grybwyll to mention
grybwyllir is/are/will be mentioned
grybwyllwyd was/were mentioned
gryf strong
gryfach stronger
gryfder strength
gryfderau strengths
gryfhau strengthen
grym force, strength, vigour (*nm*)
grymoedd forces (*npl*)
grymus mighty, powerful, strong (*adj*)
gryn tolerable
grynhoi to summarize
gryno compact
grynodeb summary
grys shirt
gu beloved
gudd hidden
guddio to hide
gul narrow
guro to beat

gw. see (*abbreviation*)

gwadd mole (*nf*)

gwadd guest, invited (*adj*)

gwaddod sediment (*nm*)

gwaddodion lees (*npl*)

gwaddoliad endowment (*nm*)

gwadiad denial (*nm*)

gwadu to deny, to disclaim (*v*)

gwae woe (*nm*)

gwaed blood, gore (*nm*)

gwaeddodd he/she/it shouted (*v*)

gwaedlyd bloody (*adj*)

gwaedu to bleed, to let blood (*v*)

gwael poor; ill, poorly (*adj*)

gwaelod bottom, depths (*nm*)

gwaelodlin base line (*nf*)

gwaelodol basal (*adj*)

gwaered descent, downward slope (*nm*)

gwaeth worse (*adj*)

gwaetha: gwaethaf worst (*adj*)

gwaethygu to decay, to deteriorate (*v*)

gwag empty, frivolous, vacant (*adj*)

gwahân apart (*nm*)

gwahaniaeth difference, disagreement, distinction (*nm*)

gwahaniaethau differences (*npl*)

gwahaniaethol differentiating, distinguishing (*adj*)

gwahaniaethu to discriminate, to distinguish (*v*)

gwahanol different, various (*adj*)

gwahanu to part, to separate, to split up (*v*)

gwahardd to forbid, to prohibit (*v*)

gwaharddiad ban, prohibition (*nm*)

gwaharddiadau bans, prohibitions (*npl*)

gwahodd to invite (*v*)

gwahoddiad invitation (*nm*)

gwahoddir is/are/will be invited (*v*)

gwahoddwyd was/were invited (*v*)

gwair hay (*nm*)

gwaith task, work (*nm*)

gwaith occasion, time (*nf*)

gwaelodol basal (*adj*)

gwalch falcon, hawk, jack, knave, rascal, rogue, scamp (*nm*)

gwall error, mistake, oversight (*nm*)

gwallau errors (*npl*)

gwallt hair (*nm*)

gwan weak (*adj*)

gwanhau to languish, to weaken (*v*)

gwanwyn spring (*nm*)

gwar scruff, nape (*nm*)

gwarant guarantee, security/securities warrant (*nf*)

gwarantau guarantees, warrants (*npl*)

gwarantu to guarantee, to underwrite (*v*)

gwarchod to babysit, to guard, to mind (*v*)

gwarchodaeth conservation, protection (*nf*)

gwarchodfa reservation, reserve, sanctuary (*nf*)

gwared to deliver, to get rid of, to save (*v*)

gwarediad deliverance, riddance (*nm*)

gwaredu to get rid of, to dispose of (*v*)

gwareiddiad civilization (*nm*)

gwarged remainder, surplus (*nm*)

gwariant expenditure (*nm*)

gwario to spend (*v*)

gwariwyd was/were spent (*v*)

gwarth disgrace, scandal, shame (*nm*)

gwartheg cattle (*npl*)

gwas boy, farm-hand, lad, manservant (*nm*)

gwasanaeth service (*nm*)

gwasanaethau services (*npl*)

gwasanaethir is/are/will be officiated (*v*)

gwasanaethu to officiate, to serve (*v*)

gwasg press, publisher (*nf*)

gwasg waist (*nm*)

gwasgar dispersed (*adj*)

gwasgaredig dispersed, scattered (*adj*)

gwasgaru to disperse, to scatter (*v*)

gwasgedd pressure (*nm*)

gwasgnod imprint (*nm*)

gwasgnodau imprints (*npl*)

gwasgu to press, to squeeze to wring (*v*)
gwastad always, constant (*adj*)
gwastad flat, level, plain (*nm*)
gwastadedd level (*nm*)
gwastraff wastage, waste (*nm*)
gwastraffu to fritter, to waste (*v*)
gwau knitting (*nm*)
gwau to knit, to twist and turn, to weave (*v*)
gwawd mockery, scorn (*nm*)
gwawr dawn, daybreak, sunrise, tinge, tint (*nf*)
gwawrio to dawn (*v*)
gwbl complete
gwblhau to complete
gwblhawyd was/were completed
gwch boat
gwddf neck, throat (*nm*)
gwe cobweb, weaving, web, woven fabric (*nf*)
gwedd appearance, countenance, sight, texture (*nf*)
gwedd harness, team, yoke (*nf*)
gweddi prayer (*nf*)
gweddïau prayers (*npl*)
gweddill remainder, residue, surplus, (the) rest (*nm*)
gweddillion remnants (*npl*)
gweddïo to pray (*v*)
gweddol fair, middling, not bad, reasonable (*adj*)
gweddu to fit, to suit (*v*)
gweddw widow (*nf*)
gweddw widowed (*adj*)
gwefan website (*nf*)
gwefannau websites (*npl*)
gwefeistr webmaster (*nm*)
gwefr charge, shock, sparkle, thrill (*nf*)
gwefus lip (*nf*)
gwefusau lips (*npl*)
gwe-gam web-cam (*nm*)
gweiddi to shout, to yell (*v*)

gweill knitting-needles (*npl*)
gweini to attend, to serve, to wait upon (*v*)
gweinidog minister, pastor (*nm*)
gweinidogaeth ministry (*nf*)
gweinidogion ministers (*npl*)
gweinydd attendant, waiter (*nm*)
gweinyddiaeth administration, ministry (*nf*)
gweinyddir is/are/will be administered (*v*)
gweinyddol administrative (*adj*)
gweinyddu to administer, to manage (*v*)
gweinyddwr administrator (*nm*)
gweinyddwyr administrators (*npl*)
gweision servants (*npl*)
gweithdai workshops (*npl*)
gweithdrefn procedure (*nf*)
gweithdrefnau procedures (*npl*)
gweithdy workshop (*nm*)
gweithfeydd works (*npl*)
gweithgar diligent, industrious (*adj*)
gweithgaredd activity (*nm*)
gweithgareddau activities (*npl*)
gweithgarwch activity, diligence, industry (*nm*)
gweithgor working party (*nm*)
gweithgorau working parties (*npl*)
gweithgynhyrchu to manufacture (*v*)
gweithiau works (*npl*)
gweithio to ferment, to operate, to work (*v*)
gweithiodd he/she/it worked (*v*)
gweithiol operative, working class (*adj*)
gweithion they worked (*v*)
gweithiwr labourer, worker (*nm*)
gweithle workplace (*nm*)
gweithlu manpower, workforce (*nm*)
gweithred action, deed, document (*nf*)
gweithrediad operation (*nm*)
gweithrediadau deeds, operations (*npl*)
gweithredir is/are/will be done (*v*)
gweithredoedd deeds (*npl*)
gweithredol acting, executive (*adj*)
gweithredu to act, to do, to implement (*v*)

gweithredwr agent, operator (*nm*)

gweithredwyd was/were done (*v*)

gweithredwyr operators (*npl*)

gweithredydd operator (*nm*)

gweithwyr workers (*npl*)

gwêl he/she/it sees, will see (*v*)

gweladwy visible (*adj*)

gwelaf I see/I will see (*v*)

gwelai he/she/it would see (*v*)

gwelais I saw (*v*)

gweld to examine, to see, to seem, to visit (*v*)

gwele you behold! (*v*)

gweled to see (*v*)

gweledigaeth brainwave, vision (*nf*)

gweledol visual (*adj*)

gwelem we would see (*v*)

gweler should be seen (*v*)

gwelid would be seen (*v*)

gwelir is/are/will be seen (*v*)

gwell better, preferable (*adj*)

gwell betters, superiors (*nm*)

gwella to get better, to improve (*v*)

gwelliannau improvements (*npl*)

gwelliant amendment, improvement (*nm*)

gwellt straw (*npl*)

gwelodd he/she/it saw (*v*)

gwelsant they saw (*v*)

gwelsoch you saw (*v*)

gwelsom we saw (*v*)

gwelwch you see (*v*)

gwelwn we see, we will see (*v*)

gwelwyd was/were seen (*v*)

gwely bed (*nm*)

gwelyau beds (*npl*)

gwen white (*adj/f*)

gwên smile (*nf*)

gwendid fault, infirmity, weakness (*nm*)

gwendidau weaknesses (*npl*)

Gwener Friday (*nm*)

Gwener Venus (*nf*)

gwenith wheat (*nm*)

gwennol shuttle, swallow (*nf*)

gwenu to grin, to shine, to smile (*v*)

gwenwyn jealousy, poison, spite, venom (*nm*)

gwenwynig poisonous, venomous (*adj*)

gwenyn bees (*npl*)

gwenynen bee (*nf*)

gwêr grease, tallow, wax (*nm*)

gwerdd green (*adj/f*)

gwerin chessmen, folk, people, pieces, proletariat (*nf*)

gwerin folk (*adj*)

gweriniaeth republic (*nf*)

gwerinol common, plebeian (*adj*)

gwern alders [trees] (*npl*)

gwern quagmire, swamp (*nf*)

gwers lesson (*nf*)

gwersi lessons (*npl*)

gwersyll camp (*nm*)

gwersylloedd camps (*npl*)

gwerth value, worth (*nm*)

gwerthfawr precious, valuable (*adj*)

gwerthfawrogi to appreciate, to value (*v*)

gwerthfawrogiad appreciation, gratitude (*nm*)

gwerthiannau sales (*npl*)

gwerthiant sale (*nm*)

gwerthir is/are/will be sold (*v*)

gwerthodd he/she/it sold (*v*)

gwerthoedd values (*npl*)

gwerthu to sell, to vend (*v*)

gwerthusiad appraisal (*nm*)

gwerthusiadau appraisals (*npl*)

gwerthuso to appraise (*v*)

gwerthwr salesman, seller (*nm*)

gwerthwyd was/were sold (*v*)

gwerthwyr sellers (*npl*)

gwestai guest (*nm*)

gwesteion guests (*npl*)

gwestiwn question

gwestiynau questions

gwesty boarding-house, guest-house, hotel (*nm*)

gweundir moorland (*nm*)
gwialen cane, rod, sapling (*nf*)
gwibio to dart, to flit, to rush (*v*)
gwifrau wires (*npl*)
gwifren wire (*nf*)
gwin wine (*nf*)
gwir truth (*nm*)
gwir genuine, real, true (*adj*)
gwir really, truly (*adv*)
gwireddu to come true, to make true (*v*)
gwirfoddol voluntary, willing (*adj*)
gwirfoddoli to volunteer (*v*)
gwirfoddolwr volunteer (*nm*)
gwirfoddolwyr volunteers (*npl*)
gwiriadau corrections (*npl*)
gwirio to check, to verify (*v*)
gwirion daft, guileless, silly, simple (*adj*)
gwirionedd truth (*nm*)
gwirioneddol genuine, real, true (*adj*)
gwiriwch you check (*v*)
gwisg clothing, costume (*nf*)
gwisgo to dress, to put on, to wear (*v*)
gwisgoedd costumes (*npl*)
gwiw excellent, fine, worthy (*adj*)
gwiwer squirrel (*nf*)
gwiwerod squirrels (*npl*)
gwlad country, countryside, nation (*nf*)
gwladfa colony, settlement (*nf*)
gwladol state (*adj*)
gwladwriaeth state (*nf*)
gwladwriaethau states (*npl*)
gwladychu to colonize, to inhabit (*v*)
gwlân wool (*nm*)
gwlân wool, woollen (*adj*)
gwledd banquet, feast, treat (*nf*)
gwledig country, rural (*adj*)
gwledydd countries (*npl*)
gwleidydd politician (*nm*)
gwleidyddiaeth politics (*nf*)
gwleidyddion politicians (*npl*)
gwleidyddol political (*adj*)
gwlith dew (*nm*)

gwlyb wet (*adj*)
gwlyptiroedd wetlands (*npl*)
gwm glue, gum (*nm*)
gwm valley
gwmni company
gwmnïau companies
gwmpas around, compass
gwmpasu to encompass
gwmwl cloud
gwn gun (*nm*)
gwn I know (*v*)
gŵn dogs
gwna he/she/it does (*v*)
gwna you do! (*v*)
gwnaed was/were done (*v*)
gwnaeth he/she/it did (*v*)
gwnaethant they did (*v*)
gwnaethoch you did (*v*)
gwnaethom we did (*v*)
gwnaethon they did (*v*)
gwnaethpwyd was/were done (*v*)
gwnaf I do/I will do (*v*)
gwnai he/she/it did (*v*)
gwnaiff he/she/it will do (*v*)
gwnânt they do/they will do (*v*)
gwnawn we do/we will do (*v*)
gwnei you will do (*v*)
gwneid would be done (*v*)
gwneir is/are/will be done (*v*)
gwnelo were he/she/it to do (*v*)
gwnes I did (*v*)
gwneud to do, to force, to make, to make
gwneuthur to make (*v*)
gwneuthurwr maker, manufacturer (*nm*)
gwneuthurwyr makers (*npl*)
gwnewch you (will) do, make (*v*)
gwnstabl constable
gwobr award, prize, reward (*nf*)
gwobrau prizes (*npl*)
gwobrwyo to award, to reward (*v*)
gwpan cup
gwr edge

gŵr husband, man (*nm*)
gwrach hag, witch (*nf*)
gwrachod witches (*npl*)
gwragedd wives, women (*npl*)
gwraidd origin, root, source (*nm*)
gwraig wife, woman (*nf*)
gwrandawiad audition, hearing (*nm*)
gwrandawiadau hearings (*npl*)
gwrandäwr listener (*nm*)
gwrandawyr listeners (*npl*)
gwrandewch you listen (*v*)
gwrando to listen (*v*)
gwrdd service
gwrdd to meet, to touch
gwreiddiau roots (*npl*)
gwreiddiol fresh, original (*adj*)
gwreiddyn origin, reason, root (*nm*)
gwres fever, heat, intensity (*adj*)
gwresogi to heat (*v*)
gwrs course
gwrtais polite
gwrthdaro to clash, to collide (*v*)
gwrthgyferbyniad contrast, opposition (*nm*)
gwrthiant resistance (*nm*)
gwrthod to refuse, to reject (*v*)
gwrthododd he/she/it refused (*v*)
gwrthodwyd was/were refused (*v*)
gwrthrych object (*nm*)
gwrthrychau objects (*npl*)
gwrthrychol objective (*adj*)
gwrthryfel mutiny, rebellion, revolt (*nm*)
gwrthsefyll to thwart, to withstand (*v*)
gwrthwyneb contrary, opposite (*nm*)
gwrthwynebiad objection, opposition, resistance (*nm*)
gwrthwynebiadau objections (*npl*)
gwrthwynebu to object, to oppose (*v*)
gwrthwynebwyr opponents (*npl*)
gwrthwynebydd adversary, objector, opponent (*nm*)
gwrw beer

gwrych hedge (*nm*)
gwrych bristles (*npl*)
gwrychoedd hedges (*npl*)
gwryw male (*nm*)
gwryw male (*adj*)
gwrywaidd masculine (*adj*)
gwsg sleep
gwsmer customer
gwsmeriaid customers
gwthio to push, to shove, to thrust (*v*)
gwtogi to reduce
Gwy Wye [river]
gwybod to know (a fact or facts) (*v*)
gwybodaeth information, knowledge (*nf*)
gwybodus enlightened, learned, well-informed (*adj*)
gwybyddus known (*adj*)
gwych excellent, magnificent (*adj*)
gwyddai he/she/it knew (*v*)
Gwyddel Irishman (*nm*)
Gwyddeleg Irish [language] (*nf*)
Gwyddelig Irish (*adj*)
Gwyddelod (the) Irish (*npl*)
gwyddoch you know (*v*)
gwyddom we know (*v*)
gwyddoniaeth science (*nf*)
gwyddonol scientific (*adj*)
gwyddonwyr scientists (*npl*)
gwyddonydd scientist (*nm*)
gwyddor rudiments, science (*nf*)
gwyddorau sciences (*npl*)
gwyddost you know (*v*)
gwyddwn I would know (*v*)
Gwyddyl Irishmen (*npl*)
gwyddys it is known (*v*)
gwydr glass, tumbler (*nm*)
gwydr glass (*adj*)
gwydrau glasses, tumblers (*npl*)
gŵydd goose (*nf*)
gŵyl festival (*nf*)
gwyliadwriaeth alertness, vigilance, wariness (*nf*)

gwyliadwrus alert, wary, watchful (*adj*)
gwyliau holidays, leave, vacation (*npl*)
gwylio to keep watch, to observe, to watch (*v*)
gwyliwch you beware!, watch (*v*)
gwyliwr guard, sentry, spectator (*nm*)
gwyll dusk, gloom, twilight (*nm*)
gwyllt raging, untamed, wild (*adj*)
gwyllt the wild (*nm*)
gwylltion wild (*adj/pl*)
gwylwyr spectators, viewers (*npl*)
gwympo to fall
gwyn blessed, darling, silver, white (*adj*)
gwyn sclera, white (*nm*)
gŵyn complaint
gwynfa paradise (*nf*)
gwynion white (*adj/pl*)
gwyno to complain
gwynt breath, smell, wind (*nm*)
gwyntoedd winds (*npl*)
gwŷr men (*npl*)
gŵyr he/she/it knows (*v*)
gŵyr wax
gwyrdd green, unripe (*adj*)
gwyrddion green (*adj/pl*)
gwyro to bend, to incline, to swerve (*v*)
gwyrth miracle (*nf*)
gwythïen seam, vein (*nf*)
gwythiennau veins (*npl*)
gychod boats
gychwyn to start
gychwynnodd he/she/it started
gychwynnol first, starting
gyd all
gyda among, with (*prep*)
gydag among, with (*prep*)
gydau bags
gydbwysedd balance
gyd-destun context
gyd-destunau contexts
gyd-fynd to agree
gydlynol cohesive

gydlynu to coordinate
gydnabod to acknowledge
gydnabyddiaeth acknowledgement
gydnabyddir he/she/it will be acknowledged
gydnaws compatible
gydol whole
gydradd equal
gydraddoldeb equality
gydran component
gydrannau components
gydsyniad agreement
gydweithio to cooperate
gydweithrediad cooperation
gydweithredol co-operative
gydweithredu to cooperate
gydwybod conscience
gydymdeimlad sympathy
gydymffurfio to conform
gyfaddas suitable
gyfaddef to admit
gyfadran faculty
gyfagos adjoining
gyfaill friend
gyfaint volume
gyfalaf capital
gyfan whole
gyfanrwydd totality
gyfansoddi to compose
gyfansoddiad composition
gyfanswm sum, total
gyfarch to greet
gyfarfod meeting
gyfarfodydd meetings
gyfarpar apparatus
gyfartal equal
gyfartaledd average
gyfarwydd familiar
gyfarwyddeb directive
gyfarwyddiadau directions
gyfarwyddo to direct
gyfarwyddwr director

gyfarwyddwyr directors
gyfarwyddyd direction
gyfateb to correspond
gyfatebol corresponding
gyfathrebu to communicate
gyfeillgar amicable
gyfeillion friends
gyfeiriad address, direction
gyfeiriadau addresses
gyfeirio to direct
gyfer acre, on behalf
gyferbyn opposite
gyffelyb like
gyffordd junction
gyfforddus comfortable
gyffredin common
gyffredinol general
gyffro excitement
gyffrous exciting
gyffuriau drugs
gyffwrdd to touch
gyfiawn just
gyfiawnder justice
gyfiawnhad justification
gyfiawnhau to justify
gyfieithiad translation
gyfieithu to translate
gyflawn complete
gyflawni to accomplish
gyflawniad accomplishment
gyflawnir is/are/will be accomplished
gyflawnodd he/she/it accomplished
gyflawnwyd was/were accomplished
gyfle chance
gyflenwad supply
gyflenwi to supply
gyflenwyr suppliers
gyfleoedd opportunities
gyfleu to convey
gyfleus convenient
gyfleuster convenience
gyfleusterau conveniences

gyflog salary
gyflogaeth employment
gyflogau wages
gyflogedig employed
gyflogi to employ
gyflogwr employer
gyflogwyr employers
gyflwr condition
gyflwyniad presentation
gyflwyniadau presentations
gyflwynir is/are/will be presented
gyflwyno to present
gyflwynodd he/she/it presented
gyflwynwyd was/were presented
gyflym fast
gyflymach faster
gyflymder speed
gyfnewid to exchange
gyfnod period
gyfnodau periods
gyfochrog parallel
gyfoedion contemporaries
gyfoes contemporary
gyfoeth wealth
gyfoethog wealthy
gyfoethogi to enrich
gyfradd rate
gyfraddau rates
gyfraith law
gyfran share
gyfraniad contribution
gyfraniadau contributions
gyfrannodd he/she/it contributed
gyfrannol contributory, proportional
gyfrannu to contribute
gyfranogi to partake of
gyfranogwyr participator
gyfranwyr contributors
gyfredol current
gyfreithiol legal
gyfreithiwr lawyer
gyfreithlon legitimate

gyfreithwyr lawyers
gyfres series
gyfrif account
gyfrifiadur computer
gyfrifiadurol computer
gyfrifiaduron computers
gyfrifir is/are/will be counted
gyfrifo to calculate
gyfrifol responsible
gyfrifoldeb responsibility
gyfrifoldebau responsibilities
gyfrifon accounts
gyfrinach secret
gyfrinachol secret
gyfrol volume
gyfrolau volumes
gyfrwng medium
gyfryngau media
gyfun comprehensive
gyfundrefn system
gyfuniad combination
gyfuno to combine
gyfunol combined
gyfweliad interview
gyfweliadau interviews
gyfwerth equal
gyfyng narrow
gyfyngedig restricted
gyfyngiad limit
gyfyngiadau limits
gyfyngu to limit
gyfystyr synonymous
gyhoeddi to publish
gyhoeddiad publication
gyhoeddiadau publications
gyhoeddir is/are/will be published
gyhoeddodd he/she/it published
gyhoeddus public
gyhoeddusrwydd publicity
gyhoeddwyd was/were published
gyhuddo to accuse
gylch circle

gylchgrawn magazine
gylchgronau magazines
gylchoedd circles
gyllell knife
gyllid revenue
gyllideb budget
gyllidebau budgets
gyllidir is/are/will be budgeted
gyllido to finance
gymaint as much
gymal clause, joint
gymdeithas society
gymdeithasau societies
gymdeithasol social
gymdeithasu to socialize
gymdogaeth neighbourhood
gymdogion neighbours
gymer he/she/it to takes
gymeradwy acceptable
gymeradwyaeth applause
gymeradwyir is/are/will be approved
gymeradwyo to approve
gymeradwywyd was/were approved
gymeriad character
gymeriadau characters
gymerir is/are/will be taken
gymerodd he/she/it took
gymerwyd was/were taken
gymesur symmetrical
gymhareb ratio
gymhariaeth comparison
gymharol comparative
gymharu to compare
gymhelliad incentive
gymhleth complex
gymhwyso to adapt
gymhwyster qualification
gymorth aid
gymryd to take
gymuned community
gymunedau communities
gymunedol community

gymwys suitable
gymwysterau qualifications
gymydog neighbour
gymysg mixed
gymysgedd mixture
gymysgu to mix
gynaliadwy sustainable
gyndyn reticent
gynefin habitat
gynefinoedd habitats
gynffon tail
gyngerdd concert
gynghanedd cynghanedd
gynghorau councils
gynghori to advise
gynghorwyr councillers
gynghorydd councillor
gynghrair league
gyngor council, counsel
gynhadledd conference
gynhaliaeth subsistence
gynhaliwyd was/were held, supported
gynharach earlier
gynhelir is/are/will be held
gynhenid inherent
gynhesu to warm
gynhwysfawr comprehensive
gynhwysion contents
gynhwysir is/are/will be contained
gynhwysol inclusive
gynhwyswyd was/were contained
gynhyrchion products
gynhyrchir is/are/will be produced
gynhyrchu to produce
gynhyrchwyd was/were produced
gynhyrchwyr producers
gynifer as many
gynigion attempts, offers
gynigir is/are/will be offered
gynigiwyd was/were offered
gynilion savings
gynilo to save

gynllun plan
gynlluniau plans
gynllunio to plan
gynlluniwyd was/were planned
gynnal to hold
gynnar early
gynnau to light
gynnes warm
gynnig offer
gynnil sparing
gynnwys to include
gynnydd growth
gynnyrch produce
gynorthwyo to assist
gynradd primary
gynrychiolaeth representation
gynrychioli to represent
gynrychiolydd representative
gynt previously, quicker
gyntaf first
gynted as soon
gynulleidfa audience, congregation
gynulleidfaoedd audiences
gynulliad assembly
gynwysedig included
gynyddol increasing
gynyddu to increase
gyrchfan destination
gyrchu to make for
gyrfa career (*nf*)
gyrfaoedd careers (*npl*)
gyrfaol vocational (*adj*)
gyrff bodies
gyrhaeddiad reach
gyrhaeddodd he/she/it reached
gyrion outskirts
gyrraedd to reach
gyrru to dispatch, to drive (*v*)
gyrrwr driver (*nm*)
gyrsiau courses
gyrwyr drivers (*npl*)
gysegredig sacred

gysgod shadow
gysgu to sleep
gyson constant
gystadlaethau competition
gystadleuaeth competitions
gystadleuol competitive
gystadleuwyr competitors
gystadlu to compete
gystal as good as
gysur comfort
gysurus comfortable
gyswllt contact
gysylltiad link
gysylltiadau links
gysylltiedig linked

gysylltir is/are/will be linked, contacted
gysylltu contact, link
gysyniad concept
gysyniadau concepts
gytbwys balanced
gytsain consonant
gytundeb agreement, contract
gytundebau contracts
gytuno to agree
gytunwyd was/were agreed
gywilydd shame
gywir correct
gywirdeb accuracy
gywiro to correct

H

a word starting with **h** printed in blue means that the root form of that word begins with the **vowel (a, e, i, o, u,** W and Y are also vowels in Welsh) **that follows it**, e.g. **hachos** root **achos**, **hoed** root **oed**

hachos case, cause
hachosi to cause
hachub to save
had seed, sperm (*nm*)
hadau seeds (*npl*)
haddasu to adapt
haddysg education
haddysgu to educate
hadeiladau buildings
hadeiladu to build
hadfer to recover
hadlewyrchu to reflect
hadnabod to know, to recognize
hadnewyddu to renew
hadnoddau resources
hadolygiad review
hadolygu to review
hadran department, section
hadrodd to recite, to report
hadroddiad report
haearn iron, (smoothing) iron (*nm*)
haeddiannol deserved, deserving (*adj*)
haeddiant deserts, merit (*nm*)
haeddu to deserve, to merit (*v*)
hael generous, lavish, magnanimous (*adj*)
hael eyebrow
haelioni generosity (*nm*)
haelodau members
haen bed, coating, layer, stratum (*nf*)
haenau layers (*npl*)
haenen layer (*nf*)
haf summer (*nm*)

hafal comparable, equal (*adj*)
hafal apple
hafaliad equation, formula (*nm*)
hafaliadau (*npl*)
hafan haven (*nf*)
hafau summers (*npl*)
hafod summer dwelling (*nf*)
Hafren Severn (river) (*nf*)
hagor to open
hagwedd attitude
haid flock, horde, swarm (*nf*)
haidd barley (*nm*)
hail second
hailgylchu to recycle
haint disease, fit, pestilence (*nm*)
halen salt (*nm*)
hallt brackish, pickled, salty (*adj*)
halogi to corrupt, to contaminate, to desecrate (*v*)
hamcanion intentions
hamdden leisure, pastime (*nf*)
hamddena to relax (*v*)
hamddenol leisurely (*adj*)
hamddiffyn to defend
hamgylch around
hamgylchedd environment
hamgylchiadau circumstances
hamlygu to reveal
hamser time
hanafu to injure
hanelu to aim
hanes account, history, report, tale (*nm*)

hanesion stories (*npl*)
haneswyr historians (*npl*)
hanesydd historian (*nm*)
hanesyddol historic, historical (*adj*)
hanfod essence, quintessence (*nm*)
hanfodion essentials (*npl*)
hanfodol crucial, essential, vital (*adj*)
hanfon to send
hangen to need
hanghenion necessities
haniaethol abstract (*adj*)
hanifeiliaid animals
hanner half (*nm*)
hannibyniaeth independence
hannog to urge
hanwybyddu to ignore
hap chance, fortune, luck (*nf*)
hapus happy (*adj*)
hapusrwydd happiness (*nm*)
harbenigedd expertise
harbwr harbour (*nm*)
harchwiliad investigation
harchwilio investigate
hardal area
hardaloedd areas
hardd beautiful, fair, handsome (*adj*)
harddangos to display
harddegau teens
harddwch beauty (*nm*)
harfer custom
harferion customs
harglwydd lord
hargraffu to print
hargymell to recommend
hargymhellion recommendations
harian money, silver
hariannu to finance
harolwg survey
harolygu inspect, review
harwain to lead
hasesu to assess
hastudiaethau studies

hastudio to study
hatal to prevent
hateb to answer
hategu to support
hatgoffa to remind
hatgynhyrchu to reproduce
hau to sow (*v*)
haul sun (*nm*)
hawdd easy, ready (*adj*)
hawdurdod authority
hawdurdodi to authorize
hawl right (*nf*)
hawl he/she/it claims (*v*)
hawlfraint copyright (*nf*)
hawliad claim (*nm*)
hawliadau claims (*npl*)
hawliau rights (*npl*)
hawlio to claim, to demand (*v*)
haws easier (*adj*)
heb not, without (*prep*)
hebddo without (him) (*prep*)
heblaw apart from, besides (*prep*)
Hebraeg Hebrew (*nf*)
hebrwng to escort (*v*)
hectar hectare (*nm*)
hedd peace (*nm*)
heddiw nowadays, today (*nm*)
heddiw today (*adv*)
heddlu constabulary, police force (*nm*)
heddluoedd police forces (*npl*)
heddwch peace, tranquility (*nm*)
heddychlon peaceful (*adj*)
hedfan to fly, to soar (*v*)
heffaith effect
heffeithio to effect
heffeithiolrwydd efficiency
hefyd also, too (*adv*)
heglwysi churches
hei hay! (*exclamation*)
heibio by, past (*adv*)
heiddo belong (to)
heini active, spry, vigorous (*adj*)

heintiad infection (*nm*)
heintiau infections (*npl*)
heintiedig infected (*adj*)
heintio to contaminate, to infect
heintus catching, contagious, infected, infectious (*adj*)
heithrio to except
hel to collect, to drive, to gather, to send (*v*)
hela to hunt, to spend (*v*)
helaeth extensive, large, plentiful (*adj*)
helaethach more extensive (*adj*)
helaethaf most extensive (*adj*)
helfa catch, hunt (*nf*)
heli briny, sea (*nm*)
helo hello (*exclamation*)
help aid, help (*nm*)
helpu to help (*v*)
helyg willows (*npl*)
helynt bother, predicament, trouble (*nf*)
helyntion troubles (*npl*)
hen ancient, former, old, stale (*adj*)
henaid soul
henaint old age, senility (*nm*)
hendre winter dwelling (*nf*)
heneb monument (*nf*)
henebion ancient monuments (*npl*)
heneiddio to age, to become old (*v*)
Henffordd Hereford
hennill to win
heno tonight (*adv*)
henoed old age, old people (*nm*)
henw name
henwau names
henwebu to nominate
henwi to be named
heol road (*nf*)
heolydd roads (*npl*)
hepgor to avoid, to dispense with (*v*)
her challenge, dare (*nf*)
herbyn against
herio to challenge (*v*)
heriol challenging (*adj*)

het hat (*nf*)
hethol to elect
heulog sunny (*adj*)
heulwen sunshine (*nf*)
hi she (*pronoun*)
hiaith language
hidlo to filter, to percolate, to strain (*v*)
hiechyd health
hil descendants, offspring, race (*nf*)
hiliaeth racism (*nf*)
hiliol racial, racist (*adj*)
hin weather (*nf*)
hincwm income
hinsawdd climate (*nf*)
hintegreiddio to integrate
hir long, tedious (*adj*)
hirach longer (*adj*)
hiraeth homesickness, nostalgia (*nm*)
hirdymor long-term (*adj*)
hirion long (*adj/pl*)
his lower
hithau even she/her, she too (*pronoun*)
hiwmor humour (*nm*)
hochr side
hoed age
hoedran age
hoelen nail (*nf*)
hoelio to nail (*v*)
hoelion nails (*npl*)
hoes age, lifetime
hoff beloved, dear, favourite (*adj*)
hoffai he/she/it would like (*v*)
hoffech you would like (*v*)
hoffem we would like (*v*)
hoffent they used to like (*v*)
hoffi to like, to wish (*v*)
hoffter affection, delight, pleasure (*adj*)
hoffwn I would like (*v*)
hoffwn we like/we will like (*v*)
hofrennydd helicopter (*nm*)
hogan: hogen girl (*nf*)
hogen girl, lass (*nf*)

hogia' lads (*npl*)
hogiau lads (*npl*)
hogyn lad (*nm*)
hôl impression, track
hôl behind
holi to ask, to inquire, to question (*v*)
holiadur questionnaire (*nm*)
holiaduron questionnaires (*npl*)
holl all, whole (*adj*)
hollbwysig all-important (*adj*)
hollol entire, quite, whole (*adj*)
hollt cleft, cranny, split (*nf*)
hollti to cleave, to split (*v*)
holodd he/she/it asked (*v*)
holwch you ask (*v*)
holwyd was/were asked (*v*)
hon this (*pronoun*)
honedig alleged (*adj*)
hongian to hang, to suspend (*v*)
honiad allegation, assertion, claim (*nm*)
honiadau allegations (*npl*)
honni to allege, to claim, to maintain (*v*)
honnir is/are/will be claimed (*v*)
honno that one (*pronoun*)
hosgoi avoid
hoyw gay (*adj*)
huawdl eloquent, loquacious (*adj*)
hud enchantment, magic (*nm*)
hudo to beguile, to conjure, to enchant (*v*)
hudol alluring, enchanting, magical (*adj*)
hudolus enchanting (*adj*)
hufen cream (*nm*)
hugain twenty
hun sleep, slumber (*nf*)
hun self (*pronoun*)
hunain selves (*pronoun*)
hunan self (*pronoun*)
hunanasesiad self-assessment (*nm*)
hunanasesu to assess oneself (*v*)
hunan-barch self-respect (*nm*)
hunangofiant autobiography (*nm*)
hunangyflogedig self-employed (*adj*)

hunaniaeth identity (*nf*)
hunanladdiad suicide (*nm*)
hunig lonely, only
hunllef nightmare (*nf*)
huno to lie at rest, to slumber (*v*)
huno to unite
hurio to hire (*v*)
hurt silly, stunned, stupid (*adj*)
hwb push, shove (*nm*)
hwch sow (pig) (*nf*)
hwn this (*pronoun*)
hwnna that (*pronoun*)
hwnnw that (*pronoun*)
hwnt away, yonder (*adv*)
hwrdd gust, ram, squall (*nm*)
hwy them, they (*pronoun*)
hwy longer (*adj*)
hwyaid ducks (*npl*)
hwyl fun, goodbye, mood, sail (*nf*)
hwyliau good mood, sails (*npl*)
hwylio to prepare, to sail (*v*)
hwyliog humorous (*adj*)
hwylus convenient, handy (*adj*)
hwyluso to expedite, to facilitate (*v*)
hwylustod convenience (*nm*)
hwyneb face
hwynebau faces
hwynebu to face
hwynt them (*pronoun*)
hwyr late, overdue (*adj*)
hwyr evening (*nm*)
hwyrach maybe, perhaps (*adv*)
hwyrach later (*adj*)
hwythau them, they too (*pronoun*)
hy bold (*adj*)
hyblyg flexible, pliable, supple (*adj*)
hyblygrwydd flexibility, suppleness (*nm*)
hybu to encourage, to promote (*v*)
hychwanegu to add
hyd length [distance], length [time] (*nm*)
hyd along, until, up to (*prep*)
hyd as long as (*conj*)

hyddysg expert, learned (*adj*)

hyder confidence (*nm*)

hyderus confident, sanguine (*adj*)

Hydref October (*nm*)

hydref autumn (*nm*)

hydrogen hydrogen (*nm*)

hyfedredd proficiency (*nm*)

hyfforddai trainee (*nm*)

hyfforddedig trained (*adj*)

hyfforddeion trainees (*npl*)

hyfforddi to coach, to instruct, to train (*v*)

hyfforddiant instruction, training, tuition (*nm*)

hyfforddwr coach, instructor, trainer (*nm*)

hyfforddwyr instructors (*npl*)

hyfryd delightful, lovely, nice (*adj*)

hyfrydwch delight, pleasure (*nm*)

hyfyw viable (*adj*)

hyfywdra viability (*nm*)

hygrededd credibility (*nm*)

hygyrch accessible (*adj*)

hygyrchedd accessibility (*nm*)

hylendid hygiene (*nm*)

hylif fluid, liquid (*nm*)

hylifau fluids (*npl*)

hyll hideous, ugly (*adj*)

hymateb response

hymchwil research

hymddygiad behaviour

hymdrechion efforts

hymestyn to reach, to stretch

hymgorffori personify

hymroddiad commitment

hymrwymiad commitment

hymweliad visit

hyn these (*pronoun*)

hŷn elder (*adj*)

hynaf elder, eldest (*adj*)

hynafiaid ancestors (*npl*)

hynafol ancient (*adj*)

hynna that (*pronoun*)

hynny that (*pronoun*)

hynod noteworthy, remarkable (*adj*)

hynt course, way (*nf*)

hynysu isolated

hyrddod rams (*npl*)

hyrwyddo to facilitate, to promote (*v*)

hysbryd spirit

hysbrydoli to inspire

hysbys evident, known, well-known (*adj*)

hysbyseb advertisement (*nf*)

hysbysebion advertisements, adverts (*npl*)

hysbysebu to advertise (*v*)

hysbysiad announcement, notice (*nm*)

hysbysiadau announcements (*npl*)

hysbysir is/are/will be informed (*v*)

hysbysodd he/she/it informed (*v*)

hysbysu to inform, to notify (*v*)

hysbyswyd was/were informed (*v*)

hysgol ladder, school

hysgolion ladders, schools

hysgrifennu to write

hystafell room

hystyried to consider

hytrach rather (*adv*)

I

i for, that, to (*prep*)
    i'ch for your, to your
    i'm for my, to my
    i'th for your, to your
    i'w for his/her, to his/her
    i'w for their, to their
iâ ice (*nm*)
iach healthy, hearty, sound (*adj*)
iachach healthier (*adj*)
iachawdwriaeth salvation (*nf*)
iachus bracing, healthy (*adj*)
iaith language, tongue (*nf*)
iâr hen (*nf*)
iard playground, yard (*nf*)
iarll count, earl (*nm*)
ias sensation, shiver, shudder, thrill (*nf*)
Iau Jupiter; Thursday (*nm*)
iau liver (*nm*)
iau younger (*adj*)
iawn very (*adv*)
iawn correct, ok, proper, right (*adj*)
iawn atonement, compensation (*nm*)
iawndal compensation, damages (*nm*)
iawnderau rights (*npl*)
ichi for (you), to you to (*prep*)
ichwi for (you), to you to (*prep*)
id id (*nm*)
Iddew Jew (*nm*)
Iddewig Jewish (*adj*)
Iddewon Jews (*npl*)
iddi for (her), to her (*prep*)
iddo for (him), to him (*prep*)
iddyn for (them), to them (*prep*)
iddynt for (them), to them (*prep*)
ie yea, yes (*adv*)
iechyd health (*nm*)
ieir chickens (*npl*)
ieithoedd languages (*npl*)

ieithyddol linguistic (*adj*)
Iesu Jesus
ieuainc young (*adj/pl*)
ieuanc young (*adj*)
ieuenctid youth (*nm*)
ieuengaf youngest (*adj*)
ifainc young (*adj/pl*)
ifanc juvenile, young (*adj*)
ig hiccup (*nm*)
ildio to relinquish, to surrender (*v*)
ill the (two etc.) of them (*pronoun*)
im for (me), to me (*prep*)
imi for (me), to me (*prep*)
inc ink (*nm*)
incwm income (*nm*)
Indiad Indian (*nm*)
Indiaid Indians (*npl*)
Indiaidd Indian (*adj*)
ing anguish, distress (*nm*)
injan engine (*nf*)
innau me myself (*pronoun*)
inni for (us), to (us) (*prep*)
integredig integrated (*adj*)
integreiddio to integrate (*v*)
iogwrt yoghurt (*nm*)
Ionawr January (*nm*)
ir fresh, juicy, succulent (*adj*)
isadran subsection (*nf*)
isaf lowest, nethermost (*adj*)
isafon tributary (*nf*)
isafonydd tributaries (*npl*)
isafswm minimum (*nm*)
is-baragraff sub-paragraph (*nm*)
is-bwyllgor sub-committee (*nm*)
is-ddeddf by-law (*nf*)
is-ddeddfau by-laws (*npl*)
isel depressed, low, menial (*adj*)
iselder depression, lowness (*nm*)

iseldir lowland (*nm*)
iseldiroedd lowlands (*npl*)
is-gadeirydd vice-chairman (*nm*)
is-ganghellor vice-chancellor (*nm*)
isio to want (*v*)

islaw below, underneath (*adv*)
isod below (*adv*)
israddedig undergraduate (*adj*)
israddedigion undergraduates (*npl*)
iti for (you), to you (*prep*)

J

jac jack (*nm*)
jam jam (*nm*)
jòb job (*nf*)

jôc joke (*nf*)
jyst just (*adv*)

L

a word starting with **l** printed in blue means that the root form of that word begins either with an **ll**, e.g. **ladd** root **lladd** or with a **g***, e.g. ***lân** root **glân**

Ll stands as a letter in its own right in Welsh. In a Welsh dictionary, unlike this list, words starting with, or containing 'll' would commence after those containing **L**:

lwc luck
lwcus lucky
lwfans allowance
llac lax, loose, slack
llach lash
llachar brilliant, dazzling, glittering

label label (*nm*)
labeli labels (*npl*)
labelu to label (*v*)
labordai laboratories (*npl*)
labordy laboratory (*nm*)
lach lash
ladd to kill
laddodd he/she/it killed
laddwyd was/were killed
laeth milk
lafar vocal
lafur labour
lai less
lais voice
lamp lamp (*nf*)
lampau lamps (*npl*)
lan up (*adj*)
*lan bank, side
lan church, church yard
*lân clean

lanc youth
landlord landlord (*nm*)
landlordiaid landlords (*npl*)
*lanhau to clean
*lanio to land
*lannau banks
lannau churchyards
lansiad launching (*nm*)
lansio to launch (*v*)
lansiodd he/she/it launched (*v*)
lansiwyd was/were launched (*v*)
lanw to fill
lanw tide
lapio to swaddle, to wrap (*v*)
larwm alarm (*nm*)
larymau alarms (*npl*)
*las blue
laser laser (*nm*)
*laswellt grass
law hand
*law rain
lawdriniaeth surgery
lawenydd happiness
lawer many
lawn full
lawnt green, lawn (*nf*)
lawr down, floor
lawysgrifau manuscripts
le place
lechi slates
led breadth, fairly
ledaenu to spread
leddfu to ease

ledled throughout
lefaru to speak
lefel level, spirit level (*nf*)
lefelau levels (*npl*)
lefydd places
leiaf least
leiafrifoedd minorities
leiafrifol minority
leihad reduction
leihau to reduce
lein line, line-out (*nf*)
leisio to voice
lem acute
lên literature
lenorion literary figures
lens lens (*nm*)
lenwi to fill
lenyddiaeth literature
lenyddol literary
leoedd places
leol local
leoli to place
leoliad location
leoliadau locations
leolir is/are/will be located
les benefit
lestri dishes
lethr slope
lethrau slopes
lety lodging
lew lion
licio to like (*v*)
lid anger, inflammation
lif flood
lifft elevator, lift (*nm*)
lifo to flow
lifogydd floods
lifrai livery, uniform (*nm*)
limrig limerick (*nm*)
linc link (*nf*)
linell line
linellau lines

liniaru to ease
litr l, litre (*nm*)
liw colour
liwiau colours
liwt lute (*nf*)
llac lax, loose, slack (*adj*)
llach lash (*nf*)
llachar brilliant, dazzling, glittering (*adj*)
lladd to deaden, to kill, to slaughter (*v*)
lladdodd he/she/it killed (*v*)
lladdwyd was/were killed (*v*)
Lladin Latin (*nf*)
lladron thieves (*npl*)
llaeth milk (*nm*)
llafar oral, vocal, vociferous (*adj*)
llafn blade (*nm*)
llafur labour, toil (*nm*)
llafur corn (*nm*)
llafurus arduous, hard, laborious (*adj*)
llai fewer, less, lesser, smaller (*adj*)
llai less, minus (*adv*)
llaid mud (*nm*)
llain plot (of land), strip, wicket (*nf*)
llais voice (*nm*)
llaith damp, moist (*adj*)
llall (the) other, (the) second (*pronoun*)
llamu to jump, to leap, to spring (*v*)
llan kirk, parish church (*nf*)
llanast mess (*nm*)
llanc lad, young man, youth (*nm*)
llannau churchyards (*npl*)
llanw flow, influx, tide (*nm*)
llanw filling (*adj*)
llanw to fill (*v*)
llath: llathen yard (measurement) (*nf*)
llaw hand, handwriting, side (*nf*)
llawdriniaeth operation (*nf*)
llawen happy, jovial, merry (*adj*)
llawenydd happiness, joy, merriment (*nm*)
llawer great deal, many (*adj*)
llawer far, lot, much (*adv*)
llawfeddyg surgeon (*nm*)

llawfeddygol surgical (*adj*)
llawlyfr handbook, manual (*nm*)
llawn complete, entire, full (*adj*)
llawn just (as), quite as, rather (*adv*)
llawnach fuller (*adj*)
llawnamser fulltime (*adj*)
llawr floor, storey (*nm*)
llawysgrif manuscript (*nf*)
llawysgrifau manuscripts (*npl*)
lle place, room, space (*nm*)
lle where (*conj*)
lle where (*adv*)
llech slate, stone, tablet (*nf*)
llechen slate (*nf*)
llechi slates (*npl*)
llechu to hide, to lurk, to shelter (*v*)
llecyn spot (*nm*)
llecynnau places (*npl*)
lled breadth, width (*nm*)
lled fairly, partly, semi- (*adv*)
lledaeniad dissemination (*nm*)
lledaenu to disseminate, to spread (*v*)
lleddfu to alleviate, to ease, to soothe (*v*)
lledr leather (*nm*)
lledu to broaden, to spread out, to widen (*v*)
llef cry, shout, wail (*nf*)
llefaru to speak, to utter (*v*)
llefarydd spokesman, spokesperson (*nm*)
lleferydd speech, utterance (*nm*)
llefrith milk (*nm*)
llefydd places (*npl*)
lleia' least (*adj*)
lleiaf least, minor, smallest, youngest (*nf*)
lleiafrif minority (*nm*)
lleiafrifoedd minorities (*npl*)
lleiafrifol minority (*adj*)
lleiafswm minimum (*nm*)
lleidr burglar, robber, thief (*nm*)
lleied so few, so little, so small (*adj*)
lleihad decrease, reduction (*nm*)
lleihau to decrease, to lessen, to reduce (*v*)
lleill others (*pronoun*)

lleiniau strips of land (*npl*)
lleisiau voices (*npl*)
lleisio to express, to sing, to voice (*v*)
lleithder dampness, humidity, moisture (*nm*)
llem acute (*adj/f*)
llen curtain, veil (*nf*)
llên literature (*nf*)
lleng host, legion, multitude (*nf*)
llenni curtains (*npl*)
llenor author (*nm*)
llenorion literary figures (*npl*)
llenwch you fill (*v*)
llenwi to fill (*v*)
llenyddiaeth literature (*nf*)
llenyddol literary (*adj*)
lleoedd places (*npl*)
lleol local (*adj*)
lleoli to locate, to place (*v*)
lleoliad location, position (*nm*)
lleoliadau locations (*npl*)
lleolir is/are/will be located (*v*)
lles benefit, good, welfare (*nm*)
llesol advantageous, beneficial (*adj*)
llesteirio to hinder, to impede, to obstruct (*v*)
llestri crockery, dishes (*npl*)
llethol overpowering, overwhelming, sweltering (*adj*)
llethr hillside, slope (*nm*)
llethrau slopes (*npl*)
llety accommodation, lodging (*nm*)
lletya to accommodate, to house, to lodge (*v*)
lleuad moon, the Moon (*nf*)
llew lion (*nm*)
llewod lions (*npl*)
llewyrch brightness, prosperity, radiance, success (*nm*)
llewyrchus flourishing, thriving (*adj*)
lleyg lay (*adj*)
lli flood (*nm*)

lliain cloth, linen, tablecloth, towel (*nm*)
lliaws host, multitude (*nm*)
llid anger, fury, irritation, wrath (*nm*)
llif current, flow (*nm*)
llif saw (*nf*)
llifanu to grind, to hone, to whet (*v*)
llifio to saw (*v*)
llifo to flow (*v*)
llifogydd floods (*npl*)
llinell line, queue, row, stripe (*nf*)
llinellau lines (*npl*)
lliniarol mitigating, soothing (*adj*)
lliniaru to alleviate, to ease, to soothe (*v*)
llinyn band, line, sinew, string, thread (*nm*)
llithro to slide, to slink, to slip (*v*)
lliw colour (*nm*)
lliw coloured (*adj*)
lliwgar colourful, vivid (*adj*)
lliwiau colours (*npl*)
lliwio to colour, to dye (*v*)
llo calf (cow); oaf (*nm*)
lloches refuge, shelter (*nf*)
Lloegr England
lloer moon (*nf*)
lloeren satellite (*nf*)
llofft bedroom, upstairs (*nf*)
llofnod autograph, signature (*nm*)
llofnodi to sign (*v*)
llofnodwyd was/were autographed, signed (*v*)
llofrudd murderer (*nm*)
llofruddiaeth murder (*nf*)
llog interest (*nm*)
llogi to hire, to lease (*v*)
lloi calves (cows) (*npl*)
llon cheerful, happy, joyful (*adj*)
llond full (*nm*)
llong ship (*nf*)
llongau ships (*npl*)
llongyfarch to compliment, to congratulate (*v*)
llongyfarchiad congratulation (*nm*)

llongyfarchiadau congratulations (*npl*)
llonydd quiet, still, tranquil (*adj*)
llonydd quiet (*nm*)
lloriau floors (*npl*)
llorweddol horizontal (*adj*)
llosg burning (*nm*)
llosg burning (*adj*)
llosgi to burn, to shine (*v*)
llu host, throng (*nm*)
lludw ash (*nm*)
llun drawing, form, photograph, picture, shape (*nm*)
Llundain London
llungopïo to photocopy (*v*)
lluniaeth fare, food, sustenance (*nm*)
lluniau pictures (*npl*)
llunio to construct, to fashion, to form (*v*)
lluniwch you draw (*v*)
lluniwyd was/were drawn (*v*)
lluoedd forces (*npl*)
lluosi to multiply (*v*)
lluosog plural (*adj*)
llusgo to drag (*v*)
llw curse, oath, vow (*nm*)
llwch dust, fertilizer (*nm*)
llwm barren, destitute, poor (*adj*)
llwy spoon (*nf*)
llwybr path, way (*nm*)
llwybrau paths (*npl*)
llwyd brown, grey, pale (*adj*)
llwyddiannau successes (*npl*)
llwyddiannus successful (*adj*)
llwyddiant success (*nm*)
llwyddo to succeed (*v*)
llwyddodd he/she/it succeeded (*v*)
llwyddwyd succeeded (*v*)
llwyfan dais, rostrum, stage (*nf*)
llwyn bush, grove, thicket (*npl*)
llwyni thickets (*npl*)
llwynog fox (*npl*)
llwyr complete, total, utter (*adj*)
llwyth burden, load; tribe (*nm*)

llwythau tribes (*npl*)
llwythi burdens (*npl*)
llwytho to load (*v*)
llydan broad, wide (*adj*)
llydanddail broad-leaved (*adj*)
Llydaw Brittany
Llydaweg Breton (*nm*)
llyfn even, level, smooth (*adj*)
llyfr book (*nm*)
llyfrau books (*npl*)
llyfrfa library, publisher (*nf*)
llyfrgell library (*nf*)
llyfrgelloedd libraries (*npl*)
llyfrgellydd librarian (*nm*)
llyfryddiaeth bibliography (*nf*)
llyfryn booklet, pamphlet (*nm*)
llyfrynnau booklets (*npl*)
llyg shrew (*nm*)
llygad eye, source (*nm*)
llygaid eyes (*npl*)
llygod mice (*npl*)
llygoden mouse (*nf*)
llygredd corruption, pollution (*nm*)
llygredig corrupt, degraded (*adj*)
llygru to adulterate, to contaminate, to pollute (*v*)
llym acute, keen, severe, sharp, strict (*adj*)
llyn lake (*nm*)
llyncu to absorb, to swallow (*v*)
llynedd last year (*adv*)
llynges fleet, navy (*nf*)
llynnoedd lakes (*npl*)
llys court, hall; slime (*nm*)
llysiau herbs, plants, vegetables (*npl*)
llysoedd courts (*npl*)
llystyfiant vegetation (*nm*)
llythrennau letters [alphabet] (*npl*)
llythrennedd literacy (*nm*)
llythrennol literal (*adj*)
llythyr epistle, letter (*nm*)
llythyrau letters [correspondence] (*npl*)
llythyren letter (*nf*)

llythyron letters [correspondence] (*npl*)
llyw helm, rudder, steering-wheel (*nm*)
llywio to pilot, to steer (*v*)
llywodraeth government (*nf*)
llywodraethau governments (*npl*)
llywodraethol governing, ruling (*adj*)
llywodraethu to control, to govern (*v*)
llywodraethwr governor (*nm*)
llywodraethwyr governors (*npl*)
llywydd dominant, president (*nm*)
lo coal
lo calf
lobïo to lobby (*v*)
loches shelter
*loes pain
*lofaol mining (coal)
lofnodi to sign
log interest,
lòg log (*nm*)
logi to hire
logio to log (*v*)
logisteg logistics (*nf*)
lolfa lounge, sitting-room (*nf*)
lon happy
lôn lane (*nf*)
lond full (of)
long ship
longau ships
lonydd quiet
lorri lorry (*nf*)
lorïau lorries (*npl*)
losgi to burn
loteri lottery (*nf*)
lu host
lun picture
luniau pictures
lunio formulate
luniwyd was/were formed
luoedd forces
lusgo to drag
lw oath
lwc luck (*nf*)

lwch dust
lwcus lucky (*adj*)
lwfans allowance (*nm*)
lwfansau allowances (*npl*)
lwybr path
lwybrau paths
lwyd grey
lwyddiannus successful
lwyddiant success
lwyddo to succeed
lwyddodd he/she/it succeeded
lwyfan stage
lwyr complete
lwyth load, tribe
lwytho to load
lydan wide
lyfr book
lyfrau books
lyfrgell library
lyfrgelloedd libraries
lyfryn booklet
lygad eye

lygaid eyes
lygredd corruption
lygru to corrupt, to pollute
***lyn** vale
lyn lake
lŷn he/she/it holds fast
lyncu to swallow
***lynu** to stick
lys court
lysiau vegetables
lysoedd courts
lystyfiant vegetation
lythrennau letters
lythyr letter (correspondence)
lythyrau letters (correspondence)
lythyren letter (alphabet)
lywio to steer
lywodraeth government
lywodraethol ruling
lywodraethu to rule
lywodraethwyr governor
lywydd president

M

a word starting with **m** printed in blue means that the root form of that word begins with a **b**, e.g. **mlwyddyn** root **blwyddyn**

a word starting with **mh** printed in blue (with asterix) means that the root form of that word begins with **p**, e.g. **mhlentyn** root **plentyn**

mab boy, son (*nm*)
mabwysiadu to adopt (*v*)
mabwysiadwyd was/were adopted (*v*)
machlud setting, sunset (*nm*)
machlud to set [of the Sun] (*v*)
madarch mushrooms, toadstools (*npl*)
maddau to forgive, to pardon (*v*)
maddeuant forgiveness, pardon (*nm*)
mae he/she/it are, is (*v*)
    mae'ch your {---} is/are
maen griddle, stone (*nm*)
maen they are (*v*)
maenor manor (*nf*)
maent they are (*v*)
maer mayor (*nm*)
maes area, field, ground, purview, square (*nm*)
maes out (*adv*)
maeth nourishment (*nm*)
maeth foster (*adj*)
maethiad nutrition (*nm*)
maetholyn nutrient (*nm*)
maethu to foster (*v*)
magnetig magnetic (*adj*)
magu to breed, to gain, to nurse, to rear (*v*)
magwyd was/were reared (*v*)
Mai May (*nm*)
mai that, that it is (*conj*)
mai blame, fault
main thin (*adj*)
mainc bench (*nf*)
maint extent, quantity, size (*nm*)

Mair Mary
maith long, tedious (*adj*)
malu to grind, to shatter, to smash (*v*)
malwod snails (*npl*)
mam mother (*nf*)
mamaliaid mammals (*npl*)
mamau mothers (*npl*)
mamiaith mother tongue (*nf*)
mamog in-lamb ewe (*nf*)
mamogiaid ewes (*npl*)
mamolaeth maternity, motherhood (*nf*)
man place, spot (*nm*)
mân fine, little, petty, small (*adj*)
mangre place, premises (*nf*)
mannau places (*npl*)
mantais advantage (*nf*)
manteisio to exploit, to take advantage (*v*)
manteisiol advantageous (*adj*)
manteision advantages (*npl*)
mantell cape, cloak, mantle (*nf*)
mantol balance (*nf*)
mantolen balance-sheet (*nf*)
manwerthu to retail (*v*)
manwl detailed, exact, precise (*adj*)
manylach more detailed (*adj*)
manylder detail, precision (*nm*)
manyleb specification (*nf*)
manylebau specifications (*npl*)
manylion details (*npl*)
manylrwydd exactness, precision (*nm*)
manylu to detail (*v*)
map map (*nm*)

mapiau maps (*npl*)
mapio to map (*v*)
marc mark (*nm*)
march stallion, steed (*nm*)
marchnad market (*nf*)
marchnadoedd markets (*npl*)
marchnata to market, to promote (*v*)
marchogaeth to ride (*v*)
marciau marks (*npl*)
marcio to mark (*v*)
marn judgement, opinion
marw to die (*v*)
marw dead deceased, lifeless (*adj*)
marwol deadly, fatal, lethal, mortal (*adj*)
marwolaeth death, mortality (*nf*)
marwolaethau deaths (*npl*)
marwoldeb mortality (*nm*)
màs mass [Phyics] (*nm*)
ma's out (*adv*)
masnach trade (*nf*)
masnachol commercial, mercantile (*adj*)
masnachu to trade (*v*)
masnachwr dealer, merchant, trader (*nm*)
masnachwyr traders (*npl*)
mater matter, subject, topic (*nm*)
materion matters (*npl*)
materol material, materialistic (*adj*)
math kind, sort (*nm*)
math sort, such (*nf*)
màth bath
mathau sorts (*npl*)
mathemateg mathematics (*nf*)
mathemategol mathematical (*adj*)
maw dirt
mawl praise, worship (*nm*)
mawn peat (*nm*)
mawr big, great, important, large (*adj*)
mawredd grandeur, greatness (*nm*)
mawreddog boastful, grand, pompous (*adj*)
mawrhydi majesty (*nm*)
mawrion prominent people (*npl*)
Mawrth Tuesday; March; Mars (*nm*)

mebyd childhood, youth (*nm*)
mecanwaith mechanism (*nm*)
mecanweithiau mechanisms (*npl*)
mecanyddol mechanical (*adj*)
medal medal (*nf*)
medd mead (*nm*)
medd he/she/it says (*v*)
medda he/she/it says, will say (*v*)
meddai he/she/it says, would say (*v*)
meddal soft, tender (*adj*)
meddalwedd software (*nm*)
medden they used to say (*v*)
meddiannu to occupy, to possess (*v*)
meddiannydd occupant (*nm*)
meddiant occupation, possession (*nm*)
meddu to own, to possess (*v*)
meddwi to get drunk, to intoxicate (*v*)
meddwl idea, (the) mind, thought (*nm*)
meddwl to intend, to mean, to think
meddwn we possess/we will possess (*v*)
meddyg doctor, physician (*nm*)
meddygaeth medicine (*nf*)
meddygfa surgery (*nf*)
meddygfeydd surgeries (*npl*)
meddyginiaeth medication, remedy (*nf*)
meddyginiaethau remedies (*npl*)
meddygol medical (*adj*)
meddygon doctors (*npl*)
meddylfryd disposition, mentality (*nm*)
meddyliau thoughts (*npl*)
meddyliodd he/she/it (*v*)
meddyliol mental (*adj*)
meddyliwch you consider, think (*v*)
medi to reap (*v*)
Medi September (*nm*)
medr ability, capacity, skill (*nm*)
medra he/she/it is able, will be able (*v*)
medrai he/she/it would be able (*v*)
medrau abilities, gifts (*npl*)
medrir is/are/will be able (*v*)
medru to be able, to know (*v*)
medrus clever, expert, skilful (*adj*)

medrusrwydd prowess (*nm*)
medrwch you can, you will be able (*v*)
medrwn we are/will be able (*v*)
medrwn I would be able, I used to be able (*v*)
megis as, like (*prep*)
Mehefin June (*nm*)
meibion sons (*npl*)
meic bike
meillion clover (*npl*)
meillionen clover (*nf*)
meincnodi to benchmark (*v*)
meinhau to taper (*v*)
meini stones (*npl*)
meintiau sizes (*npl*)
meintiol quantitative (*adj*)
meinwe gauze, tissue (*nm*)
meirch stallions (*npl*)
meirw dead (ones) (*npl*)
meistr boss, master (*nm*)
meistri masters (*npl*)
meithrin to cherish, to cultivate, to rear (*v*)
meithrinfa crèche, nursery (*nf*)
mêl honey (*nm*)
melen yellow (*adj/f*)
melin mill (*nf*)
melinau mills (*npl*)
mellt lightning (*npl*)
mellten lightning (*nf*)
melyn yellow (*adj*)
melys sweet (*adj*)
memorandwm memorandum (*nm*)
menter risk, speculation, venture (*nf*)
mentor mentor (*nm*)
mentora to mentor (*v*)
mentoriaid mentors (*npl*)
mentrau ventures (*npl*)
mentro to dare, to risk, to venture (*v*)
mentrus daring, enterprising, risky (*adj*)
menyn butter (*nm*)
menyw female, woman (*nf*)
menywod women (*npl*)
merch daughter, girl (*nf*)

merched girls (*npl*)
Mercher Wednesday; Mercury (*nm*)
Meseia messiah (*nm*)
mesul by (*adv*)
mesur measure, measurement (*nm*)
mesur to measure (*v*)
mesuradwy measurable (*adj*)
mesurau measures (*npl*)
mesuriad measurement (*nm*)
mesuriadau measurements (*npl*)
mesurydd meter (*nm*)
mesuryddion meters (*npl*)
metel metal (*nm*)
metelau metals (*npl*)
methdaliad bankruptcy (*nm*)
methiannau failures (*npl*)
methiant failure (*nm*)
methodd he/she/it failed (*v*)
Methodist Methodist (*nm*)
Methodistiaid Methodists (*npl*)
methodoleg methodology (*nf*)
methu to fail, to miss, to be unable (*v*)
metr metre (*nm*)
metrig metric (*adj*)
mewn in, in (a) (*prep*)
mewnbwn input (*nm*)
mewndirol inland (*adj*)
mewnforio to import (*v*)
mewnforion imports (*npl*)
mewnfudiad immigration (*nm*)
mewnfudo to immigrate (*v*)
mewnfudwr immigrant, incomer (*nm*)
mewnfudwyr immigrants (*npl*)
mewnlifiad influx (*nm*)
mewnol inner, inside, internal (*adj*)
mewnrwyd intranet (*nf*)
meysydd fields (*npl*)
*mha which
*mhanel panel
*mharagraff paragraph
*mharagraffau paragraphs
*mharc park

*mhell far
*mhen head
*mhennod chapter
*mhentref village
*mhlas mansion
*mhlentyn child
*mhlith amid
*mhlwyf parish
*mhob every
*mhobman everywhere
*mhresenoldeb presence
*mhrif chief, main
*mhrifysgol university
*mhrofiad experience
mil thousand (*nf*)
milfeddygol veterinary (*adj*)
miliwn million (*nf*)
miliynau millions (*npl*)
milltir mile (*nf*)
milltiroedd miles (*npl*)
miloedd thousands (*npl*)
milwr soldier (*nm*)
milwrol martial, military (*adj*)
milwyr soldiers (*npl*)
min edge, lip, point (*nm*)
miniog penetrating, pointed, sharp (*adj*)
minnau I even, I for my part (*pronoun*)
minne I too (*pronoun*)
mis month (*nm*)
misoedd months (*npl*)
misol monthly (*adj*)
miwsig music (*nm*)
mlaen front
mlaenau fronts
mlwch box
mlwydd year
mlwyddyn year
mlychau boxes
mlynedd years
mlynyddoedd years
mo no, not (*prep*)
moch pigs (*npl*)

moch cheek
mochyn pig, swine (*nm*)
mod am, are
modd means, way (*nm*)
moddion medicine (*nm*)
model model (*nm*)
modelau models (*npl*)
modelu to model (*v*)
modern modern (*adj*)
moderneiddio to modernize (*v*)
modfedd inch (*nf*)
modiwl module (*nm*)
modiwlau modules (*npl*)
modrwy ring (*nf*)
modryb aunt (*nf*)
modur automobile, motor, motor car (*nm*)
modurdy garage (*nm*)
moduron cars (*npl*)
moel bald, bare, plain (*adj*)
moel hilltop (*nf*)
moesegol ethical (*adj*)
moesol moral (*adj*)
moethus luxurious, sumptuous (*adj*)
mohono not him/it (*prep*)
mol belly
molysgiaid mollusca (*npl*)
moment moment (*nf*)
môn base, root
Môn Anglesey
monitro to monitor (*v*)
mor as, how, so (*adv*)
môr sea (*nm*)
mordaith cruise, voyage (*nf*)
mordwyo to navigate, to sail (*v*)
more early, morning
morfa fen, salt-marsh (*nf*)
morfil whale (*nm*)
morfilod whales (*npl*)
morgais mortgage (*nm*)
morglawdd breakwater, dyke, embankment (*nm*)
moroedd seas (*npl*)

morwr mariner, sailor, seaman (*nm*)
morwrol maritime (*adj*)
morwyn maid, virgin (*nf*)
morwyr seamen (*npl*)
mrawd brother
mro area
mron breast
mud dumb, mute, speechless (*adj*)
mudiad movement (*nm*)
mudiadau movements (*npl*)
mudo to migrate, to move (*v*)
mudol migrant, migratory (*adj*)
mul donkey, mule (*nm*)
munud minute (*nf*) *South Wales;* (*nm*) *North Wales*
munudau minutes (*npl*)
mur wall (*nm*)
muriau walls (*npl*)
musnes business
mwd mud (*nm*)
mwg fumes, smoke (*nm*)
mwrdeistref borough
mwy bigger, greater, more (*adj*)
mwy again, any more, more (*adv*)
mwya': mwyaf biggest, greatest, largest, major, most (*adj*)
mwyach any more, henceforth (*adv*)
mwyafrif majority, preponderance (*nm*)
mwyfwy increasingly, more and more (*adv*)
mwyn mineral, ore (*nm*)
mwyn dear, fine, gentle, mild, tender (*adj*)
mwynau minerals (*npl*)
mwynderau delights, pleasures (*npl*)
mwynglawdd mine (*nm*)
mwyngloddiau mines (*npl*)
mwyngloddio to mine (*v*)
mwynhad enjoyment, pleasure (*adj*)
mwynhau to enjoy (*v*)
myd world
myfi it is I, me myself (*pronoun*)
myfyrdod contemplation, meditation (*nm*)
myfyrio to contemplate, to ponder (*v*)

myfyriwr student (*nm*)
myfyrwraig student (female) (*nf*)
myfyrwyr students (*npl*)
mygu to smoke, to steam; to suffocate (*v*)
mymryn bit, mite, particle (*nm*)
myn kid (goat) (*nm*)
myn by (*prep*)
myn says (*v*)
mynach friar, monk (*nm*)
mynachod monks (*npl*)
mynd to become, to cease, to depart, to go (*v*)
mynd go, zip (*nm*)
myned to go (*v*)
mynedfa entrance, gateway (*nf*)
mynedfeydd entrances (*npl*)
mynediad access, admission (*nm*)
mynegai index (*nm*)
mynegeio to index (*v*)
mynegeion indeces, indexes (*npl*)
mynegi to express, to indicate (*v*)
mynegiant expression (*nm*)
mynegir is/are/will be expressed (*v*)
mynegodd he/she/it expressed (*v*)
mynegwyd was/were expressed (*v*)
mynnai he/she/it would insist (*v*)
mynnir is/are/will be insisted (*v*)
mynnodd he/she/it insisted (*v*)
mynnu to insist, to persist (*v*)
mynnwch you insist (*v*)
mynwent cemetery, graveyard (*nf*)
mynwentydd cemeteries (*npl*)
mynwes bosom, breast (*nf*)
mynych frequent (*adj*)
mynychaf most frequent (*adj*)
mynychder frequency, repetition (*nm*)
mynychu to attend, to visit regularly (*v*)
mynydd mountain (*nm*)
mynyddig mountainous (*adj*)
mynyddoedd mountains (*npl*)
mysg midst (*nm*)
mywyd life

N

a word starting with **n** printed in blue means that the root form of that word begins with **d**, e.g. **ninas** root **dinas**

a word starting with **ng** printed in blue means that the root form of that word begins with **g**, e.g. **ngeiriau** root **geiriau**

a word starting with **ngh** printed in blue means that the root form of that word begins with **c**, e.g. **nghwpan** root **cwpan**

a word starting with **nh** printed in blue means that the root form of that word begins with **t**, e.g. **nhad** root **tad**

Ng stands as a letter in its own right in Welsh. In a Welsh dictionary, unlike this list, words containing 'ng' would commence after those containing **G** (NOT N)

agosaf nearest
agwedd attitude
agweddau attitudes
angau death
angel angel
angen need
angenrheidiol necessary

na no, not (*negative particle*)
na neither . . . nor, nor (*conj*)
na that . . . not, who . . . not (*pronoun*)
na than (*conj*)
nabod to know (*v*)
nac no, not (*negative particle*)
nad no, not (*pronoun*)
naddo no (*adv*)
naddu to carve, to chip (*v*)
Nadolig Christmas (*nm*)
nag than (*conj*)
nage no (*adv*)
nai nephew (*nm*)
naid jump, leap (*nf*)
naill either . . . (or), the one . . . (the

other[s]) (*pronoun*)
nain grandma, grandmother (*nf*)
nam blemish, defect, fault (*nm*)
namau faults (*npl*)
namyn except, minus (*prep*)
nant brook, stream (*nf*)
nant tooth
naratif narrative (*nm*)
nas no, not (*pronoun*)
natur nature, temper (*nf*)
naturiol innate, natural (*adj*)
naw nine (*num*)
nawdd patronage, sponsorship, support (*nm*)
nawfed ninth (*num*)
nawr now (*adv*)
naws feel, tinge, touch (*nf*)
ne south; right
neb anyone, nobody, no one (*nm*)
nef bliss, heaven (*nf*)
nefoedd heaven (*nf*)
nefol celestial, heavenly (*adj*)
negatif negative (*adj*)
neges errand, message (*nm*)
negeseuon messages (*npl*)
negodi to negotiate (*v*)
negyddol negative (*adj*)
neidio to jump, to leap, to pounce (*v*)

neidiodd he/she/it leaped (*v*)

neidr snake (*nf*)

neilltu one side (*nm*)

neilltuo to reserve, to set to one side (*v*)

neilltuol particular, special (*adj*)

neilltuwyd was/were set to one side (*v*)

neis nice (*adj*)

neithiwr last night (*adv*)

nen sky, the heavens (*nf*)

nenfwd ceiling (*nf*)

nentydd streams (*npl*)

nepell near (*adv*)

nerfol nervous (*adj*)

nerfus nervous (*adj*)

nerth power, strength, vigour (*nm*)

nerthol mighty, strong (*adj*)

nes nearer (*adj*)

nes till, until (*prep*)

nesa next (*adj*)

nesaf nearest, next (*adj*)

neu or, or else (*conj*)

neuadd hall, hall (of residence) (*nf*)

neuaddau (*npl*)

newid change (*nm*)

newid to alter, to change (*v*)

newidiadau changes (*npl*)

newidiodd he/she/it changed (*v*)

newidiol changeable (*adj*)

newidiwyd was/were changed (*v*)

newydd news (*nm*)

newydd new (*adj*)

newyddiaduraeth journalism (*nf*)

newyddiadurwr journalism (*nm*)

newyddiadurwyr journalists (*npl*)

newyddion news (*npl*)

newyddlen news sheet (*nf*)

newyn famine, starvation (*nm*)

newynog hungry (*adj*)

words starting with '**g**'

ngeiriau words

ngeni to be born

words starting with '**c**'

nghaer Chester, fortress

nghalon heart

nghanllaw guideline, rail

nghanol middle

nghanolbarth midland

nghanolfan centre

nghapel chapel

ngharchar jail

nghariad love

nghartref home

nghastell castle

nghefn back

ngholeg college

ngholofn column

nghorff body

nghwm valley

nghwmni company

nghwpan cup

nghwrs course

nghyd joint

nghyd-destun context

nghyfarfod meeting

nghyfarfodydd meetings

nghyffiniau vicinity

nghyfnod period

nghyfraith law

nghyfres series

nghynllun plan

nghynulliad assembly

nghysgod shadow

nghystadleuaeth competition

nghyswllt context

words starting with '**g**'

ngofal care (for)

ngogledd north

ngoleuni light

ngolwg view

ngorllewin west

ngwaelod bottom

ngwaith work

ngweddill remainder

ngwely bed

ngwlad country
ngwledydd countries
ngwres heat
words starting with '**t**'
nhabl table
nhad father
nhad-cu grandfather
nhaid grandfather
nhermau terms
nheulu family
nhîm team
nhraed feet
nhref town
nhrefn order
nhw them (*pronoun*)
nhyb opinion
nhymor season, term
ni us, we (*pronoun*)
ni not (*negative particle*)
nifer number (*nf*)
niferoedd numbers (*npl*)
niferus numerous (*adj*)
ninnau we for our part, we too (*pronoun*)
nis not (*particle*)
nitrogen nitrogen (*nm*)
niwclear nuclear (*adj*)
niwed damage, harm, hurt (*nm*)
words starting with '**d**'
niwedd end
niweidio to damage, to harm (*v*)
niweidiol detrimental, harmful (*adj*)
niwl fog, haze, mist (*nm*)
niwmismateg numismatics (*nf*)
niwrnod day
niwsans nuisance (*nm*)
niwtral neutral (*adj*)
nod aim, objective, purpose (*nm*)
nodau notes (*npl*)
noddedig sponsored (*adj*)
noddfa refuge, sanctuary, shelter (*nf*)
noddi to patronize, to sponsor (*v*)
noddir is/are/will be sponsored (*v*)

noddwr patron, sponsor (*nm*)
noddwyd was/were sponsored (*v*)
noddwyr sponsors (*npl*)
nodedig notable, remarkable (*adj*)
noder (*should be*) noted (*v*)
nodi to mark, to note (*v*)
nodiadau notes (*npl*)
nodir is/are/will be noted (*v*)
nododd he/she/it noted (*v*)
nodwch you note, you will note (*v*)
nodwedd characteristic, feature, trait (*nf*)
nodweddiadol characteristic, typical (*adj*)
nodweddion characteristics (*npl*)
nodweddu to typify (*v*)
nodwyd was/were noted (*v*)
nodwydd needle (*nf*)
nodyn note (*nm*)
noeth bare, naked (*nf*)
nofel novel (*nf*)
nofelau novels (*npl*)
nofelydd novelist (*nm*)
nofio to swim (*v*)
nôl to bring, to fetch (*v*)
Normanaidd Norman (*adj*)
Normaniad Norman (*nm*)
nos night (*nf*)
noson evening, night (*nf*)
noswaith evening, night (*nf*)
nosweithiau nights (*npl*)
nwy gas (*nm*)
nwyddau goods, ware (*npl*)
nwylo hands
nwyon gases (*npl*)
nyddiau days
nyffryn vale, valley
nyrs nurse (*nf/nm*)
nyrsio to nurse (*v*)
nyrsys nurses (*npl*)
nyth nest (*nm*)
nythod nests (*npl*)
nythu to nest, to nestle (*v*)

o

a word starting with **o** printed in blue means that the root form of that word begins with **g**, e.g. **obaith** root **gobaith**

o (*prep*)
    o'ch from your, of your
    o'i from his/her/its; of his/her/its
    o'm from my, of my
    o'th from my, of my
    o'u from their, of their
o he, him, it (*pronoun*)
o oh! (*exclamation*)
obaith hope
obeithio to hope
obeithiol hopeful
oblegid because (*conj*)
oblegid on account of, owing to (*prep*)
oblygiadau implications
OC AD
och och, oh! (*exclamation*)
ochor side (*nf*)
ochr aspect, edge, facet, side (*nf*)
ochrau sides (*npl*)
ocsigen oxygen (*nm*)
od odd, strange (*adj*)
oddef suffer
oddeutu about, approximately (*adv*)
oddeutu about (you) (*prep*)
oddi from, out of (*prep*)
oddieithr except, unless (*prep*)
odid hardly, scarcely (*adv*)
odidog excellent
odl rhyme (*nf*)
odli to rhyme (*v*)
odyn kiln (*nf*)
oed age (*nm*)
oedd he/she/it was (*v*)
oeddan they were (*v*)

oeddech you used to (*v*)
oeddem we used to (*v*)
oedden they would (*v*)
oeddent they would (*v*)
oeddwn I used to (*v*)
oeddynt they were (*v*)
oedfa meeting, service (*nf*)
oedi to delay, to linger, to wait (*v*)
oedolion adults (*npl*)
oedolyn adult (*nm*)
oedran age (*nm*)
oedrannus aged, elderly (*adj*)
oen lamb (*nm*)
oer cold (*adj*)
oerfel cold (*nm*)
oergell fridge, refrigerator (*nf*)
oeri to chill, to get cold (*v*)
oerni cold (*nm*)
oes age, era, lifetime (*nf*)
oes are, is (*v*)
oesau ages (*npl*)
oesoedd ages (*npl*)
oesol perpetual (*adj*)
of blacksmith
ofal care (for)
ofalu to care (for)
ofalus careful
ofalwyr carers
ofer futile, vain, wasteful (*adj*)
offeiriad parson, priest (*nm*)
offeiriaid priests (*npl*)
offer implements (*npl*)
offeryn implement, instrument, tool (*nm*)
offerynnau instruments (*npl*)

offrwm offering, sacrifice (*nm*)

ofid worry

ofn dread, fear, trepidation (*nm*)

ofnadwy awful, terrible (*adj*)

ofnau fears (*npl*)

ofni to be afraid, to fear (*v*)

ofnus fearful, nervous, timid (*adj*)

ofod space

ofyn to ask

ofyniad question

ofynion requirements

ofynnir is/are/will be required

ofynnodd he/she/it asked

ofynnol required

ofynnwyd was/were asked

oglau scents, smells (*npl*)

ogledd north

ogleddol northern

ogof cave, grotto (*nf*)

ogoniant splendour

ogystal as well as (*adj*)

ohebiaeth correspondence

oherwydd because (*conj*)

ohirio to postpone

ohoni of (her) (*prep*)

ohono of (him) (*prep*)

ohonoch of (you) (*prep*)

ohonom of (us) (*prep*)

ohonon of (us) (*prep*)

ohonyn of (them) (*prep*)

ohonynt of (them) (*prep*)

ôl impression, mark, spoor, track (*nm*)

ôl behind (*adj*)

ola': olaf final, last (*adj*)

olau light

olchi to wash

oleuadau lights

oleuni light

oleuo to light

olew oil (*nm*)

olion tracks (*npl*)

oll all, (not) at all (*adv*)

ollwng to release

ollyngiadau releases

ôl-raddedig post-graduate (*adj*)

olrhain to follow, to plot, to trace (*v*)

olwg look, sight

olwyn wheel (*nf*)

olwynion wheels (*npl*)

olygfa view

olygfeydd sight, views

olygir is/are/will mean

olygu to edit, to entail

olygydd editor

olygyddion editors

Olympaidd Olympic (*adj*)

olyniaeth succession (*nf*)

olynol consecutive, successive (*adj*)

olynydd successor (*nm*)

ombwdsmon ombudsman (*nm*)

ond but, only (*conj*)

onest honest

onestrwydd honesty

ongl angle (*nf*)

onglau angles (*npl*)

oni has he/she not?, isn't it? (*particle*)

oni unless (*conj*)

onid unless (*particle*)

opera opera (*nf*)

opsiwn option (*nm*)

opsiynau options (*npl*)

optegol optical (*adj*)

orau best

orchmynion commands

orchudd cover

orchuddio to cover

orchwyl task

orchymyn command, commandment

ordnans ordnance (*nm*)

oren orange (*nm*)

oresgyn to defeat

orffen to complete

orffwys to rest (*v*)

orffwysfa caesura, resting place

orfod to have to
orfodaeth compulsion
orfodi to force
orfodol compulsory
organ organ [instrument/body] (*nf*)
organau organs (*npl*)
organeb organism (*nf*)
organebau organisms (*npl*)
organig organic (*adj*)
oriau hours (*npl*)
oriel gallery (*nf*)
orielau galleries (*npl*)
orlawn overflowing
orllewin west
orllewinol western
ormod too much
ormodol to excess
ornest contest

oroesi to survive
orsaf station
orsafoedd stations
orsedd throne
oruchwyliaeth supervision
oruchwylio to supervise
orwedd to lie
os if (*conj*)
osgo posture, slant, stance (*nm*)
osgoi to avoid, to elude (*v*)
osod to set
osodir is/are/will be set
osododd he/she/it set
osodwyd was/were set
osôn ozone (*nm*)
ostwng to lower
ostyngiad reduction
ots care (for), matter (*nm*)

P

a word starting with **ph** printed in blue means that the root form of that word begins with **p**, e.g. **phapur** root **papur**

pa how, what, when, which (*pronoun*)

pabell marquee, pavilion, tent (*nf*)

pac kit, pack (*nm*)

pacio to pack (*v*)

paent paint (*nm*)

pafiliwn pavilion (*nm*)

paham wherefore, why (*adv*)

paid don't (*v*)

paith pampas, prairie, range (*nm*)

palas palace (*nm*)

palmant pavement (*nm*)

pam wherefore, why (*adv*)

pan when, while (*conj*)

pan pan (*nm*)

paned cup of (*nm*)

panel panel (*nm*)

paneli panels (*npl*)

pant dell, depression, dip, hollow (*nm*)

papur paper (*nm*)

papurau papers (*npl*)

pâr pair (*nm*)

pâr he/she/it lasts (*v*)

para to last (*v*)

paragraff paragraph (*nm*)

paragraffau paragraphs (*npl*)

paratoad preparation (*nm*)

paratoadau preparations (*npl*)

paratoi to groom, to prepare (*v*)

paratowyd was/were prepared (*v*)

parau pairs (*npl*)

parc field, park (*nm*)

parch esteem, respect (*nm*)

parchedig reverend (*adj*)

Parchg Rev. (*abbreviation*)

parchu to respect, to revere, to venerate (*v*)

parchus respectable, respectful (*adj*)

parciau parks (*npl*)

parcio to park (*v*)

parent they used to last (*v*)

parhad continuation, durability, sequel, wear (*nm*)

parhaodd he/she/it continued (*v*)

parhaol continuous, permanent, perpetual (*adj*)

parhau to continue, to last (*v*)

parhaus continual, sustained (*adj*)

parlwr parlour (*nm*)

parod instant, obliging, ready, willing (*adj*)

parodd he/she/it caused (*v*)

parodrwydd readiness (*nm*)

parsel parcel (*nm*)

parth district, domain, part (*nm*)

parthau parts (*npl*)

parthed concerning, regarding (*prep*)

parti fête, party (*nm*)

partïon parties (*npl*)

partner mate, partner (*nm*)

partneriaeth partnership (*nf*)

partneriaethau partnerships (*npl*)

partneriaid partners (*npl*)

pasbort passport (*nm*)

pasbortau passports (*npl*)

Pasg Easter (*nm*)

pasio to pass (*v*)

patrwm example, pattern (*nm*)

patrymau patterns (*npl*)
pawb everybody (*npl*)
pe if, though, were (*conj*)
pebyll tents (*npl*)
pechod sin (*nm*)
pechodau sins (*npl*)
pecyn pack, package (*nm*)
pecynnau packages (*npl*)
pecynnu to package (*v*)
pedair four (*num/f*)
pedol horseshoe (*nf*)
pedwar four (*num/m*)
pedwaredd fourth (*num/f*)
pedwerydd fourth (*num/m*)
peidio to cease, to refrain (*v*)
peidiwch don't (*v*)
peilot pilot (*nm*)
peint pint (*nm*)
peintio to paint (*v*)
peiriannau engines, machines (*npl*)
peirianneg engineering (*nf*)
peiriannwr engineer, mechanic (*nm*)
peiriant engine, machine (*nm*)
peirianwaith machinery, mechanism (*nm*)
peirianwyr engineers, mechanics (*npl*)
peirianyddol mechanical (*adj*)
pêl ball (*nf*)
pêl-droed football, soccer (*nf*)
pêl-droediwr footballer, soccer player (*nm*)
pelen ball, pellet (*nf*)
peli balls (*npl*)
pell distant, far, long (*adj*)
pellach further, later (*adj*)
pellach any longer (*adv*)
pellaf furthest (*adj*)
pelled as far as (*adj*)
pellter distance (*nm*)
pelydr rays (*npl*)
pelydryn beam, gleam, ray (*nm*)
pen end, head, mouth, top (*nm*)
penaethiaid heads (*npl*)
penawdau headlines (*npl*)

pen-blwydd birthday (*nm*)
pencadlys headquarters (*nm*)
pencampwriaeth championship (*nf*)
pendant definite, positive (*adj*)
penderfynais I decided (*v*)
penderfyniad decision (*nm*)
penderfyniadau decisions (*npl*)
penderfynir is/are/will be decided (*v*)
penderfynodd he/she/it decided (*v*)
penderfynol determined, resolute (*adj*)
penderfynu to decide (*v*)
penderfynwch you decide (*v*)
penderfynwyd was/were decided (*v*)
pen draw end (*nm*)
penillion verses (*npl*)
pennaeth chief, head (*nm*)
pennaf chief, predominant, principal (*adj*)
pennau heads (*npl*)
pennawd caption, heading (*nm*)
pennill stanza, verse (*nm*)
pennir is/are/will be decided, marked (*v*)
pennod chapter, episode (*nf*)
pennu to decide, to determine, to specify (*v*)
pennwyd was/were decided, marked (*v*)
penodau chapters (*npl*)
penodedig appointed, determined (*adj*)
penodi to appoint (*v*)
penodiad appointment (*nm*)
penodiadau appointments (*npl*)
penodir is/are/will be appointed (*v*)
penodol distinct, especial, specific (*adj*)
penodwyd was/were appointed (*v*)
pensaer architect (*nm*)
pensaernïaeth architecture (*nf*)
pensaernïol architectural (*adj*)
pensiwn pension (*nm*)
pensiynau pensions (*npl*)
pensiynwr pensioner, senior citizen (*nm*)
pensiynwyr pensioners (*npl*)
pentir headland (*nm*)
pentre: **pentref** village (*nm*)
pentrefi villages (*npl*)

pentwr heap, pile, stack (*nm*)
penwythnos weekend (*nm*)
perchen owner (*nm*)
perchennog owner, proprietor (*nm*)
perchenogaeth possession (*nm*)
perchenogion owners (*npl*)
pererin pilgrim (*nm*)
pererindod pilgrimage (*nm*)
perffaith perfect (*adj*)
perfformiad performance (*nm*)
perfformiadau performances (*npl*)
perfformio to perform (*v*)
peri to cause, to induce (*v*)
persbectif perspective (*nm*)
person person (*nm*)
person parson (*nm*)
personau persons (*npl*)
personél personnel (*nm*)
personol personal (*adj*)
personoliaeth personality (*nf*)
perswadio to persuade (*v*)
perth bush, hedge (*nf*)
perthi hedges (*npl*)
perthnasau relatives (*npl*)
perthnasedd relevance (*nm*)
perthnasol pertinent, relevant (*adj*)
perthyn to belong, to be related (*v*)
perthynai he/she/it would belong (*v*)
perthynas relation, relative (*nm/f*)
perthynas connection, relationship (*nf*)
perthynol relative (*adj*)
perwyl purpose (*nm*)
peryg danger (*nm*)
perygl danger, jeopardy, peril (*nm*)
peryglon dangers (*npl*)
peryglu to endanger, to jeopardize (*v*)
peryglus dangerous, perilous (*adj*)
petaech were you to (*v*)
petaent were they to (*v*)
petai were he/she/it to (*v*)
peth some, thing (*nm*)
pethau: pethe things (*npl*)

petrol petrol (*nm*)
pha what, which
pham why
phan when
phapur paper
phapurau papers
pharagraff paragraph
pharagraffau paragraphs
pharatoi to prepare
pharc park
pharch respect
pharhad continuation
pharhau to continue
phartner partner
phartneriaethau partnerships
phartneriaid partners
phatrwm pattern
phatrymau patterns
phawb everybody
phe were
phedair four
phedwar four
pheidio to cease
pheidiwch don't
pheiriannau engines, machines
phen head
phenderfyniad decision
phenderfyniadau decisions
phenderfynodd he/she/it decided
phenderfynu to decide
phenderfynwyd was/were decided
phennaeth head
phennu determine
phenodi to appoint
phensiynau pensions
phentref village
phentrefi villages
pherfformiad performance
pherfformio to perform
pheri to cause
pherson parson, person
phersonol personal

pherthnasau relatives
pherthnasol relevant
pherthynas relation
pheryglon dangers
pheth thing
phethau things
phlanhigion plants
phlant children
phlentyn child
phob every
phobl people
phoblogaeth population
phoen pain
phoeni to worry
pholisi policy
pholisïau policies
phopeth everything
phosibl possible
photensial potential
phreifat private
phren wood
phresenoldeb presence
phridd earth
phrif main
phrifysgol university
phrifysgolion universities
phrin scarce
phriodol appropriate
phris price
phrisiau prices
phroblem problem
phroblemau problems
phroffesiynol professional
phrofi to prove, to test
phrofiad experience
phrofiadau experiences
phrofion tests
phroses process
phrosesau processes
phrosesu process
phrosiect project
phrosiectau projects

phryd when
phryder worry
phryderon worries
phrynu to buy
phum five
phump five
phwerau powers
phwnc subject
phwrpas purpose
phwy who
phwyllgor committee
phwynt point
phwysau weight (s)
phwysig important
phwysigrwydd importance
phwyslais emphasis
phwyso to weigh
phyllau pits
phynciau subjects
physgod fish (es)
piano piano, pianoforte (*nm*)
pibell pipe, tube (*nf*)
pibellau pipes (*npl*)
picnic picnic (*nm*)
pig beak, bill, point, spike (*nf*)
pig touchy (*adj*)
pigo to choose, to peck, to pick, to select, to sting (*v*)
pìn pin (*nm*)
pinc pink (*adj*)
pinc chaffinch (*nm*)
pla plague, pestilence, pest (*nm*)
plaen clear, frank, plain (*adj*)
plaen plane [for wood] (*nm*)
plaid party (*nf*)
planed planet (*nf*)
planhigfeydd plantations (*npl*)
planhigion plants (*npl*)
planhigyn plant (*nm*)
plannu to plant (*v*)
plant children (*npl*)
plas country house, mansion (*npl*)

plastig plastic (*nm*)
plastig plastic (*nm*)
plasty mansion (*nm*)
plât plate (*nm*)
platiau plates (*npl*)
pleidiau parties (*npl*)
pleidlais vote (*nf*)
pleidleisiau votes (*npl*)
pleidleisio to poll, to vote (*v*)
plentyn child (*nm*)
plentyndod childhood (*nm*)
pleser pleasure (*nm*)
pleserus enjoyable, pleasant (*adj*)
plesio to please, to satisfy (*v*)
plismon policeman (*nm*)
plismona to police (*v*)
plith midst (*nm*)
plwg plug (*nm*)
plwm lead (metal) (*nm*)
plwm plumb (*adj*)
Plwton Pluto (*nm*)
plwyf parish (*nm*)
plwyfi parishes (*npl*)
plygu to bend, to fold, to refract (*v*)
plymio to dive, to plummet, to plunge (*v*)
pnawn afternoon (*nm*)
po the (sooner) the (better), the ... the ... (*particle*)
pob all, each, every (*adj*)
pob baked (*adj*)
pobl folk, people (*nf*)
pobloedd peoples (*npl*)
poblogaeth population, populace (*nf*)
poblogaethau populations (*npl*)
poblogaidd popular (*adj*)
poblogrwydd popularity (*nm*)
pobman everywhere (*nm*)
pobol people (*nf*)
poced pocket (*nf*)
poen ache, nuisance, pain (*nf*)
poeni to bother, to fret, to hurt, to pester, to tease, to worry (*v*)

poenus aching, painful, sore (*adj*)
poeth hot, spicy (*adj*)
polisi policy (*nm*)
polisïau policies (*npl*)
politicaidd political (*adj*)
pont arch, bridge (*nf*)
pontio to bridge, to span (*v*)
pontydd bridges (*npl*)
pop mineral water, pop (*nm*)
pop pop (*adj*)
popeth everything (*nm*)
popty bakehouse, oven (*nm*)
porfa grass, pasture (*nf*)
pori to browse, to graze (*v*)
portffolio portfolio (*nm*)
porth door, lobby, porch (*nm*)
porth harbour (*nf*)
porthi to feed (*v*)
porthiant food, nourishment (*nm*)
porthladd harbour, port (*nm*)
porthladdoedd harbours (*npl*)
portread portrait, portrayal (*nm*)
portreadu to portray (*v*)
porwr browser, grazer (*nm*)
posib possible (*adj*)
posibiliadau possibilities (*npl*)
posibilrwydd possibility (*nm*)
posibl feasible, possible (*adj*)
positif positive (*adj*)
post post (mail) (*nm*)
poster poster (*nm*)
posteri posters (*npl*)
postio to post (*v*)
postiwyd was/were posted (*v*)
postyn post (*nm*)
potel bottle (*nf*)
poteli bottles (*npl*)
potensial potential (*nm*)
praidd congregation, flock (*nm*)
prawf probation, proof, test, trial (*nm*)
pregeth sermon (*nf*)
pregethu to preach (*v*)

pregethwr preacher (*nm*)
preifat private (*adj*)
preifatrwydd privacy (*nm*)
premiwm premium (*nm*)
pren wood, timber, tree (*nm*)
pren wooden (*adj*)
prentis apprentice (*nm*)
prentisiaeth apprenticeship (*nf*)
prentisiaethau apprenticeships (*npl*)
prentisiaid apprentices (*npl*)
pres brass; money, (*nm*)
Presbyteraidd Presbyterian (*adj*)
presennol present (*adj*)
presennol (the) Present (*nm*)
presenoldeb presence (*nm*)
presgripsiwn prescription (*nm*)
presgripsiynau prescriptions (*npl*)
preswyl boarding, residential (*adj*)
preswylio to dwell, to reside (*v*)
preswylwyr dwellers, residents (*npl*)
preswylydd inhabitant, resident (*nm*)
pridd earth, soil (*nm*)
priddoedd soils (*npl*)
prif chief, head, main, prime (*adj*)
prifardd award-winning poet (*nm*)
prifathro headmaster, principal (*nm*)
prifddinas capital city, metropolis (*nf*)
priffordd highway, main road (*nf*)
priffyrdd highways (*npl*)
prifwyl National Eisteddfod (*adj*)
prifysgol university (*nf*)
prifysgolion universities (*npl*)
prin deficient, few, rare, scarce (*adj*)
prin hardly, scarcely (*adv*)
prinder dearth, scarcity, shortage (*nm*)
print print (*nm*)
printiedig printed (*adj*)
printio to print (*v*)
priod married; proper (*adj*)
priod (marriage) partner, partner, spouse (*nm*)
priodas marriage, matrimony, wedding (*nf*)

priodasau marriages (*npl*)
priodasol marital, matrimonial (*adj*)
priodi to couple, to marry, to wed (*v*)
priodol appropriate, suitable (*adj*)
priodoli to ascribe, to attribute (*v*)
priodwedd property (*nf*)
priodweddau properties (*npl*)
pris price (*nm*)
prisiad valuation (*nm*)
prisiau prices (*npl*)
prisio to price, to value (*v*)
problem problem (*nf*)
problemau problems (*npl*)
profedigaeth bereavement, tribulation (*nf*)
proffesiwn profession (*nm*)
proffesiynau professions (*npl*)
proffesiynol professional (*adj*)
proffil profile (*nm*)
proffwyd prophet (*nm*)
profi to experience, to prove, to taste, to test, to try (*v*)
profiad experience (*nm*)
profiadau experiences (*npl*)
profiadol experienced, veteran (*adj*)
profion tests (*npl*)
profwyd was/were proven (*v*)
prosbectws prospectus (*nm*)
proses process (*nf*)
prosesau processes (*npl*)
prosesu to process (*v*)
prosesydd processor (*nm*)
prosiect project (*nm*)
prosiectau projects (*npl*)
protein protein (*nm*)
protest protest (*nf*)
Protestannaidd Protestant (*adj*)
protestio to protest, to remonstrate (*v*)
protocol protocol (*nm*)
protocolau protocols (*npl*)
pryd when (*adv*)
pryd complexion (*nm*)
pryd meal (*nm*)

Prydain Britain (*nf*)
prydau meals (*npl*)
pryddest poem (*nf*)
Prydeinig British (*adj*)
pryder anxiety, worry (*nm*)
pryderon worries (*npl*)
pryderu to fret, to worry (*v*)
pryderus anxious, worried (*adj*)
prydferth beautiful, handsome (*adj*)
prydferthwch beauty (*nm*)
prydiau times (*npl*)
prydles lease (*nf*)
prydlon prompt, punctual (*adj*)
pryf fly, grub, insect, worm (*nm*)
pryfed flies, insects (*npl*)
pryfyn insect, worm (*nm*)
prynhawn afternoon (*nm*)
pryniad purchase (*nm*)
prynu to buy, to purchase, to redeem (*v*)
prynwch you buy (*v*)
prynwr buyer, consumer, redeemer (*nm*)
prynwyr buyers (*npl*)
prysur busy (*adj*)
prysurdeb commotion (*nm*)
pum five (*num*)
pumdeg fifty (*num*)
pumdegau fifties (*npl*)
pumed fifth (*num*)
pump five (*num*)
punnau pounds £ (*npl*)
punnoedd pounds £ (*npl*)
punt pound £ (*nf*)
pur pure (*adj*)
pur fairly, quite (*adv*)
pŵer power (*nm*)
pwerau powers (*npl*)
pwerus powerful (*adj*)
pwll coal-mine, pit; pond, pool (*nm*)
pwmp pump (*nm*)
pwnc subject, topic (*nm*)

pwrpas aim, object, purpose (*nm*)
pwrpasau purposes (*npl*)
pwrpasol purposeful (*adj*)
pwy who (*pronoun*)
Pwyl, Gwlad Poland
pwyllgor committee (*nm*)
pwyllgorau committees (*npl*)
pwynt point, purpose (*nm*)
pwyntiau points (*npl*)
pwyntio to point (*v*)
pwys pound (lb) (*nm*)
pwys importance (*nm*)
pwysau weights (*npl*)
pwysau pressure, weight (*nm*)
pwysedd (blood) pressure, pressure (*nm*)
pwysicach more important (*adj*)
pwysicaf most important (*adj*)
pwysig important (*adj*)
pwysigrwydd importance, value (*nm*)
pwyslais emphasis, stress (*nm*)
pwysleisio to emphasize, to stress (*v*)
pwysleisiodd he/she/it emphasized (*v*)
pwyso to bring pressure to bear, to lean, to weigh (*v*)
pydru to putrefy, to rot (*v*)
pyllau pits, pools (*npl*)
pymtheg fifteen (*num*)
pymthegfed fifteenth (*num*)
pynciau subjects (*npl*)
pysgod fish (es) (*npl*)
pysgodfa fishery (*nf*)
pysgodfeydd fisheries (*npl*)
pysgodyn fish (*nm*)
pysgota to angle, to fish (*v*)
pysgotwr angler, fisherman (*nm*)
pysgotwyr fishermen (*npl*)
pyst posts (*npl*)
pythefnos fortnight (*nm*)
pytiau snippets (*npl*)

R

a word starting with **r** printed in blue means that the root form of that word begins either with an **rh**, e.g. **rad** root **rhad** or with a **g**, e.g. ***radd** root **gradd**

Rh stands as a letter in its own right in Welsh. In a Welsh dictionary, unlike this list, words starting with '**rh**' would commence after those containing **R**

rygbi rugby
rysáit recipe
ryseitiau recipes
rhad cheap, inexpensive
rhaeadr cascade, waterfall
rhaff rope, string

rad cheap
*radd degree
*raddau degrees
*raddedig graduated
*raddedigion graduates
*raddfa scale
*raddfeydd scales
*raddio to graduate
*raddol graduate
ragfarn prejudice
raglen programme
raglenni programmes
ragnodir is/are/will be prescribed
ragor more
ragoriaeth excellence
ragorol excellent
rai some
raid must
rali rally (*nf*)
*ramadeg grammar
ran part

ranbarth region
ranbarthau regions
ranbarthol regional
rannau parts
rannu to share
ras race (*nf*)
rasio to race (*v*)
rasus races (*npl*)
realaeth realism (*nf*)
realistig realistic (*adj*)
realiti reality (*nm*)
record record (*nf*)
recordiad recording (*nm*)
recordiadau recordings (*npl*)
recordiau records (*npl*)
recordio to record (*v*)
recriwtio to recruit (*v*)
red he/she/it runs, will run
redeg to run
refeniw revenue (*nm*)
refferendwm referendum (*nm*)
reg curse
reidrwydd obligation
reilffordd railway
reilffyrdd railways
reis rice (*nm*)
reit quite (*adv*)
rennir is/are/will be shared
rent rent
reol rule
reolaeth control
reolaidd regular
reolau rules

reoleiddio to regulate

reoli to rule

reoliad regulation

reoliadau regulations

reolir is/are/will be regulated

reolwr manager

reolwyr managers

res row

restr list

restrir is/are/will be listed

restru to list

restrwyd was/were listed

reswm reason

resymau reasons

resymol reasonable

rew frost

rhad cheap, inexpensive (*adj*)

rhaeadr cascade, waterfall (*nf*)

rhaff rope (*nf*)

rhaffau ropes (*npl*)

rhag against, from, lest (*prep*)

rhagair foreword, preface (*nm*)

rhagarweiniad introduction (*nm*)

rhagarweiniol introductory, preliminary (*adj*)

rhagddi before (her) (*prep*)

rhagddo before (him) (*prep*)

rhagddynt before (them) (*prep*)

rhagdyb assumption, presupposition (*nf*)

rhagdybiaeth hypothesis, preconception (*nf*)

rhagdybiaethau preconceptions (*npl*)

rhagdybio to assume, to preconceive (*v*)

rhagfarn bias, prejudice (*nf*)

rhagfynegi to foretell (*v*)

Rhagfyr December (*nm*)

rhaglen program, programme (*nf*)

rhaglenni programmes (*npl*)

rhagnodi to prescribe (*v*)

rhagnodir is/are/will be prescribed (*v*)

rhagofalon precautions (*npl*)

rhagolwg outlook, prospect (*nm*)

rhagolygon prospects (*npl*)

rhagor distinction, more (*nm*)

rhagor any more (*adv*)

rhagori to excel, to surpass (*v*)

rhagoriaeth distinction, excellence (*nf*)

rhagorol excellent, superb (*adj*)

rhagrith hypocrisy (*nm*)

rhagweithiol proactive (*adj*)

rhagweld to foresee (*v*)

rhagwelir is/are/will be foreseen (*v*)

rhagwelwyd was/were foreseen (*v*)

rhagymadrodd introduction (*nm*)

rhai some (*pronoun*)

rhaid necessity (*nm*)

rhain these (*pronoun*)

rhamant romance (*nf*)

rhamantus romantic (*adj*)

rhan lot, part, portion, role, share (*nf*)

rhan-amser part-time (*adj*)

rhanbarth region (*nm*)

rhanbarthau regions (*npl*)

rhanbarthol divisional, regional (*adj*)

rhanddeiliad stakeholder (*nm*)

rhanddeiliaid stakeholders (*npl*)

rhaniad division, parting (*nm*)

rhaniadau divisions (*npl*)

rhannau parts (*npl*)

rhannol in part (*adj*)

rhannu to distribute, to divide, to share (*v*)

rhannwch you share (*v*)

rhannwyd was/were shared (*v*)

rhatach cheaper (*adj*)

rhed he/she/it runs, will run (*v*)

rhedeg to conjugate, to flow, to run (*v*)

rhediad flow, run, slope (*nm*)

rhedodd he/she/it ran (*v*)

rhedyn bracken, ferns (*npl*)

rheg curse, swear-word (*nf*)

rheidrwydd compulsion, necessity (*nm*)

rheilffordd railway (*nf*)

rheilffyrdd railways (*npl*)

rheini those (*pronoun*)

rheithgor jury (*nm*)
rhelyw remainder, the rest (*nm*)
rheng rank, row (*nf*)
rhennir is/are/will be shared (*v*)
rhent rent (*nm*)
rhenti rents (*npl*)
rhentu to rent (*v*)
rheol rule (*nf*)
rheolaeth control, management (*nf*)
rheolaethau controls (*npl*)
rheolaethol managerial (*adj*)
rheolaidd regular (*adj*)
rheolau rules (*npl*)
rheoledig regulated (*adj*)
rheoleiddio to regulate (*v*)
rheoli to control, to govern, to regulate, to rule (*v*)
rheoliad regulation (*nm*)
rheoliadau regulations (*npl*)
rheoliadol regulatory (*adj*)
rheolir is/are/will be managed (*v*)
rheolwr manager, ruler (*nm*)
rheolwraig manager (*nf*)
rheolwyr managers (*npl*)
rheolydd regulator (*nm*)
rhes row, stripe, tier (*nf*)
rhesi rows (*npl*)
rhestr list, file, row (*nf*)
rhestrau lists (*npl*)
rhestredig listed (*nf*)
rhestri lists (*npl*)
rhestrir is/are/will be listed (*v*)
rhestru to list (*v*)
rhestrwch you list (*v*)
rhestrwyd was/were listed (*v*)
rheswm cause, explanation, reason (*nm*)
rhesymau reasons (*npl*)
rhesymedig reasoned (*adj*)
rhesymeg logic (*nf*)
rhesymegol logical (*v*)
rhesymol reasonable (*adj*)
rhesymu to argue, to reason (*v*)

rhew frost, ice (*nm*)
rhewi to freeze (*v*)
rhiant parent (*nm*)
rhieni parents (*npl*)
rhif number (*nm*)
rhifau numbers (*npl*)
rhifedd numeracy (*nm*)
rhifo to count, to number (*v*)
rhifyn issue, number (*nm*)
rhinwedd virtue (*nm*)
rhinweddau virtues (*npl*)
rhisgl bark (*nm*)
rhith form, illusion, semblance (*nm*)
rhiw hill, slope (*nf*)
rho you give! (*v*)
rhodd gift, present (*nf*)
rhoddai he/she/it gives, would give (*v*)
rhoddi to give (*v*)
rhoddion gifts (*npl*)
rhoddir is/are/will be given (*v*)
rhoddodd he/she/it gave (*v*)
rhoddwr giver (*nm*)
rhoddwyd was/were given (*v*)
rhoddwyr givers (*npl*)
rhodfa promenade (*nf*)
rhodio to stroll, to walk (*v*)
rhoes he/she/it gave (*v*)
rhoi to give, to present, to put (*v*)
rhoi you give, you will give (*v*)
rhoir is/are/will be given (*v*)
rholio to roll (*v*)
rhos heath, moor (*nf*)
rhostir heath (*nm*)
rhosyn rose (*nm*)
rhowch you give, you will give (*v*)
Rhufain Rome
Rhufeinig Roman (*adj*)
rhugl fluent (*adj*)
rhuo to bellow, to roar (*v*)
rhuthro to dash, to hurry, to rush (*v*)
rhwng between (*prep*)
rhwyd net (*nf*)

rhwydd easy, fluent, free (*adj*)
rhwydi nets (*npl*)
rhwydwaith network (*nm*)
rhwydweithiau networks (*npl*)
rhwydweithio to network (*v*)
rhwyg rift, split, tear (*nm*)
rhwygo to rip, to tear, to wrench (*v*)
rhwym bond, tie (*nm*)
rhwym bound to; constipated (*adj*)
rhwymedigaeth obligation (*nf*)
rhwymedigaethau obligations (*npl*)
rhwymo to bandage, to bind (*v*)
rhwystr barrier, hindrance, obstruction (*nm*)
rhwystrau barriers (*npl*)
rhwystredigaeth frustration (*nf*)
rhwystro to hinder, to prevent (*v*)
rhy over, too (*adv*)
rhybudd caution, notice, warning (*nm*)
rhybuddio to caution, to warn (*v*)
rhybuddion warnings (*npl*)
rhych furrow, rut, slot, trenches (*nm*)
rhychwant span (*nm*)
rhyd ford (*nf*)
rhydd exempt, free, loose (*adj*)
rhydd he/she/it gives (*v*)
rhyddfrydol liberal (*adj*)
rhyddha he/she/it frees, will free (*v*)
rhyddhad liberation, relief
rhyddhau to free, to loosen, to release (*v*)
rhyddhawyd was/were freed (*v*)
rhyddiaith prose (*nf*)
rhyddid freedom, liberty (*nm*)
rhyfedd odd, queer, strange, weird (*adj*)
rhyfeddod marvel, wonder (*nm*)
rhyfeddol amazing, marvellous, phenomenal (*adj*)
rhyfeddu to amaze (*v*)
rhyfel war (*nm*)
rhyfeloedd wars (*npl*)
rhyfelwr warrior (*nm*)
rhyfelwyr warriors (*npl*)

rhyngddo between (him) (*prep*)
rhyngddyn between (them) (*prep*)
rhyngddynt between (them) (*prep*)
rhyngoch between (you) (*prep*)
rhyngom between (us) (*prep*)
rhyngrwyd Internet (*nf*)
rhyngweithio to interact (*v*)
rhyngweithiol interactive (*adj*)
rhyngwladol international (*adj*)
rhyngwyneb interface (*nm*)
rhythm rhythm (*nm*)
rhyw sex (*nm*)
rhyw some (*adj*)
rhywbeth something (*nm*)
rhywbryd sometime (*adv*)
rhywfaint some amount (*adj*)
rhywfaint somewhat (*adv*)
rhywiol sexual, sexy (*adj*)
rhywioldeb sexuality (*nm*)
rhywle somewhere (*adv*)
rhywogaeth breed, species (*nf*)
rhywogaethau breeds, species (*npl*)
rhywrai some (*npl*)
rhywsut somehow (*adv*)
rhywun someone, somebody (*nm*)
riant parent
rieni parents
rif number
rifau numbers
rifo to count
rinwedd virtue
rinweddau virtues
risg risk (*nf*)
risgiau risks (*npl*)
*risiau steps
*ro gravel, shingle
roc rock (*nm*)
roced rocket (*nf*)
rocedi rockets (*npl*)
rodd gift
roddai he/she/it would give
roddi to give

roddion gifts
roddir is/are/will be given
roddodd he/she/it gave
roddwyd was/were given
roedd he/she/it was *(v)*
roeddech you were *(v)*
roeddem we were *(v)*
roedden they were *(v)*
roeddent they were *(v)*
roeddwn I was *(v)*
roeddynt they were *(v)*
roes he/she/it gave
roi to give
roir is/are/will be given
rôl role *(nf)*
rolio to roll *(v)*
rownd round (competition) *(nf)*
rownd around *(prep)*
rownd round *(adj)*
rowndiau rounds *(npl)*
rŵan now *(adv)*
rwbel rubble *(nm)*
rwber eraser, rubber *(nm)*
Rwsia Russia
rwy I am *(v)*
rwyd net
rwydd easy
rwydwaith network
rwyf I am *(v)*
rwymedigaeth obligation
rwymedigaethau obligations
rwymo to bind
rwystr barrier
rwystrau barriers
rwystro to hinder

rwyt you are *(v)*
rybudd warning
rybuddio to warn
rydan we are *(v)*
rydd free
ryddhad relief
ryddhau to free
ryddhawyd was/were freed
ryddiaith prose
ryddid freedom
rydw I am *(v)*
rydych you are *(v)*
rydym we are *(v)*
rydyn they are *(v)*
ryfedd strange
ryfeddod wonder
ryfeddol amazing
ryfel war
rygbi rugby *(nm)*
***rym** strength
***rymus** powerful
ryngwladol international
rysáit recipe *(nf)*
ryseitiau recipes *(npl)*
ryw sex, some
rywbeth something
rywbryd sometime
rywfaint some
rywiol sexual
rywle somewhere
rywogaeth breed, species
rywogaethau species
rywsut somehow
rywun someone

S

Saboth Sabbath (*nm*)

sach sack (*nf*)

sachau sacks (*npl*)

Sadwrn Saturday; Saturn (*nm*)

saer carpenter, wright (*nm*)

Saesneg English (language) (*nf*)

Saeson English (people) (*npl*)

saeth arrow (*nf*)

saethau arrows (*npl*)

saethu to fire, to shoot (*v*)

safai he/she/it would stand (*v*)

safbwynt standpoint, viewpoint (*nm*)

safbwyntiau points of view (*npl*)

saff safe (*adj*)

saffrwm crocus, saffron (*nm*)

safiad stand (*nm*)

safle location, position, site (*nm*)

safleoedd locations (*npl*)

safodd he/she/it stood (*v*)

safon class, form, standard (*nf*)

safonau standards (*npl*)

safoni to standardize (*v*)

safonol standard (*adj*)

saib pause, rest (*nm*)

saif he/she/it stands (*v*)

sail basis, foundation, ground (*nf*)

saim dripping, fat, grease (*nm*)

sain sound, tone (*nm*)

saint saints (*npl*)

Sais Englishman (*nm*)

saith seven (*num*)

saith deg seventy (*num*)

saithdegau seventies (*npl*)

sâl ill, poor, shoddy (*adj*)

salad salad (*nm*)

salm psalm (*nf*)

salwch illness (*nm*)

sampl sample, specimen (*nf*)

samplau samples (*npl*)

samplu to sample (*v*)

sanctaidd hallowed, holy, sacred (*adj*)

sancteiddrwydd holiness, sanctity (*nm*)

sant saint (*nm*)

santes saint (feminine) (*nf*)

sathru to ride roughshod over, to trample (*v*)

sawdl heel (*nm*)

sawl many, several (*adj*)

sawl however many, whomsoever (*adv*)

saws sauce (*nm*)

Sbaen Spain

Sbaeneg Spanish (language) (*nf*)

sbardun accelerator, spur, throttle (*nm*)

sbarduno to spur (*v*)

sbectol glasses, spectacles (*nf*)

sbectrwm spectrum (*nm*)

sbel break, period, spell, time (*nf*)

sbesimen specimen (*nm*)

sbesimenau specimens (*npl*)

sbio to look (*v*)

sbon brand new, spanking (*adj*)

sbort fun (*nm*)

sbri fun, hilarity (*nm*)

sbwriel refuse, rubbish, trash (*nm*)

sebon soap (*nm*)

sector sector (*nm*)

sectorau sectors (*npl*)

sedd seat (*nf*)

seddau seats (*npl*)

seddi seats (*npl*)

sef namely, that is (*conj*)

sefydledig established (*adj*)

sefydliad establishment, institute, institution (*nm*)

sefydliadau institutions (*npl*)
sefydliadol institutional (*adj*)
sefydlir is/are/will be established (*v*)
sefydlodd he/she/it established (*v*)
sefydlog fixed, set, settled (*adj*)
sefydlogi to fix, to stabilize (*v*)
sefydlogrwydd stability (*nm*)
sefydlu to establish, to install, to institute (*v*)
sefydlwyd was/were established (*v*)
sefyll to sit (an examination), to stand, to stay, to stop (*v*)
sefyllfa position, situation (*nf*)
sefyllfaoedd situations (*npl*)
segur idle, unemployed, unoccupied (*adj*)
seiat meeting (*nf*)
seibiant pause (*nm*)
seiciatrig psychiatric (*adj*)
seiciatryddol psychiatric (*adj*)
seiclo to cycle (*v*)
seicoleg psychology (*nf*)
seicolegol psychological (*adj*)
seicolegwyr psychologists (*npl*)
seiliau foundations (*npl*)
seiliedig based (*adj*)
seilio to base (*v*)
seilir is/are/will be based (*v*)
seiliwyd was/were based (*v*)
seiniau sounds (*npl*)
seintiau saints (*npl*)
Seisnig English (*adj*)
seithfed seventh (*num*)
sêl zeal (*nf*)
Seland Newydd New Zealand
selio to seal (*v*)
selog ardent, zealous (*nf*)
semen semen (*nm*)
seminar seminar (*nf*)
seminarau seminars (*npl*)
senedd parliament, senate (*nf*)
seneddol parliamentary (*adj*)
sengl single (*adj*)

sensitif sensitive (*adj*)
sensitifrwydd sensitivity (*nm*)
sêr stars (*npl*)
serch love (*nm*)
serch although, despite (*conj*)
seremoni ceremony (*nf*)
seremonïau ceremonies (*nm*)
seren asterisk, globule, star (*nf*)
sero nought, zero (*nm*)
serth precipitous, sheer, steep (*adj*)
sesiwn session (*nf*)
sesiynau sessions (*npl*)
set clique, set (*nf*)
setiau sets (*npl*)
setliad settlement (*nm*)
setlo to clear up, to settle (*v*)
sewin sea-trout, sewin (*nm*)
sganio to scan (*v*)
sgert skirt (*nf*)
sgi ski (*nm*)
sgil following (*nm*)
sgìl skill (*nm*)
sgil-gynhyrchion side-effects (*npl*)
sgiliau skills (*npl*)
sgio to ski (*v*)
sglein polish, shine (*adj*)
sgleinio to glaze, to polish, to shine (*v*)
sglodion chips (*npl*)
sgôr score [competition]; [musical] (*nf*)
sgori: sgorio to score (*v*)
sgoriodd he/she/it scored (*v*)
sgrech scream, screech, shriek (*nf*)
sgrechain to scream, to shriek (*v*)
sgrechian to screech (*v*)
sgrifennu to write (*v*)
sgrin screen, settle (*nf*)
sgriniau screens (*npl*)
sgrinio to screen(*v*)
sgript script (*nf*)
sgriptiau scripts (*npl*)
sgriptio to script (*v*)
sgwâr ring, square (*nm*)

sgwâr square (*adj*)
sgwennu to write (*v*)
sgwrs chat, conversation, talk (*nf*)
sgwrsio to chat, to talk (*v*)
sgyrsiau conversations (*npl*)
si buzz, hum, rumour, whisper (*nm*)
siaced jacket (*nf*)
sialens challenge (*nf*)
sialensau challenges (*npl*)
siambr chamber (*nf*)
siambrau chambers (*npl*)
sianel channel (*nf*)
sianelau channels (*npl*)
sianeli channels (*npl*)
siâp shape (*nm*)
Siapan Japan
siapiau shapes (*npl*)
siarad to speak, to talk (*v*)
siaradwr speaker (*nm*)
siaradwyr speakers (*npl*)
siaredir he/she/it speaks, will speak (*v*)
Siarl Charles
siart chart (*nm*)
siarter charter (*nm*)
siartiau charts (*npl*)
siartr charter (*nm*)
siartredig chartered (*adj*)
siawns chance (*nf*)
sibrwd to whisper (*v*)
sibrwd a whisper (*nm*)
sicr certain, sure (*adj*)
sicrhau to assure, to ensure, to fasten (*v*)
sicrhawyd was/were ensured (*v*)
sicrhewch you make sure (*v*)
sicrwydd assurance, certainty (*nm*)
sidan silk (*nm*)
siec cheque (*nf*)
siec check (*adj*)
sieciau cheques (*npl*)
sièd shed (*nf*)
sifil civil (*adj*)
sigaréts cigarettes (*npl*)

siglo to shake (*v*)
silff ledge, shelf (*nf*)
silffoedd shelves (*npl*)
silindr cylinder (*nm*)
silio to spawn (*v*)
sillaf syllable (*nf*)
sillafu to spell (*v*)
silwair silage (*nm*)
sin scene (*nf*)
sinc sink; zinc (*nm*)
sinema cinema (*nf*)
sïo to murmur (*v*)
sioc shock (*nf*)
siocled chocolate (*nm*)
sioe show (*nf*)
sioeau shows (*npl*)
siom disappointment (*nf*)
siomedig disappointed, disappointing (*adj*)
siomi to disappoint (*v*)
siop shop, workshops (*nf*)
siopa to shop (*v*)
siopau shops (*npl*)
siopwr shopkeeper (*nm*)
sipsiwn gypsies (*npl*)
sir county, shire (*nf*)
siriol bright, cheerful, pleasant (*adj*)
siroedd counties (*npl*)
sirol county (*adj*)
siwgr sugar (*nm*)
siŵr sure (*adj*)
siwrnai journey (*nf*)
siwrnai once (*adv*)
siwt suit (*nf*)
sleid slide (*nf*)
sleidiau slides (*npl*)
slyri slurry (*nm*)
sment cement (*nm*)
smotyn penalty spot, speck, spot (*nm*)
smygu to smoke (*v*)
sodiwm sodium (*nm*)
soffistigedig sophisticated (*adj*)
sofietaidd soviet (*adj*)

soia soya (*nm*)
solet solid (*adj*)
sôn to mention, to talk (*v*)
sôn mention, sign, talk (*nm*)
soned sonnet (*nf*)
soniodd he/she/it mentioned (*v*)
soniwyd was/were mentioned (*v*)
sonnir is/are/will be mentioned (*v*)
sosban saucepan (*nf*)
sownd stuck; sound, steady (*adj*)
stabl stable (*nf*)
stablau stables (*npl*)
stad estate, state (*nf*)
stadau estates (*npl*)
stadiwm stadium (*nf*)
stafell room (*nf*)
staff staff (*nm*)
staffio to staff (*v*)
stamp stamp (*nm*)
stampiau stamps (*npl*)
statig static (*adj*)
statud statute (*nf*)
statudau statutes (*npl*)
statudol statutory (*adj*)
statws status (*nm*)
steddfod Eisteddfod (*nf*)
steil style; surname (*nm*)
stêm steam (*nm*)
stiwdio studio (*nf*)
stoc stock (*nf*)
stociau stocks (*npl*)
stocio to stock (*v*)
stondin booth, stall (*nf*)
stondinau stalls (*npl*)
stop stop (*nm*)
stopio to stop (*v*)
stôr stock, store (*nf*)
storfa repository, store (*nf*)
storfeydd repositories (*npl*)
stori fib, story (*nf*)
storïau stories (*npl*)
storio to store (*v*)

storm storm (*nf*)
stormydd storms (*npl*)
straen strain (*v*)
straeon stories (*npl*)
strategaeth strategy (*nf*)
strategaethau strategies (*npl*)
strategol strategic (*adj*)
streic strike (*nf*)
stribed strip (*nm*)
stribedi strips (*npl*)
strôc seizure, stroke (of genius) (*nf*)
strwythur structure (*nm*)
strwythurau structures (*npl*)
strwythuredig structured (*adj*)
strwythuro to structure (*v*)
strwythurol structural (*adj*)
stryd street (*nf*)
strydoedd streets (*npl*)
stumog stomach (*nf*)
stwff stuff (*nf*)
sudd juice, sap (*nm*)
suddo to pot, to putt, to sink (*v*)
sugno to suck (*v*)
Sul Sunday (*nm*)
sut how, what sort (*adv*)
sw zoo (*nf*)
swigod bubbles (*npl*)
swil bashful, demure, shy (*adj*)
Swistir Switzerland
switsh switch (*nm*)
switshis switches (*npl*)
swllt shilling (*nm*)
swm amount, sum (*nm*)
swmp bulk (*nm*)
swmpus bulky (*adj*)
sŵn noise, sound (*nm*)
swnio to sound (*v*)
swnllyd noisy (*adj*)
swper supper (*nm/f*)
swydd job, position, post (*nf*)
swyddfa office (*nf*)
swyddfeydd offices (*npl*)

swyddi jobs, posts (*npl*)
swyddog officer, official (*nm*)
swyddogaeth duty, function (*nf*)
swyddogaethau functions (*npl*)
swyddogion officers, officials (*npl*)
swyddogol official (*adj*)
swyn attraction, charm, spell (*nm*)
swyno to captivate, to charm, to enchant (*v*)
swynol captivating, charming (*adj*)
sy what is, who is (*v*)
sych boring, dry (*adj*)
sychder drought, dryness (*nm*)
syched thirst (*nm*)
sychu to dry, to wipe (*v*)
sydd are, is (*v*)
sydyn abrupt, sudden (*adj*)
syfrdanol astounding, stunning, stupendous (*adj*)
sylfaen base, basis, foundation (*nf*)
sylfaenol basic, fundamental, primary (*adj*)
sylfaenu to base, to found (*v*)
sylfaenwr founder (*nm*)
sylfaenwyr founders (*npl*)
sylfaenydd founder (*nm*)
sylfeini foundations (*npl*)
syllu to gaze, to peer, to stare (*v*)
sylw attention, comment, observation, remark (*nm*)
sylwadau observations (*npl*)
sylwch you note (*v*)
sylwedd gist, matter, substance (*nm*)
sylweddau substances (*npl*)
sylweddol significant, substantial (*adj*)
sylweddoli to realize (*v*)
sylweddolodd he/she/it realized (*v*)
sylwer (*should be*) noted (*v*)
sylwi to notice, to observe (*v*)
sylwodd he/she/it noticed (*v*)
symbol symbol (*nm*)
symbolaidd symbolic (*adj*)
symbolau symbols (*npl*)

symbyliad encouragement, incentive, stimulus (*nm*)
symbylu to encourage, to stimulate (*v*)
symiau sums (*npl*)
syml simple (*adj*)
symlach simpler (*adj*)
symleiddio to simplify (*v*)
symptom symptom (*nm*)
symptomau symptoms (*npl*)
symud to budge, to move (*v*)
symudedd mobility (*nm*)
symudiad motion, movement (*nm*)
symudiadau movements (*npl*)
symudodd he/she/it moved (*v*)
symudol mobile, moveable (*adj*)
symudwyd was/were moved (*v*)
syn amazed, astonished (*adj*)
synau sounds (*npl*)
syndod amazement, surprise, wonder (*nm*)
syndrom syndrome (*nf*)
synhwyrau senses (*npl*)
synhwyro to feel, to sense, to smell (*v*)
synhwyrol rational, sensible (*adj*)
syniad concept, guess, idea, thought (*nm*)
syniadaeth conception (*nf*)
syniadau ideas (*npl*)
synnu to amaze, to astonish, to surprise (*v*)
synnwyr judgement, sense (*nm*)
syntheseiddio to synthesize (*v*)
synthetig synthetic (*adj*)
syr sir (*nm*)
syrcas circus (*nf*)
syrfëwr surveyor (*nm*)
syrffio to surf (*v*)
syrthio to fall (*v*)
syrthiodd he/she/it fell (*v*)
system system (*nf*)
systematig systematic (*adj*)
systemau systems (*npl*)
syth straight (*adj*)

T

a word starting with **th** printed in blue means that the root form of that word begins with a **t**, e.g. **thad** root **tad**

Th stands as a letter in its own right in Welsh. In a Welsh dictionary, unlike this list, words containing 'th' would commence after those containing **T**

tywyllwch dark, darkness, night

tywys to guide, to lead

tywysog prince

theori theory

therapi therapy

therapiwtig therapeutic

tabernacl tabernacle (*nm*)

tabl table (*nm*)

tablau tables (*npl*)

tabled tablet (*nf*)

tabledi tablets (*npl*)

Tachwedd November (*nm*)

tacsi taxi (*nm*)

tad father (*nm*)

tadau fathers (*npl*)

tadolaeth fatherhood, paternity (*nf*)

taenu to spread (*v*)

Taf Taff (river)

tafarn inn, pub, tavern (*nf*)

tafarnau pubs (*npl*)

tafarndai inns (*npl*)

tafarndy inn, public house (*nm*)

taflen leaflet (*nf*)

taflenni leaflets (*npl*)

taflu to discard, to throw, to toss (*v*)

tafod tongue (*nm*)

tafodiaith dialect (*nf*)

Tafwys Thames

tagfa blockage, choking, jam (*nf*)

tagfeydd jams (*npl*)

tai houses (*npl*)

tail dung, manure (*nm*)

tair three (*num/f*)

taith journey (*nf*)

tal tall (*adj*)

tâl fee, payment (*nm*)

talcen forehead (*nm*)

taleb receipt, voucher (*nf*)

talebau vouchers (*npl*)

talent talent (*nf*)

talentog talented (*adj*)

taliad payment (*nm*)

taliadau payments (*npl*)

talm period (*nm*)

talu to pay (*v*)

talwm while (*nm*)

talwrn cockpit, threshing floor (*nm*)

talwyd was/were paid (*v*)

tamaid bit, morsel, snippet (*nm*)

tan under (*prep*)

tan until (*conj*)

tân fire (*nm*)

tanat under (you) (*prep*)

tanau fires (*npl*)

tanbaid fiery, incandescent (*adj*)

tanc tank (*nm*)

tanciau tanks (*npl*)

tanddaearol subterranean, underground (*adj*)

tangnefedd peace (*nm*)

tanio to fire, to ignite, to start (*v*)

tanlinellu to underline (*v*)

tanllyd fiery (*adj*)

tano under (him) (*prep*)
tanseilio to subvert, to undermine (*v*)
tanwydd fuel (*nm*)
tanysgrifio to subscribe (*v*)
tap tap (*nm*)
tâp tape (*nm*)
tapiau taps (*npl*)
tarddiad derivation, source (*nm*)
tarddu to derive from, to originate, to spring (*v*)
tarfu to interrupt, to disrupt (*v*)
targed target (*nm*)
targedau targets (*npl*)
targedu to target (*v*)
taro to hit, to strike, to suit (*v*)
tarw bull (*nm*)
tasg task (*nf*)
tasgau tasks (*npl*)
tasglu task force (*nm*)
tatws potatoes (*npl*)
taw silence (*nm*)
taw that it is/was (*conj*)
tawel calm, muted, quiet, still (*adj*)
tawelu to calm, to placate, to quieten, to sedate (*v*)
tawelwch calm, quiet, stillness (*nm*)
te tea (*nm*)
tebyg like, similar (*adj*)
tebyg likelihood (*nm*)
tebygol likely, probable (*adj*)
tebygolrwydd likelihood, probability (*nm*)
tebygrwydd likeness, resemblance, similarity (*nm*)
tecell kettle (*nm*)
techneg technique (*nf*)
technegau techniques (*npl*)
technegol technical (*adj*)
technoleg technology (*nf*)
technolegau technologies (*npl*)
technolegol technological (*adj*)
teclyn thingamyjig, tool (*nm*)
teg fair, fairly, fine (*adj*)

tegan toy (*nm*)
teganau toys (*npl*)
tegell kettle (*nm*)
tegwch beauty, fairness (*nm*)
teiar tyre (*nm*)
teiars tyres (*npl*)
teilwng deserving, worthy (*adj*)
teilyngdod merit, worthiness (*nm*)
teimlad feeling, sentiment (*nm*)
teimladau feelings, sentiments (*npl*)
teimlai he/she/it would feel (*v*)
teimlo to feel (*v*)
teimlwn we feel, we will feel (*v*)
teip print, type (*nm*)
teipio to type (*v*)
teir three (*num/f*)
teirgwaith three times, thrice (*adv*)
teithiau journeys (*npl*)
teithio to travel (*v*)
teithiol peripatetic, travelling (*adj*)
teithiwr passenger, traveller (*nm*)
teithwyr passengers, traveller (*npl*)
teitl title (*nm*)
teitlau titles (*npl*)
telathrebu to telecommunicate (*v*)
teledu television (*nm*)
teleffon telephone (*nm*)
telerau terms (*npl*)
telir is/are/will be paid (*v*)
telyn harp (*nf*)
telyneg lyric (*nf*)
teml temple (*nf*)
temtasiwn temptation (*nm*)
tenant tenant (*nm*)
tenantiaeth tenancy (*nf*)
tenantiaid tenants (*npl*)
tenau slim, sparse, thin (*adj*)
tendr tender (*nm*)
tendro to tender (*v*)
tensiwn tension (*nm*)
teras terrace (*nm*)
terfyn boundary, end, limit (*nm*)

terfynau bounds (*npl*)
terfynol final (*adj*)
terfynu to end, to terminate (*v*)
term term (*nm*)
termau terms (*npl*)
testament testament (*nm*)
testun subject, text (*nm*)
testunau subjects (*npl*)
testunol textual (*adj*)
teulu family, household (*nm*)
teuluaidd domestic, familial (*adj*)
teuluoedd families (*npl*)
teuluol domestic, familial (*adj*)
tew fat, thick (*adj*)
teyrnas kingdom (*nf*)
teyrnasiad reign (*nm*)
teyrnasu to reign, to rule (*v*)
teyrngarwch allegiance, loyalty (*nm*)
teyrnged tribute (*nf*)
thad father
thad-cu grandfather
thaflenni pamphlets
thaflu to throw
thai houses
thaid grandfather
thair three
thaith journey
thâl payment
thaliadau payments
thalu to pay
than under, until
thân fire
tharged target
thargedau targets
thargedu to target
tharo to strike
thasgau tasks
the tea
theatr theatre (*nf*)
thebyg similar
thechnegau techniques
thechnegol technical

thechnoleg technology
theg fair
theimladau feelings
theimlo to feel
their three
theithiau journeys
theithio to travel
theitl title
theledu television
thelerau terms
thema theme (*nf*)
thematig thematic (*adj*)
themâu (*npl*)
thenantiaid tenants
theori theory (*nf*)
therapi therapy (*nm*)
therapiwtig therapeutic (*adj*)
therapydd therapist (*nm*)
therapyddion therapists (*npl*)
thestun subject, text
thestunau subjects, texts
theulu family
theuluoedd families
thi you
thîm team
thimau teams
thipyn bit
thir land
thirfeddianwyr landowners
thlodi poverty
thorri to break
thra very
thraddodiadau traditions
thraean one third
thraed feet
thrafnidiaeth traffic
thrafod to discuss
thrafodaeth discussion
thrafodaethau discussions
thrais rape, violence
thramor abroad
thraw there

thref town

threfi towns

threfn order

threfniadau arrangements

threfnu to arrange

threftadaeth heritage

threuliau expenses

thri three

thrigain sixty

thrigolion inhabitants

thrin to treat

thriniaeth treatment

thro turn

throi to turn

thros over

throseddau crimes, offences

throseddwyr criminals

throsglwyddo to transfer

throsodd over (him)

thrwsio to repair

thrwy through

thrwyn nose

thrydan electricity

thua about

thwf growth

thwristiaeth tourism

thwyll deceit

thyfu to grow

thymor term

thynnu to draw

thystiolaeth evidence

ti you (*pronoun*)

tic tick (*nm*)

ticio to tick (*v*)

ticiwch you tick (*v*)

tîm team (*nm*)

timau teams (*npl*)

tin anus, bum (*nf*)

tincer tinker (*nm*)

tipyn little, (quite) a bit (*nm*)

tir ground, land (*nm*)

tirfeddiannwr landowner (*nm*)

tirfeddiannwyr landowners (*npl*)

tiriogaeth dominion, territory (*nf*)

tiriogaethol territorial (*adj*)

tirlenwi to landfill (*v*)

tirlun landscape (*nm*)

tirlunio to landscape (*v*)

tiroedd lands (*npl*)

tirwedd landscape, relief (*nf*)

tirweddau landscapes (*npl*)

tithau even you, you for your part (*pronoun*)

tiwb tube (*nm*)

tiwtor tutor (*nm*)

tiwtoriaid tutor (*npl*)

tlawd impoverished, poor (*adj*)

tlodi impoverishment, poverty (*nm*)

tlodion poor (people) (*npl*)

tlos pretty (*adj/f*)

tlotaf poorest (*adj*)

tlws gem, jewel, medal, trophy (*nm*)

tlws pretty (*adj*)

to roof; generation (*nm*)

toc soon (*adv*)

tocyn tag, ticket, token (*nm*)

tocyn slice (*nm*)

tocynnau tickets (*npl*)

toddi to blend, to dissolve, to melt, to thaw (*v*)

toddydd solvent (*nm*)

toddyddion solvents (*npl*)

toiled toilet (*nm*)

toiledau toilets (*npl*)

toll duty, levy, tariff, toll (*nf*)

tollau tariffs (*npl*)

tom dung, manure (*nf*)

tomato tomato (*nm*)

tomen dump, dunghill, mound (*nf*)

ton billow, wave (*nf*)

tôn tune (*nf*)

tonau tunes (*npl*)

tonnau waves (*npl*)

top top (*nm*)

tor belly, litter, underside (*nf*)

tor break (*nm*)

torf crowd (*nf*)

torfol collective, mass (*adj*)

Tori Tory (*nm*)

toriad break, cut, (day) break, fracture, section (*nm*)

toriadau cuttings (*npl*)

Toriaid Tories (*npl*)

torri to break, to cut, to fell, to sever (*v*)

torrodd he/she/it broke (*v*)

tost toast (*nm*)

tost ill, sore (*adj*)

tra extremely, very (*adv*)

tra while, whilst (*conj*)

trac track (*nm*)

trachefn again (*adv*)

tractor tractor (*nm*)

traddodi to commit, to deliver (*v*)

traddodiad tradition (*nm*)

traddodiadau traditions (*npl*)

traddodiadol traditional (*adj*)

traean one-third (*nm*)

traed feet (*npl*)

traeth beach, sands (*nm*)

traethau beaches (*npl*)

traethawd composition, dissertation, essay, thesis (*nm*)

traethlin shoreline (*nf*)

traethodau dissertations, essays (*npl*)

trafferth bother, trouble (*nf*)

trafferthion difficulties (*npl*)

traffig traffic (*nm*)

trafnidiaeth traffic (*nf*)

trafod to discuss, to handle, to negotiate (*v*)

trafodaeth discussion, negotiation (*nf*)

trafodaethau discussions (*npl*)

trafodion proceedings, transactions (*npl*)

trafodir is/are/will be discussed (*v*)

trafodwch you discuss (*v*)

trafodwyd was/were discussed (*v*)

tragwyddol eternal (*adj*)

tragywydd for ever (*adj*)

trahaus arrogant, haughty (*adj*)

trais force, rape, violence (*nm*)

tramgwydd hindrance, offence (*nm*)

tramgwyddau hindrances (*npl*)

tramor foreign, overseas (*adv*)

tramwyo to traverse (*v*)

trannoeth the next day (*adv*)

tras kin, lineage, pedigree (*nf*)

traul consumption, expense, wear (*nf*)

traw pitch (music) (*nm*)

trawiad blow, stroke (*nm*)

trawiadol striking (*adj*)

traws cross (*adj*)

trawsnewid to convert, to transform, to transmute (*v*)

tre town (*nf*)

trech stronger, superior (*adj*)

trechu to defeat, to overpower (*v*)

tref home, town (*nf*)

trefi towns (*npl*)

trefn order, procedure (*nf*)

trefniad arrangement (*nm*)

trefniadaeth organisation, procedure (*nf*)

trefniadau arrangements (*npl*)

trefniadol procedural (*adj*)

trefniant arrangement (*nm*)

trefnir is/are/will be organised (*v*)

trefnu to arrange, to organise (*v*)

trefnus methodical, orderly (*adj*)

trefnwyd was/were organised (*v*)

trefnwyr organisers (*npl*)

trefnydd organiser, organizer (*nm*)

trefol urban (*adj*)

treftadaeth heritage, inheritance (*nf*)

treial trial (*nm*)

treialon trials (sheep-dog) (*npl*)

treiddio to penetrate, to permeate, to pervade (*v*)

treigl motion, passage (*nm*)

treiglo to mutate; to roll, to trickle, to trundle (*v*)

treisgar violent (*adj*)

treisiol violent (*adj*)

trên engine, train (*nm*)

trenau trains (*npl*)

treth rate, tax (*nf*)

trethadwy taxable (*adj*)

trethi taxes (*npl*)

trethiannol rateable (*adj*)

trethu to tax (*v*)

treuliau expenses (*npl*)

treulio to digest, to spend, to wear (*v*)

treuliodd he/she/it spent (*v*)

tri three (*num/m*)

tribiwnlys tribunal (*nm*)

tribiwnlysoedd tribunals (*npl*)

tridegau thirties (*npl*)

trigain sixty (*num*)

trigo to die, to dwell (*v*)

trigolion inhabitants (*npl*)

trin battle (*nf*)

trin to cultivate, to handle, to treat (*v*)

trindod trinity, Trinity (*nf*)

triniaeth treatment (*nf*)

triniaethau treatments (*npl*)

trio to try (*v*)

triongl triangle (*nm*)

trip trip (*nm*)

trist sad, tragic (*adj*)

tristwch sadness, sorrow (*nf*)

tro bend, turn, twist, walk (*nm*)

trochi to dip, to immerse; to dirty, to soil (*v*)

trodd he/she/it turned (*v*)

troed foot (*nf*)

troed base, foot (*nm*)

troedfedd foot (*nf*)

troedfeddi feet (*npl*)

troellog tortuous, twisting, winding (*adj*)

troeon occasions; turns (*npl*)

troi to stir, to turn, to twist (*v*)

trol cart (*nf*)

trom heavy (*adj/f*)

tros over (*prep*)

trosedd crime, offence (*nf*)

troseddau offences (*npl*)

troseddol criminal (*npl*)

troseddu to commit an offence, to transgress (*v*)

troseddwr criminal, culprit (*nm*)

troseddwyr criminals, culprits (*npl*)

trosglwyddiad conveyance, transference (*nm*)

trosglwyddiadau conveyances (*npl*)

trosglwyddir is/are/will be transferred (*v*)

trosglwyddo to transfer, to transmit (*v*)

trosglwyddwyd was/were transferred (*v*)

trosi to convert, to translate, to turn (*v*)

trosiant turnover (*nm*)

trosodd over (*adv*)

trosolwg overview (*nm*)

trosom for (us), over (us) (*prep*)

trosti for (her), over (her) (*prep*)

trosto for (him), over (him) (*prep*)

trostynt for (them), over (them) (*prep*)

trothwy doorstep, threshold (*nm*)

trowch you turn (*v*)

trowyd was/were turned (*v*)

truan poor fellow, wretch (*nm*)

truan poor, wretched (*adj*)

trueni pity (*nm*)

truenus lamentable, piteous, pitiful, wretched (*adj*)

trugaredd compassion, mercy (*nm*)

trugarog compassionate, merciful (*adj*)

trwch layer, thickness (*nm*)

trwchus thick (*adj*)

trwm heavy, sad (*adj*)

trwodd through (*adv*)

trwot through (you) (*prep*)

trwsio to mend, to smarten (*v*)

trwy by means of, through (*prep*)

trwyadl exhaustive, thorough (*adj*)

trwydded licence, permit (*nf*)
trwyddedau licences (*npl*)
trwyddedig licensed, qualified (*adj*)
trwyddedu to license (*v*)
trwyddi through (her) (*prep*)
trwyddo through (him) (*prep*)
trwyddynt through (them) (*prep*)
trwyn nose, nozzle, promontory, snout (*nm*)
trychineb catastrophe, disaster (*nf*)
trydan electric current, electricity (*nm*)
trydanol electric, electrical (*adj*)
trydedd third (*num/f*)
trydydd third (*num/m*)
tryloyw translucent, transparent (*adj*)
trylwyr thorough (*adj*)
trymion heavy (*adj/pl*)
trysor treasure (*nm*)
trysorau treasures (*npl*)
Trysorlys Treasury (*nm*)
trysorydd treasurer (*nm*)
trywydd track, trail (*nm*)
tu side (*nm*)
tua about towards (*prep*)
tuag about, towards (*prep*)
tudalen page (*nm*)
tudalennau pages (*npl*)
Tuduriaid Tudors (*npl*)
tuedd tendency, propensity, bias (*nf*)
tueddiad tendency (*nm*)
tueddiadau tendencies (*nm*)
tueddol inclined, liable, susceptible (*adj*)
tueddu to be inclined to, to tend to (*v*)
tun tin, tin can (*nm*)
tunnell ton (*nf*)
turio to burrow, to bore (*v*)
twf growth (*nm*)
twll burrow, hole, puncture (*nm*)
twnnel tunnel (*nm*)
twp daft, obtuse, stupid (*adj*)
twr crowd, heap (*nm*)
twrci turkey (*nm*)
twristiaeth tourism (*nf*)

twristiaid tourists (*npl*)
twrnai attorney, lawyer (*nm*)
twt dapper, neat, tidy (*adj*)
twt rubbish!, tut! (*exclamation*)
twyll deceit, fraud (*nm*)
twyllo to cheat, to deceive, to fool (*v*)
twym hot, warm (*adj*)
twyn dune, hillock, knoll (*nm*)
twyni dunes (*npl*)
tŷ house (*nm*)
tyb opinion, surmise (*nm*)
tybaco tobacco (*nm*)
tybed I wonder (*adv*)
tybiaeth presumption (*nf*)
tybiedig putative, supposed (*adj*)
tybio to presume, to suppose (*v*)
tybir is/are/will be assumed (*v*)
Tyddewi St. Davids
tyddyn croft, smallholding (*nm*)
tydi it is you, you yourself (*pronoun*)
tyfiant growth, tumour, vegetation (*nm*)
tyfodd he/she/it grew (*v*)
tyfu to grow, to increase (*v*)
tyllau holes (*npl*)
tyllu to bore, to burrow, to excavate (*v*)
tylwyth family, kindred (*nm*)
tymheredd temperature (*nm*)
tymhorau seasons, terms (*npl*)
tymhorol seasonable, seasonal, temporal (*adj*)
tymor season, term (*nm*)
tyndra strain, tension, tightness (*nm*)
tyner delicate, gentle, tender (*adj*)
tynged destiny, fate (*nf*)
tyngedfennol fateful (*adj*)
tyniad pull, subtraction (*nm*)
tyniadau attractions (*npl*)
tynnir is/are/will be drawn (*v*)
tynnodd he/she/it drew (*v*)
tynnu to attract, to draw, to extract, to photograph, to pick, to pull, to subtract (*v*)

tynnwch you draw, pull *(v)*
tynnwyd was/were drawn, pulled *(v)*
tyrd come! *(v)*
tyrfa crowd, multitude *(nf)*
tyst witness *(nm)*
tystio to testify, to witness *(v)*
tystiolaeth evidence, testimony *(nf)*
tystion witnesses *(npl)*
tystysgrif certificate, diploma *(nf)*
tystysgrifau certificates *(npl)*

tywallt to pour *(v)*
tywod sand *(npl)*
tywydd weather *(nm)*
tywyll blind, dark, obscure *(adj)*
tywyllwch dark, darkness, night *(nm)*
tywys to guide, to lead *(v)*
tywysog prince *(nm)*
tywysoges princess *(nf)*
tywysogion princes *(npl)*

U

uchaf topmost, uppermost (*adj*)
uchafbwynt climax, highlight, pinnacle (*nm*)
uchafbwyntiau highlights (*npl*)
uchafswm maximum (*nm*)
uchder altitude, height (*nm*)
uchel high; loud (*adj*)
ucheldir highland, upland (*nm*)
ucheldiroedd highlands (*npl*)
uchelgais ambition (*nm*)
uchelgeisiol ambitious (*adj*)
uchelwr nobleman (*nm*)
uchelwyr (*npl*)
uchod above (*adv*)
ufudd dutiful, obedient (*adj*)
ufuddhau to obey (*v*)
ugain twenty (*num*)
ugeinfed twentieth (*num*)
ugeiniau twenties (*npl*)
un one (*num*)
un same (*adj*)
un each, one (*nm*)
unai he/she/it would unite (*v*)
undeb union, unity (*nm*)
undebau unions (*npl*)
undod unity (*nm*)
undydd day, one-day (*adj*)
uned unit (*nf*)
unedau units (*npl*)
unedig united (*adj*)
unedol unitary (*adj*)
unfed first (*num*)
unffurf uniform (*adj*)
unfryd unanimous (*adj*)

unfrydol unanimous (*adj*)
uniaethu to identify with (*v*)
uniaith monoglot (*adj*)
unig lone, lonely, only, sole (*adj*)
unigol individual, singular (*adj*)
unigolion individuals (*npl*)
unigolyn individual (*nm*)
unigrwydd loneliness (*nm*)
unigryw unique (*adj*)
union direct, exact, precise, straight, upright (*adj*)
uniongyrchol direct (*adj*)
unioni to rectify, to redress, to straighten (*v*)
unionsyth point-blank, upright, vertical (*adj*)
unllawr one-storey (*adj*)
unlle anywhere, same place (*nm*)
unman anywhere (*nm*)
uno to amalgamate, to join, to unite (*v*)
unol united (*adj*)
unrhyw any (*adj*)
unwaith once (*adv*)
urdd guild, order (*nf*)
urddas dignity, nobility (*nm*)
urddasol dignified, noble, stately (*adj*)
ustus magistrate (*nm*)
uwch advanced, higher, senior (*adj*)
uwchben above, over, overhead (*prep*)
uwchefrydiau advanced studies (*npl*)
uwchgynghrair super-league (*nf*)
uwchlaw above (*prep*)
uwchradd secondary (*adj*)
uwchraddio to upgrade (*v*)

W

a word starting with **w** printed in blue means that the root form of that word begins with a **g**, e.g. **waed** root **gwaed**

waed blood
wael ill, poor
waelod bottom
waered down
waeth worse
waethaf worst
wag empty
wahân apart
wahaniaeth difference
wahaniaethu differences
wahanol different
wahanu to part
wahardd to forbid
wahodd to invite
wahoddiad invitation
waith work
wal wall (*nf*)
waliau walls (*npl*)
wallau mistakes
wallt hair
wan weak
war scruff
warant guarantee
warantu to guarantee
warchod baby-sit, guard
warchodaeth conservation
ward ward (*nf*)
wardiau wards (*npl*)
waredu to dispose of
wariant expenditure
wario to spend
wariwyd was/were spent
wartheg cattle
was farm-hand, lad

wasanaeth service
wasanaethau services
wasanaethir is/are/will be served
wasanaethu to serve
wasg press
wasgar scattered
wasgnodau imprints
wasgu to press
wastad constant, flat
wastraff wastage
wastraffu to waste
wawr dawn
wddf neck, throat
we web
wedd appearance
weddi prayer
weddill remainder
weddillion remnants
weddïo to pray
weddol fair
weddw widow
wedi after (*prep*)
    wedi'i after his/her/its
    wedi'u after their
wedyn afterwards, next, then (*adv*)
wefan website
wefannau websites
wefr shock
weiddi to shout
weini to serve
weinidog minister
weinidogaeth ministry (pastoral)
weinidogion ministers
weinyddiaeth ministry (secular)

weinyddir is/are/will be ministered
weinyddol administrative
weinyddu to serve
weision servants
weithdai workshops
weithdrefn procedure
weithdrefnau procedures
weithfeydd works
weithgar diligent
weithgaredd activity
weithgareddau activities
weithgarwch diligence
weithiau occasionally, sometimes
weithio to work
weithiodd he/she/it worked
weithiwr worker
weithlu workforce
weithred action
weithrediad operation
weithrediadau actions
weithredir is/are/will be carried out
weithredoedd deeds
weithredol acting
weithredu to act
weithredwr operator
weithredwyr operators
weithwyr workers
wel well!
wêl he/she/it sees
weladwy visible
welaf I see/I will see
welai he/she/it would see
welais I saw
weld to see
wele you behold!
weledigaeth vision
weledol visual
welir is/are/will be seen
well better
wella to improve
welliannau improvements
welliant improvement

wellt straw
welodd he/she/it saw
welsant they saw
welsoch you saw
welsom we saw
welwch you see
welwn we see, we will see
welwyd was/were seen
wely bed
welyau beds
wen white
wên smile
wendid weakness
wendidau weaknesses
wennol swallow
wenu to smile
wenwyn poison
wenwynig poisonous
werdd green
werin folk
weriniaeth republic
wers lesson
wersi lessons
wersyll camp
werth value
werthfawr valuable
werthfawrogi appreciate
werthiant sales
werthir is/are/will be sold
werthodd he/she/it sold
werthoedd values
werthu to sell
werthuso to evaluate
werthwyd was/were sold
westai guest
westy guest-house
wifren wire
win wine
wir truth
wireddu to realize
wirfoddol voluntary
wirfoddolwyr volunteers

wirio to check
wirion silly
wirionedd truth
wironeddol truly
wisg clothing
wisgo to dress
wiw dare not; fine
wiwer squirrel
wlad country
wladfa colony, Patagonia
wladwriaeth state
wladwriaethau states
wlân wool
wledd feast
wledig rural
wledydd countries
wleidyddiaeth politics
wleidyddion politicians
wleidyddol political
wlyb wet
wn (a) gun, I know
wna you do
wnaed was/were done
wnaeth he/she/it did
wnaethant they did
wnaethoch you did
wnaethom we did
wnaethon they did
wnaethpwyd was/were done
wnaf I do/I will do
wnaiff he/she/it will do
wnânt they do/they will do
wnawn we do /we will do
wnei you do
wneid would be done
wneir is/are/will be done
wnelo were he/she/it to do
wnes I did
wneud to do
wneuthur to do, to make
wneuthurwyr makers, manufacturers
wnewch you do

wobr prize
wobrau prizes
wobrwyo award
wragedd ladies, wives
wraidd root
wraig wife, woman
wrandawiad hearing
wrando to hear
Wranws Uranus
wreiddiau roots
wreiddiol original
wres heat
wrth because, by, towards, while (*prep*)
wrthdaro to clash, to collide
wrthi at it, from (her) (*prep*)
wrtho from (him) (*prep*)
wrthod to refuse
wrthrych object
wrthrychau objects
wrthrychol objective
wrthsefyll to withstand
wrthwynebiad objection
wrthwynebu to object to
wrthych from (you) (*prep*)
wrthyf from (me) (*prep*)
wrthym from (us) (*prep*)
wrthyn from (them) (*prep*)
wrthynt from (them) (*prep*)
wrthyt from (you) (*prep*)
wthio to push
wy egg (*nm*)
wyau eggs (*npl*)
wybod to know
wybodaeth information, knowledge
wybyddus known
wych superb
wyddai he/she/it knew
Wyddfa, yr Snowdon
Wyddgrug, yr Mold
wyddoch you know
wyddom we know
wyddoniaeth science

wyddonol scientific
wyddor alphabet, rudiments
wyddost you know
wyddwn I would know
wyddys he/she/it knows
wydr glass
wyf I am *(v)*
wyliadwrus alert
wyliau holidays
wylio to weep
wyllt wild
wylwyr viewers
wyn white
ŵyn lambs *(npl)*
wyna to lamb *(v)*
wyneb facade, face, surface *(nm)*

wynebau faces *(npl)*
wynebu to face *(v)*
wynt wind
ŵyr he/she/it knows
wyrdd green
wyrth miracle
wysg track, wake *(nm)*
wyt you are *(v)*
wyth eight *(num)*
wythdegau eighties *(npl)*
wythfed octave *(nm)*
wythfed eighth *(num)*
wythnos week *(nf)*
wythnosau weeks *(npl)*
wythnosol weekly *(adj)*

Y

a word starting with **y** printed in blue means that the root form of that word begins with a **g**, e.g. **yrru** root **gyrru**

y the, that (*definite article*)
ych ox (*nm*)
ychwaith either (*adv*)
ychwaneg extra (*nm*)
ychwanegiad addition, supplement (*nm*)
ychwanegiadau additions (*npl*)
ychwanegion extras (*npl*)
ychwanegir is/are/will be added (*v*)
ychwanegodd he/she/it added (*v*)
ychwanegol additional, extra (*adj*)
ychwanegu to add, to augment,
    to supplement(*v*)
ychwanegwch you add (*v*)
ychwanegwyd was/were added (*v*)
ychydig few, little (*nm*)
ŷd corn (*nm*)
ydach you are (*v*)
ydan we are (*v*)
ydi (*she*) is (*v*)
ydoedd he/she/it was (*v*)
ydw I am, yes (*v*)
ydwyf I am (*v*)
ydwyt you are (*v*)
ydy he/she/it is (*v*)
ydych you are (*v*)
ydym we are (*v*)
ydyn they are (*v*)
ydynt they are (*v*)
ydyw he/she/it is (*v*)
yfed to drink, to imbibe (*v*)
yfory tomorrow (*adv*)
ym in (*prep*)
yma here, present, this (*adv*)

ymadael to leave, to part (*v*)
ymadawedig deceased (*adj*)
ymadawiad departure, parting (*nm*)
ymaddasu to acclimatize, to adapt (*v*)
ymadrodd expression, phrase (*nm*)
ymadroddion expressions (*npl*)
ymaelodi to become a member, to join (*v*)
ymagwedd attitude (*nf*)
ymagweddau attitudes (*npl*)
ymaith away, hence, off (*adv*)
ymarfer to practise, to rehearse, to train (*v*)
ymarfer exercise, practice (*nm*)
ymarferiad practice (*nm*)
ymarferion exercises (*npl*)
ymarferol possible, practical, realistic (*adj*)
ymarferoldeb practicality (*nm*)
ymarferwr practitioner (*nm*)
ymarferwyr practitioners (*npl*)
ymarferydd practitioner (*nm*)
ymatal to abstain, to refrain (*v*)
ymateb to respond (*v*)
ymateb reaction, response (*nm*)
ymatebion responses (*npl*)
ymatebodd he/she/it responded (*v*)
ymatebol responding (*adj*)
ymatebwr respondent (*nm*)
ymatebwyr respondents (*npl*)
ymatebydd respondent (*nm*)
ymbelydredd radioactivity (*nm*)
ymbelydrol radioactive (*adj*)
ymborth food, sustenance (*nm*)
ymchwil research (*nf*)
ymchwiliad inquiry, investigation (*nm*)

ymchwiliadau inquiries (*npl*)
ymchwilio to explore, to investigate (*v*)
ymchwiliol investigative, research (*adj*)
ymchwiliwr explorer, investigator, researcher (*nm*)
ymchwilwyr investigators (*npl*)
ymchwilydd investigator (*nm*)
ymddangos to appear, to seem (*v*)
ymddangosai he/she/it would appear (*v*)
ymddangosiad appearance (*nm*)
ymddangosiadol apparent, seeming (*adj*)
ymddangosodd he/she/it appeared (*v*)
ymddengys he/she/it appears (*v*)
ymddeol to retire (*v*)
ymddeoliad retirement (*nm*)
ymddiddori to take an interest in (*v*)
ymddiheuriad apology (*nm*)
ymddiheuriadau apologies (*npl*)
ymddiheuro to apologize (*v*)
ymddiried to trust (*v*)
ymddiriedaeth confidence, trust (*nf*)
ymddiriedolaeth trust (*nf*)
ymddiriedolaethau trusts (*npl*)
ymddiriedolwr trustee (*nm*)
ymddiriedolwyr trustees (*npl*)
ymddiswyddiad resignation (*nm*)
ymddiswyddo to resign (*v*)
ymddwyn to behave(*v*)
ymddygiad behaviour, conduct, manners (*nm*)
ymddiswyddo to resign (*v*)
ymdeimlad feeling (*nm*)
ymdoddi to blend, to fuse, to melt (*v*)
ymdopi to cope, to manage (*v*)
ymdrech attempt, effort, exertion (*nf*)
ymdrechion efforts (*npl*)
ymdrechu to endeavour, to strive (*v*)
ymdrin to deal, to treat (*v*)
ymdriniaeth treatment (*nf*)
ymdriniwyd was/were treated (*v*)
ymdrinnir is/are/will be treated (*v*)
ymdrochi to bathe (*v*)

ymelwa to exploit (*v*)
ymennydd brain (*nm*)
ymerodraeth empire (*nf*)
ymestyn to extend, to reach, to stretch (*v*)
ymestynnol challenging, extending (*adj*)
ymfalchïo to pride oneself, to take pride in (*v*)
ymfudo to emigrate (*v*)
ymgais attempt, effort, endeavour (*nm*)
ymgartrefu to settle in (*v*)
ymgasglu to accrete, to congregate (*v*)
ymgeisio to apply, to try (*v*)
ymgeiswyr applicants (*npl*)
ymgeisydd applicant, candidate (*nm*)
ymgorffori to embody, to enshrine (*v*)
ymgyfarwyddo to familiarize oneself (*v*)
ymgymerwr undertaker (*nm*)
ymgymerwyd was/were undertaken (*v*)
ymgymerwyr undertakers (*npl*)
ymgymryd to undertake (*v*)
ymgynghori to confer, to consult (*v*)
ymgynghoriad consultation (*nm*)
ymgynghoriadau consultations (*npl*)
ymgynghorir is/are/will be consulted (*v*)
ymgynghorol advisory, consultative (*adj*)
ymgynghorwyd was/were consulted (*v*)
ymgynghorwyr advisers (*npl*)
ymgynghorydd adviser, consultant (*nm*)
ymgynnull to assemble, to gather (*v*)
ymgyrch campaign, drive, expedition (*nf*)
ymgyrchoedd campaigns (*npl*)
ymgyrchu to campaign (*v*)
ymgyrchwr campaigner (*nm*)
ymgyrchwyr campaigners (*npl*)
ymgyrraedd to strive for (*v*)
ymhel to be concerned with, to meddle, to tamper (*v*)
ymhelaethiad elaboration (*nm*)
ymhelaethu to elaborate, to expand upon (*v*)
ymhell afar, far (*adv*)
ymhellach further (*adj*)

ymhen at last, eventually *(prep)*

ymhle where *(adv)*

ymhlith amongst *(prep)*

ymhlyg implicit, intrinsic *(adj)*

ymhob in each *(adv)*

ymholi to inquire *(v)*

ymholiad enquiry, inquiry *(nm)*

ymholiadau inquiries *(npl)*

ymhyfrydu to delight in, to revel *(v)*

ymlacio to relax *(v)*

ymladd to combat, to fight *(v)*

ymlaen ahead, on, onward *(adv)*

ymlediad diffusion, dilation, expansion *(nm)*

ymledol spreading *(adj)*

ymledu to dilate, to spread, to suffuse *(v)*

ymlusgiad reptile *(nm)*

ymlusgiaid reptiles *(npl)*

ymlyniad adherence, attachment *(nm)*

ymofyn to fetch, to get, to seek, to want *(v)*

ymolchi to wash (oneself) *(v)*

ymorol to seek, to take care *(v)*

ymosod to assail, to assault, to attack *(v)*

ymosodiad assault, attack, onslaught *(nm)*

ymosodiadau attacks *(npl)*

ymosododd he/she/it attacked *(v)*

ymosodol aggressive, attacking *(adj)*

ymosodwr attacker *(nm)*

ymroddedig devoted *(adj)*

ymroddiad devotion *(nm)*

ymroi to devote *(v)*

ymron almost *(adv)*

ymrwymedig committed *(adj)*

ymrwymiad commitment, undertaking *(nm)*

ymrwymiadau commitments *(npl)*

ymrwymo to commit oneself *(v)*

ymryson contest, rivalry *(nm)*

ymryson to compete, to contend, to contest *(v)*

ymsefydlu to establish oneself *(v)*

ymson monologue, soliloquy *(nm)*

ymson to soliloquize *(v)*

ymuno to join in *(v)*

ymunodd he/she/it joined *(v)*

ymunwch you join *(v)*

ymunwyd was/were joined *(v)*

ymwadiad renunciation *(nm)*

ymwadiadau denials *(npl)*

ymweld to call, to visit *(v)*

ymweliad call, visit *(nm)*

ymweliadau visits *(npl)*

ymwelodd he/she/it visited *(v)*

ymwelwch you visit *(v)*

ymwelwr caller, visitor *(nm)*

ymwelwyd was/were visited *(v)*

ymwelwyr visitors *(npl)*

ymwelydd visitor *(nm)*

ymwneud to do with, to pertain to *(v)*

ymwrthod to abstain from *(v)*

ymwthiol intrusive *(adj)*

ymwybod consciousness *(nm)*

ymwybodol aware, conscious *(adj)*

ymwybyddiaeth awareness, consciousness *(adj)*

ymyl border, edge, side, verge *(nm)*

ymylol marginal *(adj)*

ymylon fringes *(npl)*

ymyriad intervention *(nm)*

ymyriadau interventions *(npl)*

ymyrraeth interference, intervention, meddling *(nf)*

ymyrryd to interfere, to intervene, to intrude *(v)*

ymysg among, amongst, between *(prep)*

yn at, in *(prep)*

yna then, there, whereupon *(adv)*

ynad justice, magistrate *(nm)*

ynadon magistrates *(npl)*

ynddi in (her) *(prep)*

ynddo in (him) *(prep)*

ynddyn in (them) *(prep)*

ynddynt in (them) *(prep)*

yng in *(prep)*

yngan to enunciate, to pronounce, to utter (*v*)

ynganu to enunciate (*v*)

ynghanol in the middle of (*adv*)

ynghlwm tied up (*adv*)

ynghyd together (*adv*)

ynghylch about (you), concerning (*prep*)

ynghynt quicker, sooner (*adv*)

ynglŷn with regard (*adv*)

ynni energy (*nm*)

yno there (*adv*)

ynof in (me) (*prep*)

ynom in (us) (*prep*)

ynot in (you) (*prep*)

yntau even he, he also, he too (*pronoun*)

ynteu or, then, therefore (*conj*)

ynys island, isle (*nf*)

ynysig insular, isolated (*adj*)

ynysoedd islands (*npl*)

ynysu to insulate, to isolate, to maroon (*v*)

yr the (*definite article*)

yrfa career

yrfaoedd careers

yrru to drive

yrrwr driver

yrwyr drivers

ys as (*conj*)

ysbaid respite, spell (*nm*)

ysbeidiol intermittent, spasmodic, sporadic (*adj*)

ysblander splendour (*nm*)

ysblennydd resplendent, splendid (*adj*)

ysbryd ghost, morale, spirit (*nm*)

ysbrydion ghosts (*npl*)

ysbrydol religious, spiritual (*adj*)

ysbrydoledig inspired (*adj*)

ysbrydoli to inspire (*v*)

ysbrydoliaeth inspiration (*nf*)

ysbwriel rubbish (*nm*)

ysbytai hospitals (*npl*)

ysbyty hospital, infirmary (*nm*)

ysfa craving, itch (*nf*)

ysgafn gentle, light, slight (*adj*)

ysgafnach lighter (*adj*)

ysgariad divorce (*nm*)

ysgaru to divorce, to separate (*v*)

ysglyfaeth prey, victim (*nf*)

ysgogi to impel, to move, to stir (*v*)

ysgogiad impulse (*nm*)

ysgogol stimulating (*adj*)

ysgol ladder (*nf*)

ysgol school (*nf*)

ysgolhaig intellectual, scholar (*nm*)

ysgolheictod learning, scholarship (*nm*)

ysgolheigaidd scholarly (*adj*)

ysgolheigion intellectuals (*npl*)

ysgolion schools (*npl*)

ysgoloriaeth scholarship (*nf*)

ysgoloriaethau scholarships (*npl*)

ysgrif essay (*nf*)

ysgrifau essays (*npl*)

ysgrifen handwriting, writing (*nf*)

ysgrifenedig written (*adj*)

ysgrifennodd he/she/it wrote (*v*)

ysgrifennu to write (*v*)

ysgrifennwch you write (*v*)

ysgrifennwr writer (*nm*)

ysgrifennwyd was/were written (*v*)

ysgrifennydd secretary (*nm*)

ysgrifenwyr writers (*npl*)

ysgrifenyddiaeth secretaryship (*nf*)

ysgrifenyddion secretaries (*npl*)

ysgrifenyddol secretarial (*adj*)

ysgrythur scripture (*nf*)

ysgubol sweeping (*adj*)

ysgubor barn, granary (*nf*)

ysgwyd to flap, to shake, to wag (*v*)

ysgwydd shoulder (*nf*)

ysgwyddau shoulders (*npl*)

ysgwyddo to shoulder (*v*)

ysgyfaint lungs (*npl*)

ysgytwol jolting, shocking (*adj*)

ysmygu to smoke (*v*)

ystad estate (*nf*)
ystadau estates (*npl*)
ystadegau statistics (*npl*)
ystadegol statistical (*adj*)
ystafell room (*nf*)
ystafelloedd rooms (*npl*)
ystatud statute (*nf*)
ystlum bat (creature) (*nm*)
ystlumod bats (*npl*)
ystlys flank, side, touchline (*nf*)
ystod during, in the course of, range, swath (*nf*)
ystum bend, pose, posture, stance (*nm*)
ystyr meaning, sense (*nm*)
ystyriaeth consideration, factor (*nf*)
ystyriaethau considerations (*npl*)

ystyrid would be considered (*v*)
ystyried to consider, to ponder (*v*)
ystyriodd he/she/it considered (*v*)
ystyriol considerate, thoughtful (*adj*)
ystyrir is/are/will be considered (*v*)
ystyriwch you consider (*v*)
ystyriwyd was/were considered (*v*)
ystyrlon meaningful (*adj*)
ystyron meanings (*npl*)
ysu to consume, to crave, to itch (*v*)
ysw. Esq.(*abbreviation*)
yswiriant insurance (*nm*)
yswiriwr insurer (*nm*)
ysywaeth alas, unfortunately (*adv*)
yw is (*v*)
yw yews (trees) (*npl*)

By the same author

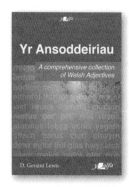

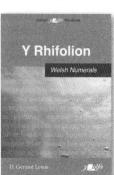

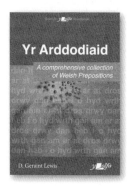

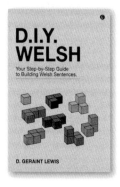

Books for beginners

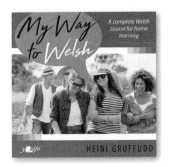

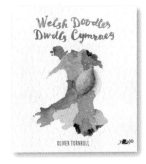

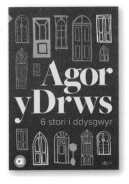

Follow
Y Lolfa
on social media platforms
for latest company news.

Visit
www.ylolfa.com/learners
to browse over 150 books
for Welsh learners of all levels.